The Stressless Brain

Kundalini Meditations for Stress and Anxiety

Madhur-Nain Webster

BALBOA.
PRESS

A DIVISION OF HAY HOUSE

Balboa Press books may be ordered through booksellers or by contacting:

Balboa Press
A Division of Hay House
1663 Liberty Drive
Bloomington, IN 47403
www.balboapress.com
1 (877) 407-4847

Print information available on the last page.

ISBN: 978-1-9822-0428-0 (sc)
ISBN: 978-1-9822-0427-3 (hc)
ISBN: 978-1-9822-0429-7 (e)

Library of Congress Control Number: 2018905793

Balboa Press rev. date: 07/06/2018

 KRI Seal Statement

This publication has received the KRI Seal of Approval. This Seal is given only to products that have been reviewed for accuracy and integrity of the sections containing the 3HO lifestyle and Kundalini Yoga as taught by Yogi Bhajan®. KRI does not review the music which accompanies meditations.

It has been argued that our modern society is undergoing a growing virtual epidemic in unmanaged chronic stress. Although our modern culture and medical system have few viable solutions, there is a recent and ongoing boom in the practice of yoga and meditation accompanied by a large and growing evidence base of rigorous biomedical research documenting the benefits of these practices on stress and mood. This book has fully described this phenomenon and has assembled a scientific rationale and a comprehensive set of Kundalini Yoga-based practices that have strong potential for improving stress and mood and overall well-being.

—Sat Bir Singh Khalsa, Ph.D.
Director of Research, Kundalini Research Institute
Assistant Professor of Medicine, Harvard Medical School

I dedicate this book to my mother and father, who have been consistently present throughout my life. For over seventy years, they have kept up and walked their talk; they are an endless source of inspiration. I love you both so much.

And to my husband of twenty-two years, Julian: I dedicate this book to you. Thank you for always loving me for me.

Contents

"Meditation is a washing machine for the brain.
Chanting is spot remover" Madhur-Nain

Preface

How many times have you proclaimed, "I am so stressed"? How many times has that phrase been casually used in conversations with friends, family members, or acquaintances?

Stress is an emotion that has become so universally accepted that it is now ingrained into our culture and society. In this fast-paced world where we face endless demands, it would be far more difficult to find someone who *didn't* feel stress on a daily basis. And because this emotion has become so normalized, many feel that it can't be changed, that chronic stress is simply part of our everyday life. It is as inevitable as waking up each day.

In the eighteen years that I have been practicing as a psychotherapist, I have encountered more patients with anxiety than any other symptom. Contrast that to eighty years ago, when society did not recognize the words *stress* or *anxiety* as common terminology. A subject that was once considered taboo to talk about, stress constantly threatens to infiltrate our lives in menacing ways: it affects our work, our household, our relationships, and our personal health (mentally and physically). It is important that we address it so that we can make good, conscious decisions to heal ourselves.

Because I had the benefit of growing up in an ashram, I was very familiar with Kundalini Yoga and became involved in it at a young age. It has followed me throughout my entire life, proving to be a useful tool of self-help in my darkest days. It is within my own journey that I discovered how important it is to build a bridge between psychology and Kundalini Yoga and meditation in a way that is easily accessible to all who need help.

I began teaching my clients meditations as a means of relieving stress and anxiety, knowing of its power due to my own experiences with this ancient yogic tool. Witnessing their positive transformations reinforced my belief that Kundalini Yoga is a gift, one that I wanted to continue sharing as often as possible. That is why I have created mantra music, available free to the masses, and why I ultimately decided to write this book: *The Stressless Brain*.

You may be asking yourself, "Why another book about anxiety and stress? There are so many self-help books out there." While that is a correct assessment, I have found that many self-help books do not give you concrete steps on what to do to successfully help yourself. Many books are sympathetic about readers' emotions, offering explanations as to why someone might feel a certain way. I have read them myself and often thought, *Yes, I do feel like that.* When it comes to advice, however, the sections are too short or confusing; in any case, I am unable to apply their advice—or lack thereof—to my personal situation. I find that at the end of the books, I still do not understand what they are asking of me.

> Although meditation can feel strange at first, creating a yogic ritual will ultimately allow you to alter your attitude and guide you into a calmer state of mind.

I want you to feel as if this book is addressing your symptoms. Through scientific research, personal stories, and meditative tools, I hope I am able to help you reach clarity of the mind. It is time, through the power of yogic practices and Kundalini meditation, to help relieve yourself of the anxiety that often coincides with untreated stress.

By employing the various yogic technology offered in this book, you will be able to unlock your potential for a positivity-led lifestyle. The trickiest aspect of this ancient form of healing is how different—and sometimes awkward—it feels to apply to the modern way of living. Although meditation can feel strange at first, creating a yogic ritual will ultimately allow you to alter your attitude and guide you into a calmer state of mind. I want to help bring you to peace.

When embarking on this journey into an anxiety-free life, you will need to give permission to yourself for honest self-reflection so that you can correct your thoughts and actions yourself. We sometimes hide emotions from ourselves because we don't want to confront them; confronting them often means dealing with them somehow.

This raw honesty can sometimes trigger very specific emotions that feel overwhelming or even unbearable. If you feel you need additional support during the meditative healing process, please consult a licensed professional who will give you the proper structure as you process and mend your anxiety or pain. It is absolutely acceptable to seek supplemental therapy.

No matter your yogic experience, Kundalini meditation can help expose deep emotions or memories that can be scary, but meditation also offers the tools to help you move through psychological pain. By keeping a journal detailing your feelings after each meditative session, you will be able to pinpoint specific emotions that you can then address through daily meditation. In addition to a journal, do not hesitate to talk to close friends about your self-healing journey; they may be able to provide a form of support that will help you feel safe and grounded.

If you ever feel flooded with emotions during your journey, remind yourself that internalized fears, anxiety, and doubt can sometimes make you feel overly sensitive. This is normal. Reaching out for added support, if needed, makes you courageous. You are showing your determination into creating a healthy life, instilling inner and outer change into your being.

In order to bring about this positive change in your life, I am going to ask you to make a commitment to meditate every day for one week after (or while) you read this book. Whether it's a new pair of shoes or learning how to paint, the best way to see if something works for you and your lifestyle is to simply try it. Because you picked up this book, I already know that you are interested in relieving the stress and anxiety in your life through a natural and pure method, such as meditation.

Once you have read through this book and consequently understand the complexities of Kundalini meditation, I would like you to try the Beginner's Meditation, even if you have practiced meditation before. This will allow you to form or reinforce a vital relationship with your breathing patterns, which is necessary to create change within yourself. Once you finish your first week, I then challenge you to meditate for forty days straight, without missing a day.

To truly experience change, you need to set a cycle of positive patterns and beliefs. Meditation is a fleeting experience until it becomes an expected practice in your life, as common as eating breakfast. When introducing it into your life, try pairing it with rituals to which you are already committed. For example, you can meditate for five minutes while your morning cup of coffee is brewing each day. Over time, your body will learn to anticipate meditation as natural behavior, and that is when you will see invigorating changes in your thoughts and life.

After you meditate (every day), please take the time to journal. Note what is different and what is the same; document your feelings, whether in great detail or by using one simple word to summarize the experience. Don't be afraid to ask yourself questions that you can address in your next session or even bring up when speaking with friends. By journaling, you will be able to observe the changes occurring within you and around you.

Yogi Bhajan—the late yogi who introduced Kundalini Yoga to the United States—stated, "Happiness is your birthright" (*The Teachings of Yogi Bhajan*, 1989). We thrive on the positivity instilled in us through endless forms of joy, and that includes having a calm, balanced mind. It is as essential to a healthy life as clean air and water.

As a wife of twenty-two years and a mother of two boys, I understand that it is difficult to stay sane and balanced. The struggles of being human are compounded by the weight of expectations. Kundalini meditation has given me a solid foundation upon which to stand, a place where I can process my emotions with clarity and instill myself with a sense of faith in the process of life. Through this, I have created contentment in my life. I hope you are able to achieve this too.

My goal is to give readers the tools and inspiration to find their inner selves. When you make this commitment, you can begin to eliminate stress and cultivate contentment, instead. Anyone can take these initial steps into self-discovery. Are you ready? If so, let's get started.

Chapter 1

My Relationship with Meditation

My relationship with meditation began before I was even born. At the time I was in my mother's womb, my parents had just started exploring a yogic and spiritual lifestyle in Tucson, Arizona. It was their path toward a deeply meaningful life. By joining an ashram—a living environment for spiritual growth—they were surrounded by like-minded people who sought to bring clarity to their life. Kundalini Yoga and meditation was an important tool in the ashram, creating balance and purpose for my parents.

Kundalini Yoga as taught by Yogi Bhajan—a form of yoga and meditation heavily focused on the use of chanting, breath, and postures— was my mother's preferred practice. I can perfectly envision my pregnant mother sitting during the waking dawn each day, her round belly containing a life that would hear her calls. The vibrations of her chanting reverberated through me in this precious stage of my development, instilling a belief system within me that I follow to this day.

Newly married and with a baby on the way, my parents relocated to the Netherlands to continue their spiritual journey at an Amsterdam-based Kundalini Yoga ashram. That is where I was born. During thirty-seven hours in labor, my mother used meditative breathing techniques to help keep her relaxed. In those days, it was not uncommon for fellow ashram members to chant and meditate in a nearby room in order to support the mother and child. It must have worked, because after a long and tedious labor, a healthy baby girl was finally born: me.

Growing up in the ashram, I felt very familiar and involved with Kundalini Yoga at a young age. Meditation and chanting were important aspects of my life. My parents also taught yoga classes in the ashram where we lived, so I would often go to their classes at night. By joining them, I was able to further surround myself with their positive spiritual energy and the optimism they projected to their students, who were searching for enlightenment. While I might not have been interested in seeking my life's purpose at the time, I loved to be lulled by the chanting. I remember often bringing my blanket to my mother's class, lying next to her, and asking her to teach a chanting meditation so that I could sleep. I would fall asleep so deeply in the middle of the class that my parents would have to carry me back to my room. My body inherently recognized the power of chanting to help bring me peace.

The chanting didn't stop at home. My mother would put me to bed with a chant while she massaged my back, face, hands, and feet. Now, most people would feel relaxed with a gentle body massage alone, but approaching it with a yogic strategy enhanced my happiness and tranquility. It made me feel safe and comfortable. At my request, my parents would recite certain mantras that I wanted to hear; perhaps, subconsciously, without yet understanding why, they were mantras my brain felt it *needed* to hear. One of my favorites then—and still to this day—is Guru Guru Wahe Guru Guru Ram Das Guru. As an adult, I now know that our bodies are perceptive to self-healing desires. If a heart requires soothing, it will attempt to seek a remedy, whether through a pint of ice cream or a calming mantra. We turn inward to try and find answers from ourselves, which then helps us to better understand and maintain balance within ourselves. By doing so, we inspire inner peace for our bodies and souls. That is a form of healing.

From Amsterdam, my parents and I moved to Hamburg, Germany. That is where my parents had their own ashram, where other families lived alongside us. Using the traditional meditative chanting support system as previously mentioned, I helped welcome other children into the world when I was eight years old. To this day, I still call these children my siblings. Even at my young age, I knew this welcoming system was a special experience, one that brought me pride and purpose. I felt that I was part of something very meaningful. I was part of the ashram community.

Just half a year later, however, my faith was severely tested.

Life, as we know, is about change and growth. How we adapt to these changes is what sets our outlook moving forward. If you face a hardship, do you become more determined? Or do you find that you settle into complacency? Does it make you angry, sad, mad? Inspired?

These are the questions I had to confront in my youth, after I was sent to live with another family in the United States while my family stayed behind in Germany. While this may seem like an alarming incident, children in the Kundalini community were often sent to boarding school—away from their parents—during this time. In fact, within a certain class in India, this tradition is very normal. Despite its commonness, this seemingly inevitable separation was still very confusing and painful for me (and many of my peers) back then. Since then, I have spent much time reconnecting to my parents and healing with them.

Although my new family was part of the same Kundalini community, they were shockingly different from my parents and the environment I grew up in. This change shook me to my core, and the trouble was that I hadn't yet developed the tools to cope with my confusion. My parents and I did spend time together on holidays and summers. I returned home and spent the last two years of high school back with my parents where we worked on healing.

For the next ten years, I suppressed a lot of that anger. Growing up in a yogic lifestyle does not necessarily mean the tools for self-healing are built within you; it just means that you might have a beneficial advantage. In fact, throughout those ten years, I still practiced a lot of meditation and yoga. I spent my summers at Kundalini Yoga camps, at Kundalini Yoga festivals, and with other Kundalini Yoga families. It was my life, when I wanted it to be.

A big turning point in my life—when meditation became a tool to release the pent-up stress and sadness within me—happened when I was nineteen years old. That was when I experienced my first real heartbreak. I felt it so strongly that I was sure my heart would never recover from the pain. Life became flat. I could not function, meaning I could not complete everyday routines that were previously small comforts. It was hard to think straight because I was asking myself a lot of questions, trying to make sense of the situation and determine what had gone wrong. I had trouble falling asleep and then staying asleep. An overactive mind kept me up at night, fueled by the fires of anxiety and sadness.

By using meditation as a healing tool, rather than treating it as an obligation, I was able to train my mind to stop overthinking. Instead, I relieved myself of worry and doubt through the use of Kundalini meditations (Anxiety Release Meditation). If anxiety started to creep up on me again, I was able to distract my mind with chanting. It brought me back to my youth and the memories of my mother's mantras before bed, which made me feel calm and protected.

Over the years, I have continued to come back to chanting to soothe myself. By doing so, I reconnect with my inner peace. Whenever my mind produces thoughts that upset me, I calm it with a mantra. It placates my emotions.

> Whenever my mind produces thoughts that upset me, I calm it with a mantra.

Sometimes, it is very easy, but it can still be difficult to quiet my mind, even after a lifetime of Kundalini Yoga experience. This is why the power of chanting—whether in your head or out loud—is so beneficial.

It is normal to struggle while meditating, especially for beginners. Don't let the frustration knock you over. Instead, focus on letting go. Trust the meditative process without expectation, and let it sweep over you. Learn from it. With time and patience, you will grow. A seed does not become a tree in a day.

Building a relationship with yourself is the first step in progressing in life and to change for the better. Life is about movement, not stagnancy. You cannot allow yourself to fall flat. You cannot accept monotony. According to the United States Geological Survey, the average adult body is composed of 60 percent water—and that energy must be kept moving. If the flow stops, disease grows. Think of it like a still pond that gets covered in algae. Allowing positive change in your life means evolving spiritually and mentally. It means speaking with your inner self.

For many people, building a relationship with yourself is not a priority when growing up. Most societies focus on forging relationships with others. The popular kid in high school, after all, is the one who has amassed the most friends. Openly expressing emotions can often be the source of ridicule, which can then harvest a feeling of uncertainty or fear over speaking out. This can eventually mutate into anxiety. Ultimately, we are told to quiet our inner voices.

Some find it difficult to tap into their inner selves, but it is a skill that anyone can master, with patience and practice. You, too, can learn to dissolve controlling thoughts from your head with the use of meditation and chanting. By exploring Kundalini Yoga, you will be able to develop your intuition, your consciousness, and your connection to a higher energy. Using this spiritual method, you can build, reconstruct, or maintain a relationship with yourself.

When I rediscovered meditation at nineteen, I still had teenage angst. I still had issues with my parents, and I still questioned everything. But with serious practice, over many years, I was able to become someone with self-worth and strength. My current worrying thoughts and internal stress—which includes being a woman, a wife, a mother, and a therapist— can all be tamed with meditation. I learned how to stay centered and calm as life carried me up and down. I learned how to build and maintain a relationship with myself. I learned how to find inner peace.

Our intellect "releases one thousand thoughts per wink of the eye," according to spiritual teacher Yogi Bhajan, who introduced Kundalini Yoga to the United States. "These thoughts are released … automatically as breath comes to you automatically" (*Yogi Bhajan Lecture: The Pranic Body*, 1982). Licensed physician and noted alternative medicine advocate Deepak Chopra has raised the argument that the average person thinks about sixty to eighty thousand thoughts per day ("Why Meditate?" 2007). That's a lot of potential distraction.

With all these confounding thoughts in our head on a daily basis, there are endless opportunities for us to face stress and anxiety. But these emotions can affect our health, mentally and physically. They can alter our relationships with people, shift how we handle our careers, and deteriorate our bodies. Deep, oppressive stress is not something we can live with our whole life. It needs to be tamed. By doing so, we can eventually learn to let go of it.

Helping people achieve this seemingly unattainable goal of a pacified state of mind became my priority in the winter of 1993. Up until then, I was enrolled at the University of Oregon with every intention of receiving a degree in international business marketing. Having witnessed my parents build several businesses in my youth (in Germany, they started Yogi Tea in their basement), becoming a businesswoman seemed like my path, at first.

As I was studying, it dawned on me that a career in such a cutthroat industry was not what I wanted. I knew, through my studies, that it was not going to fulfill me emotionally.

On a family vacation to Mexico in the winter of 1993, I told my mother that I did not want to lead the lifestyle of a businesswoman. Although we experienced a complicated relationship in my youth, my mother and I had since grown close after I returned to Hamburg for my last two years of high school. It was no surprise, then, that she wanted to help me realize my potential, both personally and professionally. She wanted to help guide me toward a career I would love.

So together, we made a list: all that I knew, all that I wanted to learn, and all that interested me. Over this Mexican vacation, we figured out that counseling was my future. I wanted to help people in the way others—including the ashram community, Yogi Bhajan, and my own parents—had helped me discover my path and purpose in life.

I revisited my enrollment at the University of Oregon, where I eventually acquired a master's degree in marriage and family therapy. This has since provided me with the opportunity to assist people in some of the darkest moments of their lives, shepherding them toward levity and lightness. My advice is not always about salvaging a relationship (sometimes the healthiest thing we can do is to let go of our bonds) but rather to have my clients focus on gaining clarity in life. This is often difficult because the pressure of stress or anxiety clouds their minds from the most dominant issues that need to be directly addressed.

Clients often ask me, "Why is stress a problem for me now?" After feeling fine for many years, they are suddenly burdened with stress or anxiety. It is because, when we were young, we were able to deal with adolescent mental stress on different levels; unable to fully comprehend our fears or worries, we naturally suppressed any anxiety that might have otherwise flourished. This natural phenomenon created an internal habit on a cellular level, impacting our subconscious minds. Over time, this repeated suppression further stressed the body and mind because we were not consciously addressing the internalized discomfort. Ultimately, as we become fully aware adults, our worries often become expressed through external stress.

Luckily for us, more and more scientific studies are concluding that meditation is a key method in recovering from anxiety and its various forms, including depression. It often serves as an even better form of therapy than medication.

A Harvard Medical School-affiliated research team from Massachusetts General Hospital used MRI technology to monitor brain activity during meditation. Results found that meditation activates the sections of the brain in charge of the autonomic nervous system, which governs the functions in our bodies that we cannot actively control. Stress, triggered by uncontrollable forces, affects this system (Hölzel, et al., 2011).

Our thoughts affect how we feel. Meditation trains the brain to feel relaxed by creating new neurological pathways. When we practice meditation with specific sounds and rhythms—as Kundalini celebrates through the use of breathing techniques and chanting—our brainwaves adjust and consequently restructure our emotions. Along with a group of colleagues, Russian biophysicist and molecular biologist Dr. Pjotr Garjajev concluded that our DNA can be reprogrammed by words and frequencies (*Vernetzte Intelligenz*, 2001). Therefore, a repetition of mantra, as exercised through Kundalini meditation, can alter your thought patterns.

I fully believe that meditation will help support you in becoming a healthier and happier person. But as I have already mentioned, you need to routinely practice—and have patience.

A client I once worked with had an especially difficult time finding inner faith and self-worth. She felt lost in her life and was uncertain about which direction to take next in order to feel fulfilled. She might sound like a familiar figure to you: she would go to work, maintain friendships, and even enjoyed romantic dates from time to time, but none of the relationships were bringing her joy. She often felt so worried that she experienced panic attacks.

At the time I met with this client, I was a licensed psychotherapist who had not yet integrated meditation into my professional career. When she sat in my office for our first consultation, I could see the pain within her, yet her eyes were brimmed with hope. I knew she was serious about her mental health and that she was determined to create real change in her life. I asked her if she would be willing to meditate.

Her answer was simple: "Yes."

Her first assigned meditation was Kirtan Kriya, a very powerful form that has been scientifically suggested to aid in depression and memory loss

(Alzheimer's Research & Prevention Foundation). It was a foreign practice to her; it felt a little weird. Adamant about making those positive changes in her life, however, she persisted despite how different and strange it was to her. She practiced … and practiced … and practiced. Between our therapy sessions and her at-home meditations, she was able to make the changes in life that she sought. Talk therapy and meditation allowed her to achieve her goals of happiness and self-worth. To this day, she continues to practice Kundalini meditations.

This client helped me understand that I needed to share and integrate meditative technology with others because of how powerful it can be for healing the body, mind, and soul. She helped me unearth an unopened box within me that contained ancient secrets of self-help and realization inside me to share with others. When I opened that box, I discovered that meditation can be an amazing method to guide clients away from stress and anxiety. It seemed natural to then implement it into my psychotherapy practice. I was able to bridge my two worlds: my knowledge of healing through Kundalini meditation with my acquired skills of psychotherapy.

The profound life changes resulting from meditative therapy continue to astound me. I see it on a daily basis in my profession, and I even see the fruits of my labor on the internet. Wanting to share meditation with as many people as quickly as possible, in 2016, I started broadcasting live meditation classes via Facebook. The positive impact was instantaneous.

"I have to thank you a million times over," a message read on Facebook. "I saw your post about antianxiety meditation last night and tried it. I went from crying and feeling out of control to feeling so much more grounded. Thank you!"

When I read these words, my heart instantly opened. I could feel their gratitude. With tears in my eyes, I turned to my husband, Julian, and said, "This is why I do what I do." Even if I never hear from this person again, I am satisfied to know that I helped them with their situation.

Meditation is about creating an experience within yourself that changes how you process emotions, how you control thoughts, and ultimately how you feel. When you have a positive experience by exploring this ancient yogic technique, you are more likely to continue practicing. The ritualistic cycle encourages positive changes to occur, regularly. Don't forget: it is about maintenance.

Chapter 2

Meditation's Cultural and Spiritual Impact

A Brief Lesson on Yoga and Meditation

A common image of the United States in the 1960s is one of daisies, doves, and long-haired adolescents promoting love and peace. It was a time when a small yet mighty counterculture society sought to connect to themselves, seeking an inner-truth. My parents in particular were looking for something to awaken their soul and for that something to usher in a deeper meaning to their lives.

This inherently Eastern philosophy of acknowledging the inner self was seen by many as a strange practice. Some might have disregarded it as an eccentric fad; it was behavior kept hidden in basements or celebrated among park-dwellers with peculiar recreational habits. But those who were like my parents—who discovered Kundalini Yoga and meditation as an answer to their calls for help—knew that this state of mind was not a trend. They recognized it as a way to find their path and purpose in life.

To this day, people are looking for directions toward this path. Most of my clients who come to me aspire to find inner peace, clarity, and support: the basic tools that Kundalini meditative technology can provide. With the modern world becoming wilder and scarier, full of unbridled expectations, it is no surprise that people continue to turn toward this ancient form of healing in order to seek a natural balance within themselves.

As we all know, life can be a challenge. Meditation provides you with a safe space to feel and process the ups and downs that you experience daily; it allows you to understand yourself on a spiritual level, resulting in a self-made sanctuary in which you can seek shelter. What I remember best about Kundalini Yoga and meditation growing up—and it is a belief I still hold—is that it helps you make sense of life. It refuses to let you feel defeated. It refreshes you so you can keep moving.

The cultural history and societal impact of meditation and yoga is a rich and varied topic. It spans regions, religions, and even eras. To delve into the complexities of its deep-rooted history would take quite some time to explore, but if you wish to practice Kundalini, it is especially helpful to at least have a brief lesson on its background.

First, it is crucial to understand that Kundalini is an energy within us. ("Kundalini" is a Sanskrit word that translated as "coiled," so Kundalini is understood as the coiled energy located at the base of our spines.) We all have the ability to tap into this energy, helping us to release tension and giving us a stark sense of self-awareness. Kundalini is being actively conscious of who we are in this human life so that we can, as a result, live to our highest potential. This potential lives within all of us, at all times.

Kundalini Yoga and meditation is the process of transcending the waves of the mind and body (which contain distractions) by teaching the mind to serve as your soul's consciousness. Essentially, throughout its history, this yogic technology has found a way to tap into the human body on a deep, spiritual level. It changes how the body operates so that it can support a basic life with all of its highs and lows, including moderating pain and suffering. Kundalini practitioners consider it a form of technology because it functions as a specific tool for everyone to use in daily life.

With the use of mudras (symbolic hand and body postures), Kundalini meditation helps us create an understanding and connection among body, mind, and spirit. When we chant while practicing, we are feeling physical vibrations through our body, while each breathing technique gives us a moment to reflect and connect with the inner self. It is the patterns instilled within these steps that teach, strengthen, and ultimately awaken the mind. Our minds then learn to serve our highest selves, our Soul Selves.

When the mind connects to the soul, we are able to experience life with lucidity. With this radiant perspective, we become able to fully grasp life and subsequently face obstacles with newfound strength. This does not mean that we become immune to life's hardships, of course, but we will possess tools to defeat the demons that try to bring us down.

If we did not experience any pain or struggle in life, we would not grow as human beings. Even with Kundalini technology surrounding me since conception, I still feel anger and bereavement. But I also know that those moments will pass; that the here and now of life's conflicts—whether internal or external—is an opportunity for me to learn. Meditation gives me the tools to view these conflicts with clarity so that I can self-correct in my future endeavors.

Ancient yogic scriptures imply that yogic healing existed among its civilizations from over forty thousand years ago. Due to weather-related migration patterns, these healing tools were dispersed across regions, culminating in different forms of practice.

Kundalini's essence—that it is not *found* but rather *experienced*—mirrors its history: there is no single founder of Kundalini Yoga. The earliest mention of the practice was in the Upanishads, which traced the practice to 1600 BCE. Then, traditional classes were between teacher and student and shared through oral recitation, although it was initially only taught to kings or those considered part of a special lineage. King Janaka, who was a master of Kundalini Yoga (Raj Yoga), ruled in Videha (an ancient kingdom in Vedic India) during this time period.

Yogi Bhajan, who became a master of Kundalini Yoga at the age of sixteen under the tutelage of Sant Hazara Singh, helped introduced Kundalini to the West in the late 1960s. In an era of questioning, seeking, and experimenting in the sixties, Yogi Bhajan provided people—like my parents—with clear yogic values, techniques, and support to incorporate into their lives.

As a big part of my family's life and my upbringing, I viewed Yogi Bhajan as a god-father, part of the family. He was my parents' spiritual teacher, offering opportunities to become self-aware and options on how to obtain that awareness—the essentials of Kundalini Yoga. This state of acknowledging and honoring the conscious self is where we find inner peace, calmness, and happiness. It is a feeling of coming home to our own true nature. It establishes our identity.

Because Kundalini Yoga was viewed as a form of Raj Yoga, or royal yoga, intended to be performed by ascetics, Yogi Bhajan initially received threats from yogis in India when he brought the practice to the West in 1968. He felt, however, that this yogic technology was also meant for the householder: average people in society, individuals who have families and a job.

Kundalini Yoga and meditation gives *everyone* the resilience to awaken their soul, ultimately guiding us toward inner and outer happiness. I teach it to my clients because they are the conventional householders, living and sometimes suffering in the real world. Using their inner resources, my clients can create change within themselves. The energy of Kundalini, or awareness, is inside all of us, and we all have the potential to experience it.

Following your own higher-conscious path is a key component in Kundalini meditation. When I was sixteen years old, I was dealing with a difficult time in my life. Depressed and feeling lost, I knew I had to speak with Yogi Bhajan.

He asked me, "What do you need?"

"I am tired of you making all the decisions in my life," I told him. "When things don't work out, I'm just mad at you. I am not learning from the experiences."

"Okay," he said. "You make the decisions. What do *you* want to do?"

"I want to go home."

I self-reflected. I listened to myself. Then, I initiated my own life.

We are no longer bound by the teacher-student code as practiced in ancient times. In fact, in this day and age, I believe we have to be our own teachers and masters. Yogi Bhajan—and the philosophy behind Kundalini Yoga—says that we must listen to our inner voice. We have to tap into our own reservoir of strength to walk ourselves out of the darkness and into the light; this is the true meaning of guru. This is hard for so many because we, as humans, have become quite lazy; we want a magic cure-all pill for a quick remedy, no skill or effort required.

You have to take the first step and do the work to better yourself. No life coach, inspirational speaker, or spiritual influencer will be able to change you and your life. But you—yes, *you*—have the power to start and maintain the transformation within yourself.

Achieving spiritual awakening through Kundalini is not an experience limited only to yoga classrooms. Despite its Eastern philosophy, scholars such as Carl Jung were not afraid to attach the ancient tool of Kundalini philosophy to modern psychology. During a seminar presented to the Psychological Club in Zurich in 1932, Jung presented the concept of Kundalini, serving as a framework in which to best understand the human mind and our yearning to seek inner happiness (*The Psychology of Kundalini Yoga: Notes of the Seminar Given in 1932*, 1999). This is another reason why I felt comfortable using it as an intervention device in psychotherapy.

Since its inception and introduction to the West, Kundalini has grown in many ways. It has become a popular yogic practice for many in the United States as well as Germany, Sweden, Iceland, China, Taiwan, and a multitude of other countries. I have been blessed enough to bring Kundalini Yoga and meditation courses to many of these international communities.

In a world that is becoming increasingly more hectic and unstable, with people desperate to find inner happiness, it is no surprise that meditation as a form of therapy continues to flourish across the world. Connecting with the soul—especially through the use of simple mantras—gives us greater mental strength. Chanting in particular creates an inner connection to your higher self, the big self, also known as the soul. This is why I teach my clients Kundalini meditations.

Kundalini, however, isn't the only form of meditation that one can turn to for guidance. Depending on your needs—including differing religious beliefs—you may want to supplement Kundalini technology with other forms of meditation.

Transcendental Meditation

Started by Maharishi Mahesh Yogi in the mid-1950s, Transcendental Meditation (often referred to as simply TM) is a technique in which one detaches from discomfort and pain by clearing the mind. The basic belief is to sit in silence for twenty minutes twice each day in a conscious effort to promote inner harmony. It is one of the most popular forms of meditation in the West.

Despite its popularity, TM can be a very difficult form of meditation for individuals who have anxiety or some forms of mental illness. I hear this often from my own clients. By sitting quietly for an extended period of time, the haunting thoughts of emotional pain have the ability to transcend and take over the mind. This is called relaxation-induced anxiety (RIA). I teach clients Kundalini meditation instead because it provides explicit tools (like breathing exercises and mantra chanting) to break the patterns of stress and anxiety.

Buddhist Meditation

Like the name implies, Buddhist meditation is connected to the religion and philosophy of the Buddha. The objective is to meditate in order to achieve enlightenment, or nirvana: a transcendent state that is the final goal of a Buddhist's cycle of rebirth. It uses a variety of techniques that support the development of mindfulness, concentration, tranquility, and insight.

To reach enlightenment is to attain awareness, freeing the soul and eliminating the ego state. This is a major difference between Buddhist meditation and the Kundalini belief system. In Kundalini, we strive to teach the ego to serve your soul, not to get rid of it altogether. Ego has a purpose: to keep the self alive. For example, the ego prevents you from walking into the street when a big truck is coming because you don't want the truck to kill you. It helps keep us safe and mentally sound, due to its link between the positive and negative mind.

Guided Meditation

Under the direction of a spiritual leader, guided meditation asks practitioners to engage in mental imagery provoked by sensory descriptions. This can include sights, sounds, tastes, and smells that culminate in a simulated perception that helps to ease the mind. This can be a helpful technique for those who feel confused or lonely when getting involved in the meditative process.

Contrary to Kundalini Yoga, guided meditation by its nature requires its practitioners to listen to another voice for healing. For those suffering with a mental illness, an attachment to the healer's voice can occur, resulting in a dependency on the spiritual leader's guidance to suppress anxiety and other stressors. For complete mental health and healing, I believe you must empower yourself from within. By doing so, you build a spiritual and emotional connection with yourself instead of with another person and with that person's voice.

Religious Meditation

Religions each have their own form of meditation, some more than others. Meditating in conjunction with religion is a way to sit with God. This often occurs in a church or synagogue or any other place where there is a pre-established presence of God. This a different concept than what Kundalini meditation philosophizes, which is the belief that the God essence is already inside us.

Despite that difference, those with a religious moral code can still support their lives with Kundalini Yoga and meditation. In fact, I created a World's Religion Meditation CD that explores this possibility. I asked religious teachers of various faiths about their prayers and then created mantra chanting based off of the prayers. Regardless of your faith, you can chant your beliefs and be instilled with inner peace.

Meditation and the Spiritual World

When I was growing up in the ashram, it seemed to me that no one outside of my yogically minded world knew about (or had even heard of) chakras. Today, everyone seems to know what they are, even if only at a basic level. At the very least, it has been accepted as part of common vernacular among those who wish to explore their spiritual side through meditation.

According to yogic belief, chakras are energy centers in our body which can affect our lives on a physical, emotional, and behavioral level. We have seven chakras in our body, each correlating to a specific energy within the body that influences emotions. One of the ways Kundalini Yoga and meditation differs from other forms of yoga is that Kundalini actually believes that there are eight chakras within us. This eighth energy center is our aura, viewed yogically as a significant aspect of who we are. Our true essence is reflected through our aura.

The importance of chakras in meditation is the energetic focus placed on our mental and physical state. Most of the chakras are stimulated through yoga, but the fourth, fifth, sixth, seventh, and eighth are more directly activated through meditation. The additional physicality that Kundalini offers—including hand postures, breath control, mantras, and other body movements—further helps to awaken these energy centers within us.

Each chakra reflects inner qualities; once activated, they each serve a purpose within our bodies that helps bring us toward spiritual enlightenment. This can also be beneficial when healing our bodies, including relieving ourselves of the burden of stress and anxiety.

Before we continue toward this path of self-discovery through Kundalini meditation, let's explore each chakra and the impact it will have on your journey.

First Chakra: Muladhara (root, earth, red)
Represents: Foundation, survival, security, self-acceptance.

Qualities: Grounded, centered, secure, loyal, stable, healthy functions of elimination.

Shadow side: Fear, insecurity, life feels like a burden, feelings of not belonging (on earth, in one's culture, or within family).

Location: The end of the spine, between the anus and sexual organs.

Influences: Organs creating elimination.

The first chakra has a very important job: elimination. Because of all the toxins surrounding us on a daily basis, this aspect is especially crucial to focus on in today's environment; we need to rid ourselves of the pollutants in our bodies and return them to the earth. Despite the visceral description, this chakra covers the process of elimination physically, mentally, *and* emotionally. For example, obsessive thoughts and lingering sadness are both intangible states that need to be purged from the body. With the help of the first chakra, this negative energy can be eliminated.

When our first chakra is open and functioning with the upper six (or seven) chakras, it gives us security, universality, and a sense of purity.

However, problems arise when the connection and synchronization with the other chakras is not open; this causes the functions of the first chakra to become exaggerated. Improper elimination and inappropriate feelings of attachment accelerate, leading to insecurity. These inappropriate feelings could manifest in the attachment to someone else with the belief that they will provide safety and security. Not everyone will take care of you, nor will everyone protect you. We must build that security within ourselves. When the first chakra (and our heart center) is out of balance, we may find ourselves attracted and attached to other people who do not have our safety as a priority.

Because it represents strength and foundation, the first chakra aids in reducing complex things (situations and feelings) to their common elements. It can ground us. Each idea, feeling, and substance within us is boiled down to the basics. When we lose this grounding, we can face unwanted compulsions and fixed behaviors, so it is vital to connect to this chakra. By opening the first chakra, we can engage with our natural expressions and build our own true identities.

Second Chakra: Syadisthana (water, creativity, orange)
Represents: Feelings, desires, creation.

Qualities: Positive, relaxed attitude to sexual functions, patience, creativity, responsible relationships.

Shadow side: Rigid emotions, frigidity, guilt, no boundaries, irresponsible relationships, problems with reproductive organs or kidneys.

Location: The sexual organs.

Influences: The sexual organs, reproductive glands, kidneys, and bladder.

Unlike the first chakra, the second chakra requires balance with the other energy centers within you. With the second chakra open, we know what we like and what we don't like; we don't lack contrast or contours. It allows us to feel desire and pleasure, and gives us the strength to express ourselves creatively.

When the second chakra is balanced and connected with the other chakras, our sexuality becomes varied, joyful, expressive, and rarely has the connotations of confusion, struggle, pain, or perversion that is often seen in today's culture. If overstimulated, however, everything becomes sexual; you live in a sexual mania.

Taste is the sensory system for the second chakra. When you are able to experience great passion, you'll find that the taste in your mouth will change. When practicing Kundalini Yoga, we unite with the infinite; our brains produce what is yogically called sweet nectar, also known as *amrit* (which some can actually taste in their mouth). If the second chakra is weak, the world seems flat and uninspired. You feel little or no passion. Food does not taste as good, or you find you don't really have an opinion either way. Without taste, life lacks a certain vitality.

Third Chakra: Manipura (fire, action, and balance, yellow)
Represents: The will of the spiritual warrior.

Qualities: Personal power and commitment, self-esteem, identity, judgment.

Shadow side: Anger, greed, shame, despair, finding obstacles everywhere, lack of strength and spontaneity, conforming in order to be recognized, refuting one's own wishes and emotions; physically, there are problems with digestion, the liver, gallbladder, and pancreas.

Location: The area of the navel point, the solar plexus.

Influences: The solar plexus, liver, gallbladder, spleen, digestive organs, pancreas, and adrenals.

The third chakra is the center of energy, willpower, and the sense of control and coordination. It is where our inner balance, inspiration, and good health are developed. The lower triangle of chakras—the first, second, and third—are the driving force to conceptualize and act on actions in life. When we are able to master the third chakra, we are able to initiate and complete these actions. This is why it is associated with the spiritual warrior: someone who is able to know their life mission and follow through with it.

Spiritual warriors are connected with their consciousness (meaning they are deeply connected to themselves) but may not necessarily be connected with the upper chakras. Their abilities are fearlessness and acting with integrity, regardless of the conditions they face. When the third chakra is strong, you have a clear idea of your life and what you would like to see in it. By becoming a spiritual warrior, you will be able to make life what you desire it to be; you can affect the quality of your life by your actions.

Situated at the navel point, the third chakra is fed by the solar plexus through its association to the adrenals and kidneys. This energy helps with the coordination and development of sight and vision. The navel point is the first place where you are fed in the womb; it is the location where you were given life. Once the umbilical cord is cut from your mother, you begin to gather energy from the cosmos. This gives you the strength to move.

Fire represents the third chakra. This element is what helps you initiate and move forward in life. When in your third chakra, you are rarely still; you are exuberant and expressive. When the third chakra is weak, you might feel the need to overcompensate. By lacking energy to finish a task, you might turn to food or drugs or some other form of addiction. Having a weak third chakra means having unrealized ideas. Strengthen this chakra, and your intentions will bloom, stirring the desire to move and inspiring you to create (and complete) actions.

If you experience doubt in the first chakra, hold onto your old habits. If you experience doubt in the second chakra, find your feelings and follow your passions. But if you experience doubt in the third chakra, *act*. Utilize your energy to do something: find a vision, project your point, and make necessary changes. As long as you are adhering to your higher self when following through on a course of action, you will be spiritually rewarded.

In Kundalini Yoga, it is believed that your energy starts in the navel point, known as the reserve pool. It travels down to your root (at the first chakra) and then back up your spine until it moves out of your body. As this energy courses through you, it arouses and awakens each chakra. This opens the doorway to the fourth chakra: the heart chakra, or the beginning of consciousness.

Fourth Chakra: Amahata (air, love and compassion, green and rosy-pink)

Represents: Love, awaking from "me" to "we."

Qualities: Compassion, kindness, forgiveness, service, love, recognizing these qualities in others, and understanding them.

Shadow side: Grief, attachment, closed to surroundings, easily hurt, dependent on love and affection from others, fear of rejection, helper syndrome, heartlessness.

Location: The middle of the chest, on the breast bone and at the level of the nipples.

Influences: The heart, lungs, and thymus gland.

The fourth chakra is the realm of the heart center, home of the soul. It opens us to feelings, compassion, and the capacity to love. The heart center is the balance point of the flow of Kundalini energy. It is situated between the lower chakras (first, second, third: representing earth) and the upper chakras (fifth, sixth, seventh: representing heaven). Because it is ruled by the element of air, it stimulates prana, or our breath. Any blocks in the diaphragm or in our breathing mechanism has a deep effect on this particular chakra.

When the heart chakra is open, we are able to self-reflect. This gives us awareness. When we are able to see ourselves through the eyes of others, we are able to see others the way we view ourselves; it is, as the phrasing goes, like walking a mile in another person's shoes. Consequently, in the fourth chakra, we learn to fully grasp the concept of "I am we."

Forging relationships with your feelings is a subtle yet important quality that is attainable when the heart center is open. Being conscious with our feelings means we are able to properly deliver their intended message to others in our lives. When we speak from our heart, we show vulnerability; others can feel our words and are touched as a result.

Just because our heart center is open does not mean that anyone or anything can slip into our vulnerable state. When engaged with the fourth chakra (and upper chakras in general), we also have the grounding to create boundaries for ourselves. However, if the heart center is overactive, we can be subjected to too much sympathy. This is seen in people who are always worrying about others and taking care of others, sometimes to the detriment of their own health. If the heart center is not active enough, we can form dependency and witness a diffusion of a sense of ourselves.

Fortify your heart center, and you may strengthen relationships throughout your life, as well. For at the heart center, there is no conflict. It is where heaven and earth come together. Speaking to a romantic partner from the heart, gives each person the feeling of being truly present with the other. In turn, this allows us to experience real intimacy. Awakening the heart center allows us to have conviction in what we say. Yogi Bhajan once said that when one speaks truth in fear, then it is a lie, but if one speaks the truth from the heart, then that truth has an element of kindness to it, even if it is something difficult to say (*The Mind: Its Projections and Multiple Facets*, 1998).

Fifth Chakra: Vishuddha (ether, projective power of the world, light blue)
Represents: The center for truth.

Qualities: Knowledge and the ability to communicate effectively, authenticity, healthy self-expression and interactions, embodying God's will, hearing and speaking the truth.

Shadow side: Lethargy, weakness in expressive and descriptive abilities, shyness, voice problems, insecurity, fear of other people's opinions and judgments; physically, there are problems with the throat, neck, and thyroid.

Location: The throat.

Influences: The trachea, throat, cervical vertebrae, thyroid, and parathyroid gland.

At the fifth chakra—representing the element of ether—we move into the mysterious and the miraculous. Ether is the element between space and time that allows everything to exist. It is the beginning of the process of manifestation: the twinkle in the eye of a future mother and father when they first meet. From there, it goes to the heart connection (fourth chakra), then fire sweeps them into action (third chakra), and finally the energy of the earth grounds the relationship (first chakra).

Through the fifth chakra, the seed of communication is planted. The power of our words is born in the throat and moves outward from there. How that seed (our words) manifests itself in our lives is determined by our connection with the other chakras. Opening the other chakras, we are able to become clear-minded and can plant positive seeds. Projecting our words in such a way means that they will be taken by the *maya* (material things and the stuff around us) of the universe and begin to manifest themselves. Once they are out there, they cannot be taken back; like the laws of Newton, the energy is already in motion.

We must be aware, focused, and in tune with our higher consciousness when projecting our words. After all, words have shaped and transformed all of our lives. Words have consequences. The messages that our children hear as infants will stay with them for life; these words become part of their karma (the cause and effect of behavior and attachment in the present or the past). Words are an important facet of how we express ourselves and communicate in this world. They can uplift us, demoralize us, and make us happy or sad. They can wound us so deeply that we spend our entire lives trying to heal ourselves. So be mindful when projecting your words.

Connecting to the ether, we have the ability to align our words with the word of God. What is your message that you want to share with others? What is your destiny on this planet, and how will you achieve it? By meditating and chanting, we are able to clear our minds and heal ourselves. We learn to trust. We are able to see ourselves for who we are—as entities of God—and embrace this wholesome realization. Like each grain of sand forming the beach, we are each a component of God that forms his whole image.

Sometimes, in trying to cure ourselves of haunting thoughts, we revisit painful past experiences. By recalling our stories, we can wound ourselves again. Through the act of meditation, we can learn to trust ourselves and let go of these feelings. We have the power to heal our bodies, minds, and souls, but we must tap into ourselves and learn to let go. Moving forward can only be accomplished by trusting ourselves. Through mastering the fifth chakra—acknowledging the impact of our words and honing our skills of the word—we are able to speak directly from our souls. By opening our souls through the ether element, we walk ourselves down the path between earth and heaven.

Sixth Chakra: Ajna (intuition, wisdom and integrity, indigo)
Represents: Center of intuition.

Qualities: Clairvoyance, concentration and determination, self-intuition, power of projection, understanding your purpose.

Shadow side: Confusion, depression, rejection of spirituality, over-intellectualizing.

Location: At the brow point, between the eyebrows.

Influences: The brain and pituitary gland.

At the sixth chakra, we see the union of opposites: there will always be two sides of every thought, every action, every thing. Any time there is light, there is also darkness. The third eye—centered between the eyebrows—gives us insight into the subtle worlds, while the two eyes that we use to see give us sight into the everyday world in which we live.

People who are able to connect with the spirits, or otherwise have what is known as a sixth sense, have mastered a connection with their sixth chakra. Because the sixth chakra gives us an inner light to the flow of our mind, these spiritually connected beings are able to experience a greater dimension beyond the normal world.

By being connected to the sixth chakra, we are also able to master the duality of the mind. After all, *Ajna*, the name of the sixth chakra, means "to command." It is where we reach integrity and integration of our personality. By opening this chakra, we are able to recognize any and all polarities of life; we are able to read between pre-established lines. This is where we get our intuition of where we want to move in life, whether physically, emotionally, or mentally.

When we meditate and focus on the third eye, we activate the pituitary gland. With the use of chanting and strong breath control, we can affect the function of the pineal and pituitary glands, as well as the hypothalamus. In particular, the pituitary gland regulates the secretion of hormones from the thyroid, adrenals, and reproductive glands. These hormones influence blood pressure, milk, contraction of the uterus, ovulation, bone maturation and growth, protein synthesis, and use of fat reserve. Some of these hormones are related to feelings of connectedness and social bonding. Regulating our immune system also influences our emotions and the flexibility—as well as overall effectiveness—of our actions. Keeping our pituitary glands healthy positively affects our entire internal system.

Seventh Chakra: Sahasrara (crown, humility, and vastness, violet)
Represents: Transcendence, connecting to the infinity, wholeness.

Qualities: Connection to the highest self, unity, elevation, relationships to the unknown, enlightenment.

Shadow side: Grief, the feeling of being separated from existence or abundance, fear of death.

Location: Crown of the head.

Influences: The brain and pineal gland.

Surrendering is the key element of the seventh chakra. Through this connection, we reach a point of being content to let go of attachments. We bow to the infinite. You might have observed that many different spiritual and religious groups incorporate bowing, and this is because they all embrace the aspect of surrender in their practice. In terms of the seventh chakra, the physical act of bowing causes our blood flow to direct itself to our head and circulate to the crown. This gives us a new sense of openness and strength.

Along with the brain, the seventh chakra is connected to the pineal gland. This gland influences levels of sex and thyroid hormones that affect our brain activity. In Kundalini Yoga, breath work (as well as chanting and mantra) can greatly enhance the effectiveness of the pineal gland. As a result, sound is a powerful trigger for the seventh chakra. When we meditate and allow ourselves to move beyond our inner and outer fears, we give up control. An opening forms in the head, the third eye, and the self. Through this opening, we are able to feel more connected to something larger than ourselves; this creates safety and security. It is through sound currents that we are able to transform our feelings.

If we are not able to open ourselves and connect with the seventh chakra, we are more likely to experience the energy from only the third and sixth chakras. This can lead to problems. By remaining unconnected from the seventh chakra, the power established from the third and sixth starts to develop into a spiritual ego. The seventh chakra gives us humility. We must open ourselves to information from the unknown, but we must consciously process our knowledge. Chanting from the heart allows us to accomplish this act.

Many people who meditate stop before they reach the seventh chakra. They find that the sixth chakra provides them with enough openness. Some even find it difficult to proceed because their nervous system is being challenged; they are afraid to let go of control, and they are wary to trust the process. This is part of the natural fight-or-flight phenomenon we experience as human beings. In meditation, we might feel like we had enough, panic, and run away from the emotions we are confronted with. You, too, might feel triggered when you start practicing, but challenge yourself and persist. Reaching the seventh chakra is a momentous accomplishment: it allows us to build integrity and wholeness. Finding this connection is possible through meditation and contemplation. Like whispering a magic word, we can use sound currents to open the gate and connect to our crown.

Eighth Chakra: The Aura (radiance, white)
Represents: Projection and protection.

Qualities: The aura combines the effects of all the chakras and constitutes their total projection.

Shadow side: Shyness, vulnerability, being withdrawn.

The eighth chakra is also known as the aura. This is where all the effects of the other chakras are combined and funneled down into one area. If you were to float out of your physical body and observe it from afar, you would be able to see an oval or circle of light around your body. This is our aura, and it is where we hold the universal energy. Many children are able to see auras while young, but we often lose the capacity to do so by the age of seven. Once in a while, adults are able to redevelop this ability through meditation and self-awareness, but it is not that common.

When the aura is strong, negative energy is unable to penetrate through us. The other seven chakras work better, and the electromagnetic fields surrounding our bodies is more vibrant. When healthy, our auras look round and

> When the aura is strong, negative energy is unable to penetrate through us.

symmetrical. When the aura is weak, on the other hand, it loses its luster and can have various dimples or pockets in its appearance. We are also prone to feeling vulnerable to everything that passes near or within us.

Our aura gives us sensitivity, which allows us to feel connected to the universe. It is no surprise, then, that our soul enjoys the effects of being in the eighth and fourth chakras: being balanced, compassionate, and expressing love helps to lift the spirit. Our souls also benefit from the sense of vastness and impersonal reality (with me becoming we) that we experience through these two chakras.

When all chakras are aligned and functioning, your presence alone will direct energy into the universe with an effortlessness that allows you to open up spaces for your own desires and needs. When you establish trust through chakras and learn to let go of your attachments, the universe will serve you. It is what the universe, with its collective conscious, wants to do.

————

A major reason why people started meditating in its earliest conception was to achieve an inner sense of peace and deep enlightenment. They sought a way to connect to God and be closer to heaven. Progressing through the chakras was—and still remains—a method to reach this sort of spiritual enlightenment. It allows us to fully connect with ourselves and create the change in our lives that we desperately need or want, emotionally or spiritually.

In today's day and age, most people meditate to create calmness and establish clarity in their lives. Stress, anxiety, fear, and worries—which so many of us experience daily—have prompted a great percentage of the population to explore this ancient Eastern healing tradition. Stress and anxiety can be so debilitating that some people can no longer function in their everyday lives, but meditation can help. By stimulating the body and mind, we learn to adjust our emotions in a safe and healthy way. It gives us that sense of peace and enlightenment.

Because we as a society have moved so far from religion, we have lost an overall connection to a higher power. Meditation helps us to rebuild this lost relationship. Faith is an aspect in our lives that can give us foundation in everything we think, say, and act on. It also gives us a sense of security, especially when our connections to other people are lacking or even nonexistent. By grounding us, faith paves the way toward peace. In that regard, it has the very same intention as meditation: to guide us toward *good*.

Whether you practice Christianity, Islam, Hinduism, Sikhism, Buddhism, Judaism, or any other religion in the world, meditation can have a place in your life. By adapting Kundalini methods to your lifestyle, you will actually find that you can strengthen your faith. Even those who do not necessarily believe in a deity—such as atheists and agnostics—find meditation beneficial. By opening the chakras, this yogic technology enhances physical and emotional healing from the inside out. This can help *anyone* practicing meditation to reach a heightened sense of self, which includes your underlying desires and purpose in life.

The word "God" in Kundalini is an acronym for "GOD," which stands for Generate, Organize, and Deliver (or Destroy). We all have this God energy within us. We can all do good (Deliver: like service) or bad (Destroy: like wars), depending on the energy we tap into. Meditation allows you to connect to your ability to best serve yourself and others.

I once worked with a Catholic client who felt uncomfortable practicing Kundalini meditations because of the Eastern belief system. In particular, chanting Sanskrit mantras was too extraordinary for him. Because Transcendental Meditation didn't quiet his inner monologue, he found that it didn't relieve him of the pain he felt. The silence during TM actually triggered his anxiety, causing relaxation-induced anxiety. Still, I was determined to help him.

My priority in guiding him toward good health was his faith. I asked him about some of his favorite verses from the Bible, those that bring him joy and peace or otherwise make him feel calm. We discussed these verses, including their meaning and personal significance to him. Together, we decided on one that spoke to him: "I am in your hands, Lord." I asked him to recite this verse every day, out loud, for seven minutes.

A few weeks later, during one of our sessions, I decided to check up on his meditation homework. I asked him how it was going. I'll never forget the way he looked at me, with a sweet smile and hope in his eyes. "Good," he said. "I don't know how or why, but I feel different."

His reaction remains another reinforcer in why I keep encouraging people to meditate. No one can make you feel happier and at peace, or give you purpose in life, than what you can discover for yourself. The essence of God is already within you.

Since then, that client has introduced a Kundalini chant into his therapy, despite his Christian beliefs. The chant is simple, yet universal: "God and me, me and God, are one."

Chapter 3

The Benefits of Meditation

As you will learn throughout this book, Kundalini meditation and yoga can help relieve your stress and anxiety. It gives you the tools to sharpen your mind, tapping into your inner truth in order to reveal strengths and weaknesses to your conscious self. By using meditation, you can determine what thoughts and behavioral patterns are healthy and which you should alter to best support your life.

Connecting to *chitta*, the universal mind, is an important undertaking we should all work toward accomplishing. The sense of unity that it evokes brings forth an idea of mass consciousness, a collective mind that wards off feelings of loneliness. Through this, we find endurance to bend our own thoughts and feelings. We become the masters of ourselves, including all our mental processes. When we can achieve this mastery, we can find a deep form of wisdom: one that leads us down a path to the yogic view of devotion, ultimately awakening our connection to the soul.

Meditation is the process of transcending the waves of the mind, teaching it to serve our soul's consciousness. When the mind connects to the essence of our spirit in this way, we are able to live our lives through a reflection of radiance and grace. We become the best versions of ourselves, stimulating our neutral mind to help us reach our highest potential.

By using breath, sound (mantras), and body poses (mudras), Kundalini meditation gives us the ability to create harmony between body, mind, and soul. Through various yogic techniques, we can learn to vanquish the bad habits formed by unwelcome commotion in our heads by triggering old patterns of feeling or thinking and creating new neurological pathways to create change. Inevitably, this builds up our intuition to respond rather than react. Responding is when you think before you act, and reacting is when you act before you think. These new patterns established throughout meditation strengthen our mind, optimizing our understanding of life and the interconnectedness we share with the universe. This clarity results in less anxiety.

Meditation's relevance throughout history gives it credence to its endless benefits. For thousands of years, people have been practicing meditation in order to achieve calmness and clarity in life. Here is what that this ancient craft can provide for us, even in the modern age:

Enhances the Neutral Mind

Meditation activates our negative and positive mind, encouraging them to work together. This brings forth the neutral mind. When we are in our neutral mind, we are able to be an active participant in life-defining choices. This does

> Kundalini meditations allow you to be more creative in all areas of your life.

not mean that we are always aware that we are making these choices, so much so that the thoughts become distracting. On the contrary, with the neutral mind, we are more calm and relaxed. When faced with an issue, we can naturally use the neutral mind as a lens to assess the situation and choose whether or not to engage. A negative mind allows us to recognize danger, while the positive mind gives us the processing capacity to determine possible outcomes. When both minds are utilized efficiently, we are able to make decisions that are best for us during any circumstance.

The neutral mind is an especially amazing tool in your career and work decisions. Through this mind-set, you can tap into the creative mind. This builds your confidence to step outside the box. With this viewpoint, you can see new solutions to old problems. Kundalini meditations allow you to be more creative in all areas of your life, and creativity often harbors joy.

Shifts Us from "Little Me" to "Soul Me"

Especially in this modern time, we should strive to be in the Soul Self: the collective consciousness. I believe there is an inherent loneliness felt in the Western culture that is a direct result from not having this deep connection to ourselves. If we did, we would achieve Soul Self, our higher selves.

Meditation builds this relationship to the Soul Self. It takes you out of the little me and connects you to your soul me. This means that we also shift from the finite (small view) to the infinite (open and secure) view of our reality.

When we feel that deep connection to the infinite, that is the Soul Self. This is experienced through Kundalini meditation; the energy frequency that carries you throughout your day is caused by tapping into the Soul Self through mindful practice. This connection ebbs and flows like a tide, so it is important to keep practicing meditation in order to maintain clarity.

Allows Us to Understand Devotion

Your inner *bhakti*—also yogically known as devotion—is built up by utilizing Kundalini technology. This is something that is being lost in our modern society. We simply don't want to worship someone. You must remember that you are worth being adored. Kundalini gives us the confidence to embrace the concept of bhakti, which is when we bow to our highest self: the Soul Self.

Through devotion, we find the guidance to let go of self-imposed control; therefore, we become less anxious. This particular meditative step is a big aspect on the release of anxiety in all its nefarious forms. Kundalini meditation enhances our connection with devotion, instilling us with the bhakti necessary to direct us toward a life with inner and outer grace.

Creates Mental Awareness and Clarity

Part of being connected to the aforementioned Soul Self means that we have a deep understanding of ourselves and the world around us. The neutral mind—or meditative mind—is the pathway to experiencing the

Soul Self. It is a mental state that we can be in once we cultivate the relationship with ourselves and inspire inner awakening.

With all of its chants, postures, and eye focuses, Kundalini meditation holds an incredible influence over our body, mind, and soul. Through these various techniques, it guides us to live in the here and now instead of dwelling on uncontrollable circumstances.

Kundalini meditation stimulates the glands in your body, primarily those in your brain. It increases blood flow, which also brings more spinal fluid to the brain; this is scientifically said to increase memory and brain function (*Frontiers in Aging Neuroscience*, 2013). As a result, we create self-awareness and clarity through meditation. It is a natural tool to activate the mental part of us to serve the emotional part of us.

Develops Intuition

Kundalini meditation—and, in particular, eye focus—helps develop your intuition. This is the trusting instinct that will allow you to best process your life. You will intrinsically know when to make changes and how to accomplish your goals.

I am a mother, and it can be hard to disengage with my sons when they are arguing with me. Teenagers especially aren't afraid to get in your face, and because they're your children and know you better than anyone, they also know which buttons to press. Being human, I sometimes engage even when I know I shouldn't. Life can get in the way, leaving me stressed and tired and vulnerable. But I try my best to keep up through meditation, which helps restrain my tendency to get involved with an argument. This is part of intuition stepping in. I know when I am needed to step in, and I know how to set boundaries.

Releases Fears, Real or Imagined

I often say that Kundalini meditation is the cheapest therapy you will ever receive. You can meditate for free on your own, but you can even find an extremely affordable class dedicated to yogic technology. Kundalini meditation changes how we look at the past, present, and future. Not only will it change how you look at your life, it will also help heal your fears.

With anxiety, not all fear is real; some is imagined. Kundalini meditation creates a consciousness to be able to recognize what is real and what is merely a mind game (imagined fear), giving you the courage to look at your fear through a different lens. By utilizing a calmer lens to assess your thoughts and emotions, you are given the strength to conquer these fears through meditation.

Sometimes, it is difficult to be rational when we are experiencing anxiety or panic, but Kundalini meditation can give us mental fortitude. It enhances our brain's functions, giving us new tools to deal with the stress and pressures of life. We are able to develop inner stability, leading to calmness and contentment.

Resolves Core Stress and Anxiety

When we practice Kundalini meditation over a prolonged period of time, we can resolve stress and anxiety. The first step is committing to making the necessary changes in your life. This means promising yourself that you will practice daily. By altering patterns in the brain, we can shift the old patterns of stress and anxiety into something life-affirming, so it is important for you to devote yourself to regular practice.

One of my favorite benefits of Kundalini meditation is that it sparks rampant creativity inside your body, empowering you to make changes, both big and small. It directs your mind to focus on a specific task. To release and heal anxiety, you can't be afraid to get creative.

In our society, we often tell people to stop worrying or just relax. Someone suffering from stress or anxiety can't just relax, so these commands are largely ineffective. This is why Kundalini meditation is ideal for those seeking reprieve from their mental issues. It gives us the proper tools to work on ourselves; by wielding a wrench, we can fasten the bolt in our minds to make good choices. We are given the wisdom to make necessary changes in life. This makes us self-sufficient and efficient.

Changes Brain to Respond instead of React

Meditation works to activate the frontal lobe, causing us to be more responsive. When our frontal lobe is too weak or small, we tend to be more reactive; this results in hot-headedness or temperamental behavior. In some of the earliest brain scans of Buddhist monks—who meditate a lot, some even all day—it was revealed that their frontal lobes are quite large (*Proceedings of the National Academy of Sciences of the United States of America*, 2014). By stimulating our frontal lobe, we are able to be more conscious in our thought processes and actions, whereas being unconscious makes us feel out of control with ourselves.

I have found that people are more reactive in today's society than they were just forty years ago. We are losing that sense of control within ourselves, which is then expressed to society at large. By turning on the news, you can see the worldwide phenomenon of extreme reactions. This in itself can cause anxiety. Many people have told me that they've stopped watching the news altogether; it gets into their heads and threatens to distort their self-made clarity. This is why I want to teach the world to meditate: so that we can all learn to respond, instead of react, and build the collective conscious to accept mindful stability, inner peace, and happiness.

Meditation can enhance our personality by creating gray matter, which helps us to feel overall much more calm and at peace. Those Buddhist monks with the large frontal lobes were longtime meditators who were free from anxiety. Wouldn't you like to see less stress in your life too?

————

Meditation is a tool that teaches your brain to serve your higher self. If you don't train your mind to focus on your higher consciousness, then you are more likely to experience stress, anxiety, drama, trauma, fear, pain, and more. Sometimes, you might not even understand why you feel these intense emotions. You are like a chameleon and shift your colors, depending on your surroundings: the beliefs, feelings, and thoughts from the people around you. Through outside influence, you can become like the people you spend extended time with. This is why it is important to build a relationship with yourself, first and foremost. By doing so, you will be able to understand who you are, on a deep level.

By changing the structural neural pathways to interact differently, meditation creates more inner calmness and peacefulness; it instills a sense of balance within yourself. This allows you to make easier choices, be less stressed and anxious, and feel happier overall. Meditation creates space between each thought, giving you the means to improve the quality of these thoughts. It strengthens you mentally, which reflects on you, physically and spiritually.

Often, people come to me feeling demoralized because they can't shut their brains off when they try silent meditation. I explain to them that we, as human beings, are not meant to quiet our minds. The function of the brain, after all, is to think. Breathing patterns and chanting helps entertain the mind as you slow it down, giving you better insight on both the quality and quantity of your thoughts. Even if you shouldn't silence them completely, you can turn down their volume in your head. Meditation strengthens your nervous system so these thoughts are no longer overwhelming. Like our stomach, we don't want our brain's inner workings to stop, lest the contents rot. We want to digest food—or information, like thought processes—in a healthy way, so that our bodies don't have to work as hard. Working too hard for too long is what causes chronic anxiety.

Scientific research has confirmed that our DNA can be influenced and reprogrammed by the repetition of mantras, without cutting out or replacing a single gene. Vibrations from chanting create a pattern that affects the neurological pathways in the brain: hearing your own voice stimulates the hypothalamus, helping to calm you down (*Brain and Behavior*, 2015). DNA and language come from the same structure or frequency. So when we practice meditation with specific sounds and rhythms, an adjustment of our brainwaves occurs; this attunes our thought patterns to work in conjunction with our body and mind's deepest needs, directly affecting our emotions.

There are three parts to meditation that we all must follow in order to feel its total impact and reach our fullest potential. First, we must poke and provoke our minds. This is the process of getting over the hump of uncomfortable feelings, whether it's unwanted emotions brewing as a result of meditation or the odd sensation of introducing chanting into your life. The second aspect is healing. We must find peace with past events in our lives in order to make amends with ourselves, mentally. This means letting go of our attachments to a painful event, allowing us to let go of the story.

Our history will always be there, but it will no longer haunt or impact us. When we successfully accomplish this, then we can reach stage three: change. If a certain behavioral pattern is not serving you in a positive way, then your life—including all your goals and dreams—suffers as a result. Changing the patterns of how we deal with difficult experiences will help guide us into making healthy decisions in life.

Patterns are incredibly important in meditation, especially in the Kundalini technique. But it is important to reiterate that regular practice is necessary in order to see the full benefits of meditation and all that it offers. We need to continually repeat the experience to thoroughly understand its consequences, including positive results and life-affirming changes.

Eventually, if you devote yourself to the regular practice of meditation, you may even reach the *Simran* state: when the mind is continuously connected to the soul. When we reach this state, we are able to feel that life is a blessing in a continuous frame of mind.

Reaching this relationship with our mind gives us the ability to connect with the universal mind, the chitta. We feel that we are a part of everything, that the universe exists inside us as much as it exists away from us. This forges a deep and stable self-identity that serves us, opening the doors for prosperity, happiness, and fulfillment. As we practice meditation, we may experience a subtle connection that gives us greater trust in the meditative process as a whole. Over time, we will learn to feel confident about opening ourselves in such a vulnerable way because we will also feel more trusting of life. By harnessing our mind, we become more fully realized versions of ourselves and can master our reactions to life.

I caution you to always remember that it is not about controlling your mind. This is what most people try to do. In fact, throughout our lives, we try to control many things: our minds, our children, our partners, our coworkers, and so on. You must learn to let go and be observant of the experience. This will inspire calmness and a sense of peace because we garner a better understanding of the universe and its functions, including our place in it.

Wisdom is knowledge and experience. I hope that you combine the education you will receive while reading this book with the practice of Kundalini meditation and yoga. Through introspection and discovery, you will be bestowed with an unparalleled sense of wisdom—including self-worth, which will usher you away from stress and anxiety's domain.

Chapter 4

Stress versus Anxiety

The Differences between Stress and Anxiety

As you read through this book, you may notice that I often interchange the words *stress* and *anxiety*. Although the exact symptoms differ, these two states of mind are directly related to one another. I have previously mentioned how stress has become a common feeling in modern society; it is almost accepted as a natural part of life or, at least, not abnormal. While it is true that some stress is expected throughout life, the amount we face on a daily basis can leave many of us feeling debilitated. If left untreated, these feelings of worry can become anxiety.

Anxiety can be expressed in many forms, such as agitation, anxiousness, apprehension, fear, and nervousness. It is persistent, unrelenting. The anxious feeling before taking a test or delivering a presentation to your colleagues might feel intense, but for some people, those emotions don't subside after the task is completed. It's like being nervous about kissing someone for the first time and then remaining nervous for the duration of that relationship.

With stress, our anxious feelings are intense but fleeting. With anxiety, the symptoms linger, threatening our mental and physical health.

Take some time to think about the things you worry about. This might involve a paycheck that will cover the monthly rent, making sure you arrive at the theater before a play starts, or wondering if you have found the person you'd like to spend your life with. The opportunities for stress are endless. Now, write these worries down. Do they consume your thoughts to the point of being an unwelcome distraction? Do your symptoms of anxiety disappear after each event passes? Do you find yourself presently worried about a past concern?

If you still feel an inherent pressure from a worry that has already been addressed in your life, you are experiencing prolonged anxiety.

Thankfully, because you are reading this book, you are already reaching out for help. With the use of appropriate meditative tools, you can recognize and rationalize the apprehension you feel when stressed or anxious. In doing so, you can learn to tame your mind and regain a sense of control in your life.

For many of us, stress is an average daily experience, like listening to music or eating dinner. We believe our normal functions cooperate with this ongoing pressure. For certain people, that stress is actually

> For many of us, stress is an average daily experience, like listening to music or eating dinner.

embraced as positive pressure. Finishing a project an hour before the deadline, for example, might be the most efficient method for some to achieve their goals.

Stress can appear in many different ways, arriving at different points in our lives. We worry about the past and why something happened, even if it was out of our control. We worry about the present, second-guessing every decision and action we make in our lives. We worry about the future because it carries the greatest unknown of all: potential.

This kind of thought might feel normal. You might think, *By remaining on alert, I am staying on top of the issues and keeping myself protected.* In the yogic philosophy, however, we find that inhibiting your feelings with overthinking only promotes the negative—or protective—mind. While it may feel safe, this mentality of plotting and preparing for various scenarios only prevents you from living your life as intended. It generates anxiety within you because you are constantly bracing yourself to deal with possible situations. Over time, this becomes very tiring.

We all view stress differently, and consequently, we treat it differently, but we are not designed to handle the immense symptoms it can bring on a long-term basis. At a certain point, this pent-up stress will result in deep psychological and physiological consequences. We need a release.

Physical stress is different from psychological stress. Those with Type

A personalities are more likely to experience the physical disruptions caused by stress, as they are prone to high-blood pressure. With high stress levels, the body can see an increased heart rate and blood flow, causing a release of cholesterol and triglycerides in the blood. Because it increases the risk of heart attack or stroke, this physical manifestation of stress is potentially fatal.

Sudden amounts of emotional stress can trigger serious cardiac problems, like heart attacks. It can even lead to death. Stanford neuroscientist Robert Sapolsky explored this truth in his documentary, *Stress: Portrait of a Killer* (2008). For those suffering from a congenital heart problem, it is imperative to minimize stress on a day-to-day basis. It can literally be lifesaving.

Stress can also lead to dangerous habits, such as smoking and overeating. The stereotype of binging on chocolate after a breakup is not one invented from lack of circumstance. When stressed—as one might feel after a broken relationship—many of us turn to food for comfort. Sugars and carbohydrates are often our snack of choice because they stimulate serotonin (that feel-good sensation) in the brain. The sucrose in sugary and carb-laden foods also trigger the release of dopamine, which impairs our hippocampus, the section of the brain that relates to memory and communication. We might eat to forget, but ignoring our feelings by tapping out doesn't help our situation. When stressed, we need to reconnect with ourselves so that we can pinpoint the problem and fix it.

As a result of the high levels of stress and anxiety in our culture, overweight persons have a tendency to gravitate toward the wrong foods; after all, many unhealthy options are comforting to our bodies due to that aforementioned serotonin. This can cause the digestive system to incorrectly process foods. In addition to misguided food consumption, cortisol hormones released during stress affect the weight around the waist. If you want to complement a weight-loss diet and exercise routine, I would suggest incorporating meditation into your life because of its stress-lowering properties.

Gastrointestinal problems—which have become quite common in Western society—are yet another symptom of stress (*Journal of Physiology and Pharmacology*, 2011). Irritable bowel syndrome and gastro-esophageal reflux disease (also known as chronic heartburn) are exacerbated through stressful situations. When you are stressed—occasionally or regularly—a tightness is formed in the body, usually around the stomach. This aggravates your system, causing physical stress such as heartburn.

Often, doctors are unable to find a specific reason a patient is suffering from digestive issues. They try to fix the obvious, physical symptoms without exploring the underlying cause: stress and anxiety. Because stress is often a secret perpetrator, it is important to self-reflect and recognize it within yourself so that you can properly address the issue.

Another dangerous habit that is used as a temporary cure for stress is smoking. It can lead to too many various long-term problems to be a beneficial stress-relieving tool, even temporarily. (Asthma, for example, is agitated by smoke—and by stress.) I once worked with a teenaged client who had turned to cigarettes in order to feel relaxed. "It takes the edge off," he told me, waving off his habit by using the excuse that he only needed one a day.

I found this heartbreaking. Not only was this teen feeling extreme anxiety in his young life, but he also happened to be drawn toward an unhealthy intervention. I tried to get him to meditate, instead. While he enjoyed the experience when we practiced Kundalini together, he had trouble meditating on his own; like so many boys his age, he was worried about what his friends and family would think (in this instance, about the chanting). It gave me a new goal: introduce meditation to as many people as possible to create understanding and acceptance of the act.

If meditation—including the custom of chanting—was common in our society, then children and adults alike would feel more comfortable bringing this yogic technology into their lives. It would no longer feel different or strange. It is why I am so keen on bringing Kundalini Yoga to more people: together, we can create healthy habits. In doing so, we can avoid unintended consequences of a clouded mind, like the terrifying reality that the effects of stress can be transferable.

Researchers at the University of Southern California found that overly stressed parents can actually trigger asthma in their children ("Parental Stress Increases Kids' Risk of Asthma," 2009). Scientists discovered that children with self-described stressed parents were 50 percent more likely to develop asthma than children with non-stressed parents. It is just one of many reasons why pregnant women should be as stress-free as possible during pregnancy. As a mom, I know that's asking a lot out of any parent. But it is important to at least try to keep stress levels low, which is possible through the use of meditation and chanting. This will benefit both the pregnant mother and the baby growing inside her.

Stress affects more than our organs, however; it can also show on our faces.

According to Zion Market Research, the global antiaging market was estimated to be worth $140 billion as of 2015. Expensive face creams, pills promising miracles, and unsustainable diets are all methods that society promotes as quick fixes to our aesthetics. We experience immense pressure to *look* younger and healthier; actually *being* healthier is not necessarily the priority. Happily, this mentality is changing.

While it might not be an instant remedy the first time it is practiced, incorporating meditation into a lifestyle seeking to reduce the aging process would be a wise investment. Because stress also accelerates aging—just look at any US president (who receives access to some of the best doctors and health advisors) before and after their term; it is important to moderate it for permanent results. Meditation also costs far less than a trip to a cosmetic surgeon's office. In fact, meditation doesn't have to cost anything at all.

Some of the most painful consequences from untreated stress are not the physical repercussions we experience over time, however. Psychological symptoms can cause a lot of damage to ourselves and to the people around us.

In a study conducted by the University of California, Berkeley researchers found that rats exposed to chronic stress suffered from acute brain lesions due to malfunctioning stem cells (*Molecular Psychiatry,* 2014). Daniela Kaufer, UC Berkeley associate professor of integrative biology, worked with colleagues to conclude that excessive cortisol (aka the stress hormone) can hijack the body's natural fight-or-flight system. Chronic stress decreases the number of stem cells that mature into neurons, altering the connection between the hippocampus and amygdala. In doing so, it can prime the brain for later mental illness; stress becomes an expectation of our brain's inner workings.

When stress weakens and destroys stem cells, our brain's capacity shrinks. If we don't use it, we lose it; it's why people learning a new language must constantly practice their skills. Our brains are affected by the aging process, which can be accelerated through stress. As we grow older, we lose muscle mass, which affects memory and body stability. This can eventually lead to immense problems, such as Alzheimer's disease.

Stress is a real thing. It is not something to be ashamed of, nor is it an emotion that we should simply accept in our lives. Although we are unable to physically grab it, science is able to measure stress levels and determine how bodies react. Through research, we are learning more and more about the strong link between untreated stress and health problems, including anxiety and, in severe cases, depression.

Like the chicken and the egg, it is sometimes hard to determine what came first: anxiety or depression. Over time, untreated anxiety will lead to depression. But if you suffer from this heavy feeling, you don't need to feel stuck forever. Meditation can help lift you up. Even a simple breathing meditation—like Beginner's Meditation—will spark a relationship between you and your body. Through this, you can start to lower your stress and usher yourself away from the dark path of anxiety.

How Stress Can Become Anxiety

It is often difficult for people to pinpoint whether they are dealing with stress or its sinister cousin, anxiety. After all, both have many of the same symptoms, including increased heart rate, tense muscles, and rapid breathing. The easiest way to determine which affliction you might be suffering from is to note the source of your worry or fear. What causes stress is different from what causes anxiety.

To put it simply: when we are stressed, we are aware of its trigger. It could be an imminent work deadline or a sinking feeling after hearing the words "We need to talk." On the other hand, we are usually less aware of what is causing our anxiety. It is often from an internal monologue— negative self-talk like "I am stupid," "I will never get it right," or "No one loves me"—that we produce unfounded feelings of pessimism. This is a direct result from overthinking.

When using Kundalini meditation techniques, it is imperative that you understand your relationship with stress first. Because we all experience some form of stress (even from conception), I believe this book will serve everyone as a helpful guide to ease the mind, body, and soul.

Determining whether you are suffering from stress or anxiety is the first step in healing yourself. If you cannot self-reflect, then you cannot self-correct.

Although the line between the two is very narrow, there are many aspects that are different. Take a moment to reflect. Are you currently feeling stressed about something? Can you identify exactly what the source is, whether it's a tangible thing or event? If you can't, it's time to explore how anxiety is affecting your life, and it's time to work on releasing this deep manifestation of stress.

Anxiety is governed mostly by fear, which directly affects how we think and act. In order to avoid confronting this emotion, we often try to evade situations that would further aggravate our symptoms. This can cause certain people to become very dominating as they desperately try to control their environment or other people. Others turn inward as an avoidance tactic, blocking out their surroundings and relying on distractions to serve as an escape. The difference can be seen in an employee bullying coworkers into submission (pressuring them to complete extra tasks) versus employees who put their heads down and obey unauthorized orders (even if completing those orders is detrimental to their physical or mental health).

Holding this stress in your body is toxic, as it can eventually become a chronic issue. Your body learns to behave in this particular manner to temporarily make yourself feel better. Like the rats in Kaufer's experiment, your body will learn to be in a constant state of alertness, which may lead to further mental complications. When the pressure of anxiety is not released in some form, it can lead to chills, hot flashes, headaches, chest pain—and, possibly, culminate in a panic attack. If you experience any of these symptoms, it is time to find a healthy release for the stress that threatens to control you and your life.

Ask yourself: Do you feel helpless overall? Another difference between stress and anxiety is how the body can adapt to any circumstance, whether it's a physical act (pumping the brakes on a car to avoid impact) or a mental feat (preparing yourself before a job interview). When you are anxious, however, you tend to feel as if you are incapable of providing the change needed in order to neutralize the situation.

Allow me to give you a personal example:

One time when I was in Santa Barbara, California, I decided to go boating. Now, some people can tolerate being on the ocean, but I became very seasick on this particular trip. Standing on the deck of the boat, I could see the land and was desperate to get back to that solid ground. I started thinking of swimming to the shore, if only it would relieve my sickness and feelings of panic a minute sooner than actually sailing back to the marina.

Gut-wrenching fear can lead us to dangerous thoughts and actions. Riddled with anxiety, some people suffer consequences that are harmful or even deadly. If I had been a truly anxious person at the time, my fears might have been acted upon in desperation. I might have concocted various scenarios in my head: the boat sinking, an inadequate number of life-preservers, a wild storm rolling in. These all would have been a direct result of an overactive mind, prompting my body to enter into a flight response in order to avoid the stress.

Thankfully, I recognized that my experience on the boat was a tangible event that could be directly addressed. I did not try to swim back to the shore that day. Instead, using my years of meditative practice, I was able to remind myself that I needed to confront the source of my fear. I used my inner strength and diffused the stress that emerged from my seasickness. I had already established a sensation of security by the time we reached land, but I was still pretty glad that I no longer had to worry about my nausea manifesting itself.

Tapping into the spirituality of meditation does not make us immune to the potential of pain and suffering. But using meditative techniques—and incorporating mantras or hymns into self-reflection—allows us to connect to our inner, authentic soul. When we can acknowledge what we seek to feel and be our best, we can learn to cope with the ups and downs of human life (and, in some cases, the ups and downs of ocean waves).

On the outside, anxiety is silent. Those who suffer from this affliction, however, know that the symptoms can run deep—and that it doesn't leave any room for a quiet and still mind.

Some of the symptoms of anxiety can affect a person's life to the point where it is unbearable. Typical functions, like meeting friends for coffee or even reading a book, become difficult, annoying, maybe impossible. The internal thoughts are too loud.

Heart palpitations, excessive trembling and sweating, nausea and dizziness, chest pain, headaches, weakness in limbs or throughout the body, muscle tension, rashes, self-doubt after eating, and sensations of choking are all physical manifestations of anxiety. This is in addition to psychological symptoms like compulsive worrying, irrational fears, and trouble branching out socially. With so much distraction for the body and mind, it is no wonder that anxious people feel so much despair.

Unfortunately, this population is increasing, as demands and expectations grow in modern society. In a 1981 paper written after a twenty-year Kaiser-Permanente study, Dr. Nicholas Cummings concluded that 60-90 percent of all trips to the doctor's office were related to stress (*The Value of Psychological Treatment*, 2000). Today, the American Institute of Stress estimates that 75-90 percent of physician visits are stress-related, due to the different scales and degrees to which people feel its symptoms. As our knowledge and understanding of mental health grows, more tools are being discovered to help treat stress and anxiety-induced disorders.

To this day, it is not uncommon for most Western doctors to prescribe pharmaceuticals to reduce the symptoms of stress and anxiety. Feelings of self-doubt, fear, and worries can be suppressed with the use of a prescription drug, but drugs also force people to stop connecting with their feelings. These pills are essentially treated as numbing agents. For some, the symptoms can actually worsen with this chemical dependency.

More recently, some doctors are looking beyond the chemistry lab for remedies to their patients' ailments. Alternative supports—including yoga/meditation, herbal supplements, and aromatherapy—are on the rise. Studies have shown that meditation and yoga in particular cause physical changes in our bodies and brains, positively affecting our lives.

While under the influence of meditation, the brain can undergo a life-affirming transformation. This is because prolonged meditation can actually increase the volume of gray matter in our brains, as researchers at UCLA observed in a 2015 study (*Frontier Psychology*, 2015). Neuroscientist Sara Lazar—who was part of an aforementioned Massachusetts General Hospital research team at Harvard Medical School—agrees with UCLA's findings. Her team concluded that individuals who practice meditation regularly have more gray matter in the prefrontal cortex, and this matter is preserved in spite of aging. Usually our frontal cortex shrinks as we grow older, limiting our knowledge retention. Because of her study, Lazar was able to make a striking discovery: "50-year-old meditators had the same amount of gray matter as 25-year-olds" ("Meditation Not Only Reduces Stress," 2015).

These findings are invaluable because of their focus on the brain's gray matter, which is our information processing power plant. The more dense it is, the more neurons are available to store and access information. With increased gray matter, we are generally more intelligent and introspective; this self-awareness is what gives us insight. When you are dealing with stress and anxiety, it is necessary to reflect on yourself and your situation(s) in a truthful way. By being mindful of your needs, you will be able to further address them through Kundalini technology.

Meditation can also aid in physical stressors. Dr. Fadel Zeidan, assistant professor of neurobiology and anatomy at Wake Forest Baptist Medical Center, also reached powerful conclusions about meditation. In his study published in 2011, he found that "meditation reduces [physical] pain through multiple brain mechanisms" (*Journal of Neuroscience*, 2011). Not only that, but he and his team discovered that the benefits of meditation could be realized after just four days of twenty-minute practice sessions.

Alternative therapy may not be an instantaneous as a pill, but it does encourage you to have a conversation with yourself. It gives you the knowledge and understanding of what should be evaluated in your life so that you can make necessary changes. A natural approach to healing is ultimately a way to build and maintain a relationship with the inner soul. That means *you,* the authentic you. It helps you embrace a deeper and more peaceful inner feeling.

I am not saying that doctors, and even medications, should be disregarded and that natural healing tools should be used exclusively. I am simply stating that we need to acknowledge when medicine is mandatory and when it is not. For many mental illnesses, there are targeted symptoms that need to be treated; this often means changing behaviors and healing past pain.

Unfortunately, many prescription drugs for mental illnesses cover these symptoms and numb the self. Kundalini (and other meditative techniques) does the opposite: it opens us up. Occasionally, this can result in emotionally fragile states. While using Kundalini meditation, trauma can be magnified as you first become exposed to your innermost emotions. This is why I suggest having a support system, whether it is a therapist or helpful friends/family members.

While I hope you find this book useful in your daily life, do not hesitate to reach out to a licensed mental health professional if you find your emotions are too overwhelming. A therapist will be able to guide you while you work on releasing the pain felt from anxiety.

Kundalini meditation is a technology. It works on the brain, nervous system, glandular system, and even more aspects of the body. It will help support your healing process, strengthening you from the inside out.

For many, talking about your feelings isn't enough; you need to physically address them, which can be accomplished by using ancient methods of self-reflection. Certain meditation techniques—like breathing and chanting exercises—allow you to confront your issues because you are poking at your subconscious mind. This allows your mental waste to float to the top so that you can see it clearly using your neutral mind. Using this meditative mind-set, you can filter these thoughts out to find purity of the mind. From there, you can begin to heal yourself.

Different Forms of Anxiety

As touched upon earlier, anxiety is just the beginning of certain disorders. The self-doubt and subsequent hopelessness you may experience as a result of anxiety can turn into deeper issues, such as panic disorders, phobias, obsessive-compulsive behaviors, and even depression.

When your mental health affects your life so much that it is a challenge to function at work or socialize with friends and family, then it is time to evaluate what your body and mind need. Because you have picked up this book, I am assuming that stress and anxiety are affecting your life. Please know that I am proud of you for taking the initiative to seek guidance. Sometimes, admitting that you need help is the hardest step to take. It means you have incredible courage.

To best release yourself of potentially paralyzing thoughts, fears, and actions caused by anxiety, it is important to know what form you may be suffering from. When you can identify the structure of your anxiety by looking at its symptoms, you can acknowledge the triggers, determine how it manifests itself in your life, and decide how to approach the healing process.

I implore you to read about the following forms of anxiety, including generalized anxiety disorder (GAD), panic disorder, social phobia, agoraphobia, other specific phobias, post-traumatic stress disorder (PTSD), obsessive-compulsive disorder (OCD), and depression/anxiety. Even if you don't relate to all the symptoms of any single disorder, you might still find the suggested meditative tools helpful to relieve your stress and anxiety. You can find all of these meditations at the end of the book.

Generalized Anxiety Disorder

Symptoms include feeling on edge, worry, physical and mental stress, restlessness, irritation, fatigue, lethargy, low energy (even if you have slept well), tense muscles (especially in your back, neck, shoulders, and jaw), trouble keeping focused on tasks, helplessness.

Generalized anxiety disorder (GAD) is the most common mental disorder in our society, affecting millions of people of all ages, backgrounds, and economic situations. Although its symptoms are not typically constant, those suffering from GAD find that many symptoms are persistent; they appear sporadically—sometimes without a trigger—on a daily, weekly, or monthly basis.

Many people diagnosed with GAD have what is called catastrophic thinking (or haunting thoughts). This is the act of obsessing over negative, upsetting, or anxious ideas. If unaddressed, this sort of uncontrollable mental behavior can result in a multitude of other symptoms that can severely affect the quality of life.

Meditations to Help
- Silent: 4/1 Segmented Breathing Meditation Page 166
- Chanting: Anxiety Release Meditation Page 216

Panic Disorder

Symptoms include heart palpitations, hot or cold flashes, tingling sensations or feelings of numbness, depersonalization (feeling like you are outside of your own body), difficulty breathing, dizziness or light-headedness, chest pains, stomach pains, digestive issues or discomfort, continuous and unfounded worry.

It is important to note the difference between experiencing panic and suffering from panic disorders. It is natural to feel distressed if a truck approaches when you're crossing the street, but the worry normally subsides after the moment passes. Panic disorder is a debilitating form of anxiety that has such severe feelings of doom that the physical and mental symptoms are life-threatening. Some people are in a constant state of panic, part of an everyday life where helplessness abounds.

At times, physical symptoms—such as ear pressure, headaches, or stomach pain—can trigger the mental symptoms of a panic attack (worry, fear, catastrophic thinking). When there is no explanation for a new bodily sensation, a doom-and-gloom reaction can quickly set in, exacerbating the feeling of an attack. The symptoms of panic disorder are often not clearly observable when seeking medical attention, making it difficult to properly diagnose.

Meditations to Help
- Silent: 4/4 Segmented Breathing Meditation Page 168
- Chanting: Master's Touch Meditation Page 226

Social Phobia

Symptoms include hopelessness, fear of unfamiliar people or situations, excessive worrying over being watched and judged by others (friends and strangers alike), overwhelming anxiety or fear in any social situation, severe fear of public speaking, anxiousness while merely thinking of being involved in a social situation, fear about meeting new people or speaking up when in a group.

Those with social phobia will avoid many typical events in life—like large gatherings of people (weddings, conventions, concerts)—due to excessive, irrational fear of social situations. The anxiety is so intense that socializing is shunned or pared down significantly, eventually developing into avoidance behaviors that can negatively impact life.

Social phobia is different from feeling nervous before public speaking or feeling shy when meeting someone for the first time, both of which are common occurrences. Rather, people with social phobia view public settings as especially distressing. There is an obsession with feeling judged, in particular, and being regarded by others in a negative light. While most people would feel briefly embarrassed if they tripped and fell in a crowd, people with social phobia would actively avoid socialization altogether due to a potential, imagined fear of being relentlessly mocked and ridiculed.

Meditations to Help
- Silent: Negative Mind Meditation Page 160
- Chanting: Inner Conflict Resolver Page 178

Agoraphobia

Symptoms include intense fear of socializing (in groups or individually), severe stress when leaving your comfort zone or routine, severe stress when feeling out of control in your environment, obsession with self-protection from external harm (with no sign of danger).

For many people, having a set routine in life is a daily comfort, and that is perfectly acceptable, as long as trying new foods, meeting new people, or traveling to new destinations doesn't cause a crippling fear. Those with agoraphobia are so fearful of new experiences that they become imprisoned within themselves; stepping outside of the established routine or safe place is impossible because of all the uncontrollable variables they might encounter.

It is not uncommon for a traumatic event to prompt agoraphobia, a form of anxiety especially seen in adults. That is why those suffering from agoraphobia often don't want to leave their own home; doing so might result in fear and panic due to the loss of control felt from losing the attachment of the safe place. If you have a severe case of agoraphobia, I recommend that you use this book in conjunction with a therapist or psychiatrist for optimal results.

Meditations to Help
- Silent: Meditation for Beginners Page 158
- Chanting: Master's Touch Meditation Page 226

Specific Phobias

Symptoms include excessive and constant fear of specific situations or events, terror when confronted or dealing with the phobia (and an inability to control this fear), avoidance behavior to negate the chance of confronting the phobia, restricting life due to internalized fears.

Phobias are intense feelings of fear due to made-up beliefs about situations, people, events, or objects. The catastrophic thinking associated with GAD is amplified, causing "What if?" scenarios—which have no real proof or basis—to overrule rational thought. Like those with social phobia and agoraphobia, phobic people avoid situations that might present a trigger.

Phobias can come in many forms; a common example is arachnophobia, or a fear of spiders. While many people don't like spiders, they can continue living their lives even with the possibility of encountering one while on a walk outside. An arachnophobe, on the other hand, might refuse a nature hike on the chance that they might see a spider, even if there is no threat. With training, those diagnosed with specific phobias can live a manageable life, with no disruption from their distrust of specific places, things, or events.

Meditations to Help
- Silent: Breath of Fire with Lions Paws Page 192
- Chanting: Keeping you Steady and on the Path Page 210

Post-Traumatic Stress Disorder

Symptoms include replaying/reliving the trauma (emotionally and physically), anxiety that the event will happen again, trigger responses that intensify fear (can be noises or a familiar setting that can set off a replaying of the event), emotional disruptions (constant upsetting thoughts, which cause a disinterest or detachment to good feelings), quick to anger.

Post-traumatic stress disorder (PTSD) is commonly seen when talking about war veterans; however, it can also stem from physical or emotional abuse, witnessing a traumatic event, or experiencing some kind of severe pain. Similar to those suffering from phobias, many with PTSD have "What if?" thoughts and emotions. Living in fear of the trauma happening again, people with PTSD construct avoidance behaviors to build a shield around themselves for protection.

Sometimes, past trauma doesn't affect a person until years after the event, which can be very confusing. PTSD can be aggravated with time as pent-up pain and exposure to triggers prompt the trauma to surface once again. The mind is not unlike a pressure cooker in that way. Often, those with PTSD feel guilt or shame about the upsetting event they experienced, so they close themselves off. Thinking they will be misunderstood, they remain silent about their struggle, which further establishes isolation and a keen sense of loneliness.

When you witness or experience a traumatic event, it is important to talk about how you feel. A conversation establishes a connection with the self and with others, neutralizing the sensation of feeling alone or helpless. With time, talking and listening also helps to relieve the painful occurrence. Because it is such a serious affliction that can lead to depression, those with PTSD should seek professional support to best release their stress and anxiety.

Meditations to Help
- Silent: 8/8 Segmented Breathing Meditation Page 174
- Chanting: Gunpati Meditation Page 222

Obsessive-Compulsive Disorder

Symptoms include feeling out of control, consuming thoughts or fears that cannot be shaken off and therefore cause disruptions in life, obsessive worrying, compulsive behavior, repeated uncontrollable actions (behavior patterns that briefly suppress worry and anxiety).

Obsessive-compulsive disorder (OCD) is a behavior disorder that is often self-diagnosed based on high-strung actions. The "gotta make things right" sensation of organizing a closet by color or fixing a photo frame brings instant gratification to most. Someone with OCD, however, would remain unsatisfied even after the fix. It is normal to be concerned about a burglary, for example, but people with OCD behavior would lock and check the car door five times as part of a set routine before stepping away from their vehicle. Distress would overshadow rational emotions if this pattern was not followed each time they locked their car.

While obsessions and compulsions are similar, they are not the same. Obsessions are thought-oriented. This is when a haunting thought creates fearful or negative emotions that can't be explained or stopped. It culminates in powerlessness. Compulsions, on the other hand, have to do with behavior. It feels like a certain act *has* to be performed in exactly a certain way. This action is perceived to be unavoidable, even when acknowledged as irrational, resulting in helplessness. Those with OCD do not necessarily experience both symptoms, though it is common.

Meditations to Help
- Silent: Mental Control Meditation Page 182
- Chanting: Laya Yoga Kundalini Meditation Page 224

Depression/Anxiety

Symptoms include excessive worry, physical and mental stress, restlessness, irritation, helplessness.

Not everyone who experiences anxiety also suffers from depression, but those who are depressed often have symptoms similar to an anxiety disorder. This includes nervousness, finding it difficult to focus or concentrate, irritability, and difficulty sleeping. Although similar, each has their own emotional and behavioral symptoms.

When you suffer from depression/anxiety, the two illnesses become blurred. It might be hard for someone to differentiate which state they are experiencing, but this confusion happens often. In fact, many doctors prescribe antidepressants to those with acute anxiety because its symptoms present as depressive. Because it is hard to find a sense of control in life (including thoughts and feelings), those with anxiety often feel that distinct melancholy that depression evokes.

Meditations to Help
- Silent: Sodarshan Chakra Kriya Page 206
- Chanting: Kirtan Kriya Meditation Page 204

Chapter 5

Society's Contributions to Stress and Anxiety

The Fight-or-Flight Response

All animals—including human beings—are born with a tool to deal with stress: the fight-or-flight response. This natural response releases adrenaline into our bodies, which can be liberating and even addicting. It is a feeling that humans adore and sometimes seek out, such as through the act of riding a thrilling roller coaster or hiding under the covers during a horror movie. Understanding the intricacies of the fight-or-flight response is important if you want to understand how stress and anxiety can negatively affect us in the modern world.

The control board for the body consists of two parts: the central nervous system (the brain and spinal cord) and the peripheral nervous system (consisting mainly of nerves). By working together, humans are able to operate multiple bodily functions at the same time, like breathing and walking simultaneously (or practicing mudras and mantras in harmony). Our peripheral nervous system is further broken down into the somatic nervous system (voluntary actions and reflex movements) and autonomic nervous system (involuntary actions; bodily functions like breathing and the heartbeat).

When a person becomes afraid, their brain is alerted. The autonomic nervous system begins to work with the endocrine system, which includes the adrenal gland (the organs above the kidneys), in order to be aroused. They will then begin to breathe heavily and sweat more profusely. As their heartbeat increases, they might start to tremble as well. Because this reaction is for survival, the excess blood within the cerebral cortex is directed to outer body parts for energy. This preparation for fight-or-flight is caused by the hormones released from the adrenal gland: norepinephrine and epinephrine (aka adrenaline).

Epinephrine prepares us for exertion as the blood pumps through our bodies at an increased rate. This fight-or-flight response was once necessary to humankind, in days when we were faced with predator attacks or other dangerous predicaments; we had to make decisions and act on them with great speed. Nowadays, humans don't need this instinct as often as our ancestors. Despite that, it has stuck with our biology throughout time.

While the release of adrenaline can still be beneficial (allowing one to become alert in times of crisis), too much of it can lead to negative consequences. If an excess of epinephrine is released in a short period of time, it can increase our stress levels. In the long run, this can lead to severe health problems, including high blood pressure. Because our early ancestors were much more physical, they often worked off the adrenaline released into the body in a natural manner; exertion through fighting or hunting was enough to burn off the hormone. In our current technological world, many people do much less physical, dangerous, or stressful work. Adrenaline often remains fixed within our bodies, resulting in side effects like insomnia, stress, and anxiety.

In small doses, we can find pleasure in the release of adrenaline, much like that of serotonin, which controls mood. The issue in today's world is that we experience this stress reaction weekly (or even daily). Although we typically do not encounter animals that are threatening to us, we now deal with problems such as rush hour traffic or a dispute with a partner. Instead of using exertion to deal with the release of epinephrine, however, humans now tend to become more aggressive, resulting in an even more stressful situation.

Adrenaline brings us to our most pure, primitive state: the fight-or-flight response. It is an innate reaction built within us, normal and necessary for survival. We have a natural dependency for some stress in our lives. The problem is that our bodies do not understand that many of our worries in the modern age are mostly mind games; we often make up thoughts about a situation based on our biased interpretation, which may not always be correct. We have deep physiological reactions due to the fight-or-flight response, affecting how we handle our stress on both a physical and an emotional level. We get too into our heads and cannot find the proper method to release the hormones caused by stress. This is where meditation can help.

Meditation encourages our minds to relax, compelling our bodies to back down from the stressful fight-or-flight response in a healthy, gentle manner. It works with the mind to power through past pain—including thoughts and feelings—by creating a sense of inner depth and understanding with the self.

Using aspects of Kundalini technology (such as posture, eye focus, mantras, and breathing patterns), we can train our bodies to release specific emotions (such as worry, fear, and anxiety) by decreasing the epinephrine in our systems. This cathartic yogic tool is an invaluable form of therapy for many, and it is a much safer way to relieve ourselves of our suppressed adrenaline than our ancestors' method of running away from a sabertooth tiger.

Managing Life with Constant Stimuli

In the modern world, we constantly seek ways of improving our lives. From securing the latest high-tech gadgets to buying off-season fruits and vegetables, we know what we want in life in order to make us happy (or at least we think we know).

Don't get me wrong: I, too, enjoy many of the new and improved aspects of life, such as the convenience of smartphones and airplanes. Whether I'm traveling for pleasure or to spread the good word of Kundalini Yoga and meditation's benefits, being able to fly around the world in a plane is an amazing privilege I have access to in this modern age.

However, I am also aware that all of this comes at a cost. The overabundance of stimulation affects us in a negative way. The saying "Everything in moderation" is not a cliché; it is a mantra worth applying to all aspects of your life. After all, even consuming too much water can cause hyponatremia (a severely low level of sodium in the blood) and be fatal. If an excess of our very own life source can be detrimental to our health, then so can the constant and varying stimuli we face every single day. Indulge only in moderation.

Feeling pressured that we need something—the latest fashionable shoes, a pill advertised on TV—causes us to experience more stress. By obtaining whatever it is that we desire, we believe that we will be able to manufacture happiness. Psychologists Tim Kasser and Michael M. Ryan talked about this in the *Journal of Personality and Social Psychology*. In a 1993 study called "A Dark Side of the American Dream," these two researchers found that individuals who had a priority for acquiring wealth or notoriety were less happy than individuals whose goals focused on self-acceptance and stronger community affiliation.

Notoriety is an especially prevalent aspiration among modern society, evidenced through the widespread desire of attaining popularity on the internet (whether through a viral video or followers on social media). Artist Andy Warhol warned us about this epidemic in 1968, ruminating, "In the future, everyone will be world-famous for fifteen minutes." It seems he was right: nowadays, many people aspire to create those fifteen minutes in their lives, but it comes with a cost.

A 2017 study published in the *American Journal of Epidemiology* discussed how social media in particular can compromise our well-being. "We found that the more you use Facebook over time, the more likely you are to experience negative physical health, negative mental health, and negative life satisfaction," concluded Holly Shakya, social media researcher at the University of California, San Diego. When we compare our lives— or "lack thereof"—to the perceived wonderful lives of others, our negative mind is triggered.

For some, this overconsumption of social media can lead to stress and even anxiety. Another 2017 study looked specifically at eighteen- to twenty-two-year-olds and how social media influenced their lives. Researchers concluded that higher (daily) social media use directly correlated with "greater [...] anxiety symptoms and an increased likelihood of having a probable anxiety disorder" (*Journal of Affective Disorders*, 2017). This, they argued, could sometimes be the result of cyberbullying. In fact, it has been observed that cyberbullying on social platforms like Facebook can activate our physiological stress response (*Cyberpsychology, Behavior, and Social Networking*, 2011), which can result in fight-or-flight.

Valuing wealth, status, or material goods over relationships (both with the self and with others) is an unhealthy mentality to have, in part because it can never be appeased; there will always be a "Fear Of Missing Out" (aka FOMO) by not satisfying these wants. It is like trying to fill a bucket with a hole on the bottom: it will never be full. We will always be searching for the latest and greatest. We want that supersized satisfaction and instant gratification.

When we feel miserable, we want a doctor to prescribe us medication to make the pain go away as quickly as possible. But despite the medical breakthroughs of certain medications, we are more unhappy than ever. (In a 2015 study published in the journal *Social Psychology and Personality Science*, researchers looked at the surveys of 1.3 million Americans and found that people over thirty were less happy in the 2010s than other adults in previous decades.) With the tools that I know and trust through Kundalini, I have to wonder why more people don't want to spend time with themselves in order to self-heal. Part of what is wrong with our society is that we have lost the art of patience.

It takes a musician—even someone with extraordinary talent—hours of practice in a single sitting to be able to perform at

> What could I feel instead of stress and anxiety?

Carnegie Hall in New York City. The time and dedication these artists spend on their craft is astonishing, and it should be inspiring to us all. We need to have that same drive within us to rid ourselves of the stress and anxiety that haunt our lives. We need to dedicate time to ourselves, and we need to exercise patience as our bodies learn to heal. And in the meantime, we can focus on the pockets of happiness in life as we begin to build contentment within the self.

Maybe it helps to have a passion to turn toward, like the musician at Carnegie. Ask yourself, What could I feel instead of stress and anxiety? What do I want to fill my life with, instead of this dread? Recognizing your strengths and interests will allow you to direct your attention to healthy life goals. Put in the effort to peel back your own layers; you will discover that you have the guts within you to open yourself up for real change.

This sort of introspection can be a difficult process for many. Finding the courage to seek help is an enormous step, and so is the self-reflection required in order to challenge stress and anxiety. I understand if your pain or anger or confusion makes it seem impossible to move forward in life, but I promise you, it *is* possible. I know this from personal experience.

I have been practicing Kundalini meditation my entire life, and I know that I would be lost if I hadn't followed this spiritual path. The times I have strayed caused enough grief to remind me that it is a journey worth following. Maintaining the routine of meditation eventually gave me a sense of inner strength to face life, and I have maintained this strength. This is because I was pushed to sit with myself on a constant basis. I got to *really* know myself. You can do this too. Just be kind and patient with yourself, and trust the process of self-discovery.

You are bombarded with constant stimuli—cell phones, television, traffic—every waking moment of your life. Without realizing it, these stimulants might have already affected you in a negative way. You might find that you're already prone to seeking out distractions for your mental anguish. Checking out by mindlessly watching television or using the computer every night might sound harmless, but it can hurt relationships with other people as well as yourself, including your inner creativity.

This particular form of distraction is a distinctly difficult dilemma to deal with because many people use these mediums a way to decrease their stress levels. I often hear from teenagers who tell me that they will watch something on an electronic device when they feel they cannot fall asleep. I am sure many adults do the same. Maybe you do, too.

Burdened with stress and anxiety, you turn toward various forms of entertainment to unwind from the day. This is not bad behavior to indulge in occasionally. But it does aggravate the issue when you start to depend on these external factors to treat the stress and anxiety in your life. They are only temporary amusements and cannot give you the proper support that your body requires for good, stable mental health.

I am not discouraging outside stimulation of all kind; it is not always bad or hurtful to you and your life. However, if you seek additional stimulation to check out from stress and anxiety on a constant basis (e.g., daily or nightly), then it becomes a problem. You lose your sense of self. Eventually, you might find that you feel distant from the people you love; you might even feel distant from yourself. You may wonder what happened to spur this disconnect. Feeling lost and bewildered, any mental anguish you've previously suffered from might become agitated. Your anxiety can increase, you may become more frustrated, and your overall health will deteriorate.

If you are already under duress, turning toward something like social media can exacerbate your stress or anxiety levels. Its intended use may be as a coping mechanism for stress when, in actuality, social media engagement can result in feelings of inadequacy, uncertainty, and a pressure to validate your self-worth. There is a natural inclination to compare your life with the lives you see on a screen, lives that seem bigger, better, happier, and more fulfilled. You may feel you need to catch up to the lavish, upbeat lifestyles seen on the web.

There are so many things you could be doing instead of scrolling through your social media feeds: baking with friends and family, going on a walk with your dog, learning how to play an instrument. Reading a book or watching a movie can be a great source of pleasure, too, as long as you don't leave your mind in the artificial worlds that are presented through fiction. Similarly, in moderation, social media can still be a great method of communication and connecting with other people. Just remind yourself that posts and pictures shared on social networks are edited articles of someone's life. We are often seeing "the best of," the highlight reel. As such, it will always be unfair to compare your life to another person's, even when theirs is perceived to be perfect. It is important to be mindful of your own happiness in life. Take a moment to count your blessings.

Remain aware of what is important to you—including relationships, a good job, material goods you already possess—and remember to focus on how these aspects in your life bring you joy. This reflection will help you appreciate all that you have. Not only will this neutralize the craving to obtain more, but it will also help bring contentment to your life. Meditation can give you the clarity to achieve this awareness, guiding you toward peace by building a connection within yourself and a relationship with the self. You will ultimately find that you are less inclined to turn toward distractions for stress and anxiety. Instead, you will turn to yourself.

By turning inward, you can discover that you are an indomitable spirit; you have the capability to enact change in your life. Your body, after all, was made to handle mental crises. Remember the fight-or-flight response: we have a dependency on stress and an urgency to relieve our systems of suppressed adrenaline. Using meditation can harness your mind and encourage it to serve you. In doing so, you purify your body of toxins formed by stress and anxiety.

I would like you to reflect on the following questions, writing down answers in your journal as you view helpful:

Are you in a relationship? When you come home from work every day, do you check out on an electronic device (the television, computer, smartphone)? If so, how does this affect your intimate relationship? Do you feel close to your partner? Do they feel close to you? If you are stressed, do you confront the issue with your partner in an attempt to help them understand? If so, do you find that this helps or hinders your healing process?

Do you have children? If so, how close do you feel to them? Do they see you relaxing with an electronic device? Are they cognizant of your anxiety or stress? If so, are they also afflicted by stress? Do they also use electronics as a method to check out? How do you think your behavior affects them, whether in a negative or positive way?

Children learn by example. Unfortunately, many of us don't know how to relax in a manner that is best for our bodies, minds, and souls. We pass these unhealthy habits to our own offspring, which has caused a mental health crisis among children. It saddens me to see so many youths who feel paralyzed in their lives, unable to cope with social issues, family issues, or school. As a result, they form unmanageable stress and anxiety at very young ages. As many as 44 percent of children ages eight to twelve experience stress, according to the American Psychological Association's 2009 survey on stress in America ("APA Study Raises Concern," 2009).

Hope is not lost, however. Another reason why I love meditation is that it gives me the tools to relax, recharge, and heal, which I have helped pass onto the next generation. You have this capability, too. If you are a parent, it is your responsibility to be a positive influence for your children. They are, after all, a reflection of you. Start practicing healthy life habits, and your children will follow in your path.

Take one of my sons as an example. My family is not free from the weight of stress and anxiety just because I practice and promote Kundalini meditation. My son has experienced his own inner pain and depression, which caused me to work very closely with him and his use of meditation. In the times I haven't been physically available for him (often because of my travels), my husband and my mother have both sat with my son to work through his troubles. He probably wouldn't have done this on his own, and it's not because he's a rebellious teenager; it's because young people his age often don't know what to do or how to help themselves. As adults, we have to step in and teach them. We teach not only by sharing self-healing methods with them but by practicing what we preach and acting as positive role models.

Real-World Applications of Meditation

Whether we've burnt our toast in the morning rush or are dealing with a loved one's terminal health diagnosis, we experience various degrees of stress in our lives on a daily basis. How we handle this stress greatly determines how we handle our lives in general, including the decisions we make and actions we take. You can see why having a clear and levelheaded outlook is important: it allows us to respond coherently rather than react irrationally.

Anyone can meditate. Better yet, anyone can meditate *anywhere* at *any time.* If you feel that you need a moment to yourself, then take a moment. Because it is an internalized act that can take as little as three minutes, no one should be inconvenienced by you recharging yourself. Like a new update on your smartphone, you'll actually be able to function better if you give yourself the time to tap into yourself, clear your mind, and refocus your energy. Any of the meditations provided at the end of this book can help you recharge.

One aspect of our lives we often overlook as being a source of major stress and anxiety is travel. Whether we are flying eight hours for an international vacation or driving forty minutes to work each day, travel can be extremely strenuous. Over time, this pent-up stress can turn into body anxiety that hinders you from fully relaxing. Luckily, as I said, meditation can be practiced anywhere: in an airport, on public transit, at work, and in the comfort of your home. You can even utilize Kundalini technology in the car; chanting helps to support an overactive mind, which is helpful if you are an anxious driver.

Many years ago, I worked with a pilot. He came to me filled with stress because of his chaotic schedule and the anxiety that formed from flying all the time. I learned from him that many pilots suffer from anxiety and even depression. He alerted me to the natural phenomenon of cosmic radiation, which aircrew are exposed to at nearly double the levels we experience on the ground. NASA recently researched the effects cosmic radiation has on humans, which includes DNA breakdown and the production of free radicals ("NASA Studies Cosmic Radiation," 2017). In my eagerness to ease this pilot's mind, I taught him the Kirtan Kriya meditation. He later reported back to me that it actually helped.

A good family friend turns to pranic breathing—an energizing breathing technique that focuses on rhythm and retention—to assist in her stress. She has a teaching career in Asia and often has to hop on a plane and cross many time zones. This, of course, comes with a price: jet lag. My friend has shared that the Breath of Fire Meditation aids her in the preparation of changing times.

Breath of Fire is a fast-paced breathing exercise that is often used in Kundalini Yoga. It asks you to inhale and exhale powerfully through the nose—using your diaphragm muscle—while the mouth remains closed. It cleans the blood and rejuvenates the body, so it is perfect for travelers. While on a flight, my friend will visit the bathroom every two to three hours and practice Breath of Fire for three minutes. When she lands, she will practice again for another twenty minutes. She swears that it grounds her (no pun intended).

There may be times when you are not at home and find that you need to meditate. As long as you can find the strength to listen to your conscious self, it doesn't matter where you practice meditation. Even crowded situations or noisy settings can provide opportunities for you to check into yourself. (I never let a middle seat on a plane deter me from meditating.) Don't be shy to practice anywhere—even in public spaces— if you feel you need to calm your mind. If you find outside influences distracting, treat them as a challenge as you try focusing on your breath, the mantra in your head, or the mudra of your hands. These are all tools that can help bring you back to *you*.

Sometimes, those outside influences need to be addressed and tamed in your mind so they don't become distractions, like when you're at work and want to be productive.

Meditation can help with a world of problems that we encounter every single day as we operate in the real and complex modern world. One of the biggest aggravators of stress is career-oriented. A huge aspect of our culture is our status in society, which includes not just having a job but making a career out of it. We are often viewed by our occupational success.

Our careers are determined by our drive for stability, identity, adventure, and (of course) money. Whether we are out in the workforce or raising children at home, we yearn to have a profession that enriches our lives. Even when we have our dream job, however, stress can threaten to throw us off course by diluting our confidence. A baker might achieve her dream of opening a cupcake shop, only to find the workload overwhelming. The stress can cause a backlog of problems, both within the workplace and within the spirit. It can discourage you, making you feel as if you are inadequate or incapable, despite your hard work.

As I mentioned in the history of Kundalini, its meditation techniques are meant for the householder. People who actively engage within society, functioning in a job and interacting with peers, can benefit from this yogic tool. When you engage with the real world, you want to operate from a place of stability, strength, and vitality. By channeling your inner frequency (through the use of breathing patterns and chanting), meditation can provide you with the support you need in your career, especially creative support.

Stress and anxiety are by-products from life and its experiences. Your career in particular is a huge influencer on your inner self; it is a symbiotic relationship that needs to be taken care of for optimal performance. By maintaining your level of stress and anxiety, you become better at your job. It gives you direction. All it takes is some time to stop, sit, and meditate.

When I started teaching live Kundalini meditation classes on Facebook, I encouraged people to pause their lives for a moment and join me for a short lesson. For seven to ten minutes, I wanted them to reconnect with themselves via meditational exercises before moving on with their lives, whether they were in their offices or at home. Folks who tried this little break have told me how much they love it because they tend to be more productive and calmer as an immediate result.

By realigning ourselves through meditative healing techniques, we can become more proficient at work. But it can do more than that. We can also become better parents (as suggested above by being a positive influence to our children), and we can also strengthen our romantic relationships.

I believe in the yogic marriage perspective: that it is the unification of two bodies into one soul. If one person changes in any way, then the other person will also shift. Unfortunately, that means that if you really want to work on yourself yet your partner refuses to engage, then your relationship may suffer. It may even end due to the lack of cohesion.

If you find this distance happening to you, I want to reassure you that it is not shameful. Relationships are all about growth, which takes the action of two separate and consenting people to achieve. We often believe that our relationships are meant to last forever, but I don't believe this to be true. In fact, it could be your relationship that is leaving you stressed and filled with anxiety. Luckily, meditation is a handy tool that can give you clarity. By instilling you with inner wisdom—which includes all of your experiences and knowledge—you can ask yourself which changes are necessary in your relationship and have the understanding to make those changes in a healthy way.

The topic of handling relationships could be an entire book on its own. If you are interested in seeking more information on this subject, I recommend Terrence Real's book, *The New Rules of Marriage.* It will offer you guidance and support in your relationship, giving you the tools to be a more conscious partner. I have studied with Terry for over five years and find that his philosophies are very much in alignment with Kundalini relational beliefs.

As for me, I have been married for over twenty-two years. I know, without a shadow of a doubt, that my own practice of Kundalini meditation has saved our marriage. It has helped me become a less insecure and reactive person. When I was a newlywed at twenty-three years old, I was a nagging wife who felt very insecure. But meditation helped me rediscover my own self, quieting my fears so that I could heal myself. It increased my inner awareness and, thus, my own power. It gave me confidence. I learned to stop looking for my husband to be everything to me; instead, I learned to complete myself.

Chapter 6

Thinking Differently about Stress and Anxiety

How Thoughts Control Our Stress Levels

Many years ago, I had the opportunity to take a wonderful course about cognitive behavioral therapy (CBT) from David D. Burns, MD. During the lesson, he drove home the concept that your thoughts create your emotions because of one simple fact: your thoughts *influence* your emotions. Because influence is such a powerful tool, utilizing different CBT interventions can actually change your thoughts and self-beliefs.

Not surprisingly, this inspired me. After all, due to the teachings of Kundalini technology, I've known all my life that our thoughts are a by-product of life and that they do not necessarily represent who we truly are. I know, from my own positive influence on myself, that we can alter what we believe to be true. Actively experiencing this radical notion of self-control is visceral and addictive. Because our body has a physical reaction to intentionally altered thoughts, we—as human beings—become fixed on this potential.

When you can see how you think, then you can change how you think. Journaling is a major component in training your mind because it allows you to physically see your thoughts and feelings. This is why I encourage you to document your spiritual discoveries as you embark on your meditative journey. By seeing your thoughts, you are wholly acknowledging them. This is when you can challenge yourself.

This challenge comes in the form of self-reflection. It might be difficult at first, but it is why I love meditation so much. It allows us to see our authentic selves, including the damaged parts that need repairing. It is similar to CBT because you must work on changing your thinking by actively reflecting on the self. Through this yogic process—incorporating chanting, mudras, eye focus, and a goal—you can metamorphosis to a fully aware state of mind. This gives you inner security.

Seizing this opportunity for change, we can lean away from the oppression of stress—an oppression that can be so heavy, it can be life-threatening. This is supported by American neuroendocrinologist Robert Sapolsky, who has explored the impact stress can have on the human body. I often recommend his short documentary, *Stress: Portrait of a Killer*, to my clients to encourage them to lower their stress levels (with the use of meditation, of course).

According to Dr. Sapolsky, our thoughts are so powerful that our bodies—including our organs and glands—react to them as if they are real. Our thoughts can create a belief that we are in danger, causing our bodies to spring into action through the fight-or-flight response. If not properly regulated, this can lead to anxiety and panic.

With our overactive thought processes, we are constantly creating new realities in our minds. Think of how we recall memories. Each time we think back on an experience or a person or a favorite meal, we subconsciously go back to the original event or memory and craft a new narrative based on what we remember in that moment. Moods can shift our outlooks, which may cause a detail in the memory to be remembered, altered, or forgotten altogether. Our memories, therefore, are never quite identical.

As human beings, so much of what we do, say, and think is influenced by feelings and memories, especially as we grow older. When we are younger, we usually don't think in remembrance; we are in the here and now. It's a wholesome perspective that is, sadly, lost over time as our experiences start to fabricate our essence. We begin to form expectations of ourselves, generally based on our peers. This phenomenon is particularly evident in teenagers, who often feel as though they need to gather as many life experiences as quickly as possible.

With an enormous amount of pressure to grow up faster, deep anxiety can settle into impressionable youths who do not fit the expected mold. I once worked with a client—a teen girl—who felt confused and anxious because she did not see herself like her peers. A lot of her friends were having sex, but she didn't feel the same desire to be sexually active. As a result, she felt as if something was wrong with her.

This young woman asked me, "Why aren't I like the other girls?" It was heartbreaking to hear her question herself in such a way, and I became determined to help her find her voice.

We spoke about the process of life and slowing down; adulting can come later. I also addressed social pressures and societal issues, hoping to wean her away from her self-made expectations that caused stress and anxiety. It was important for me to armor her with confidence and strength so that she could stand by her beliefs rather than idly stand aside in doubt.

To create an internal shift toward her own untapped power, I taught her the Me within Me meditation: "Me within me is the purity. Me within me is the reality. Me within me is the grace. I am the master of the space." My words could offer love and support, but the deep healing that she required had to be created from within herself. Establishing internalized patterns through yogic techniques, her mind strengthened and her principles became unfettered. By achieving that internal shift, she was able to discover her self and support her thoughts with fearlessness.

As a parent, I believe that self-reliance is one of the most important qualities we can teach our children. Because it sharpens our mind's response mechanism, learning how to be self-soothing during life's biggest obstacles is an invaluable lesson. Who we are as a person is reflected in the way we react or respond to negative experiences. In the case of my client, her feelings of inadequacy led her to stress and anxiety; left untreated, this could have been wildly damaging to her psyche and mental health in the long term.

Kundalini meditation helps to broaden our understanding of the self, including what our authentic self is experiencing throughout life. By tapping into this true identity, we become instilled with clarity and a newfound sense of reality. This gives us the courage to truly *live*.

Controlling Thoughts through Meditation

In my eighteen years as a therapist, I have encountered more clients who wish to change and heal themselves than anything else. They come to me with great expectations, hoping that a professional will be able to give them the tools or wisdom to generate change in their lives. Psychotherapy is primarily about talking; through this method, my clients can process and understand the thoughts in their heads in relation to their lives. They can see what is working and what is not. Meditation gives clarity to these thoughts so that appropriate changes can be made. It teaches your mind to serve you, rather than being commanded by your thoughts.

I often tell my clients that we make up about 98 percent of what we think (I don't say 100 percent because there is always someone willing to challenge me). Of course, some of our thoughts are fact-based—scientific studies included in this book, for example—and those are real. The thoughts that are created from the experiences around you, however, can be skewed with bias and ultimately alter your perception of reality.

Our feelings come from our interpretation of the situation we are faced with. Within a nanosecond, we make up in our minds and we react with our feelings. Remember: even our memories can be falsely recalled. As a result, it is hard for some people—especially those with clouded minds due to mental disorders—to determine what is authentic and what is a fabrication in their lives.

Terry Real, founder of Relational Life Therapy (RLT), discussed the breakdown of reality in *The New Rules of Marriage*. Conflicts happen between couples because of a disruption in the cycle of communication, a six-step process in polishing and clearly delivering your intended message. When this occurs, we often jump to conclusions of what we believe the other is thinking or wanting. A common example of this is when one skeptical partner accuses the other of cheating, an opinion that might have been pre-established based on a hunch but was bias-confirmed because of a glance that lingered a second too long.

You must understand that you can create your own reality, but this is not always good or healthy. When thinking a thought, your body learns to behave as though that thought is real. This can lead to dire consequences if you allow your negative thoughts to take control of your mind. If you are experiencing this, find solace in the fact that it is not a lost cause. You can still take back the reins of control and fix your mind. Take me and my young marriage, for example.

When I was newly married, I was worried that my husband was

attracted to other women. My brain started to form scenarios of this potential, which haunted me. These images would play in my head like a broken record, over and over again. It caused such a visceral reaction in me that I could feel it in my gut. It resonated throughout my body. Everyone speaks of the direct relationship of the gut to the mind (that "follow your instinct" drive motivates so many of us), but being mindful of that connection only exacerbated my plight.

Every time my mind drifted to an insecure thought, I would feel it in the pit of my stomach. This only reinforced the mentality that it must be true. My poor husband was faced with too many arguments with me as a result of my own internal fear. But as I soon learned, hope was not lost. There was a perfectly good tool I already had in my pocket that I could use to help salvage my marriage and my mind.

It was through the use of meditation, of course, that I started to understand my thoughts better. With logic on my side, I recognized that my insecurity was drawn from old, unresolved pain. Because I hadn't properly addressed this pain in the past, it threatened to override my thoughts and project itself outward in a way that affected my whole life, not just my head.

Through the use of meditation, I was able to change my internal dialogue from "Others will hurt me" to "I can trust him"; this altered my view of my marriage and, thankfully, put me at peace regarding my husband's fidelity. It also gave me the mental space to learn from my husband because I was no longer on the offensive. Being eager to ask questions and willing to listen assisted in repairing the damage caused by my own fear and insecurities. Meditation encouraged me to remain open, calm, and clear-headed so that my husband could hear me and help me. And I could hear him clearly too. With this mutual respect and understanding, we could listen to one another and offer each other the support we both needed during this trying time.

As you can see, meditation helps support us in our relationships, both romantic and platonic. It gives us more clarity, raises our self-worth, and keeps us grounded. It fosters confidence. It encourages conversations. It can change your mind and your life.

Creating Rituals to Establish Self-Control

Looking back at the history of humanity, it is evident that rituals have often been a cornerstone of civilization. We often see this in religious communities. If you live in a predominately Jewish town, you would see its population regularly go to temple. Christians receive the Eucharist as part of a rite that is repeated during Mass. Sikhs, Muslims, Hindus, and others all have rituals to govern their lives. These activities help us to regulate our mental selves or our psyches. It gives us peace. A sense of security is granted when we know what is required of us as human beings, especially when it comes to the meaning of life.

Free thought and free will, of course, can upend this ritualistic behavior. We have seen the effects of society (through technology, for example) steering us away from the personal attachments of certain ceremonial behaviors. Instead of going on a walk with a friend, we connect through screens on computers and phones. We might opt to go online shopping, but focusing on three-month goals—especially financial goals—could be a more fulfilling use of your time. I've even challenged traditional behaviors in my own life.

Growing up in the Western Sikh community, I was a rebel. As a teenager, I made the active choice to wear a turban when most of my friends did not. Additionally, the custom then was to wear all white. Again, I challenged conventions by wearing a black turban instead. In the late 1980s and early 1990s, this was very frowned upon. Breaking the norm meant breaking away from tradition.

I am proud that I stood up for myself and created my own customs. In doing so, I believe I was able to move into the authentic self by embracing my true identity. I think it is important to question our expectations within life and from life, even deep-rooted traditions. As long as this curiosity comes from a genuine source, rather than out of spite or fear or anger, then we can stand to benefit from the knowledge we acquire as a result.

Questioning a certain ritual is not the same as questioning the *power* of rituals. An act that is repeated again and again becomes a potent force in your life, whether it is an act of defiance or one that follows the status quo. Much like how thoughts shape your emotions, all repetitions you experience in life affect your mind through your DNA.

Ann Graybiel, professor of neuroscience in the Department of Brain and Cognitive Sciences at the Massachusetts Institute of Technology, led a 2005 study about how old habits die hard (*Nature*, 2005). In an experiment conducted with rats and maze runs, Graybiel and her team confirmed that neural activity in the brain shifted when habits were formed. After the rats learned the path to their reward, the neurons became quiet as the brain adjusted to an autopilot mode. They also discovered that the slow firing patterns of the neurons reversed once the reward in the maze was removed. The neurological pathways of the rats lit up again as they attempted to establish a new expectation. Eventually, the rats stopped searching for the missing reward; they gave up the habit.

This finding emphasizes how important it is to create and maintain good habits. Once your brain learns a certain cue—like the expectation to meditate daily—it will operate in an instinctive manner. The experience becomes the norm. This means that bad habits are also deeply ingrained in the brain through neurologically determined expectations. They can be reversed, but it takes time, patience, and training of the mind.

Graybiel's study made one last remarkable observation: once the reward was returned to the rats, the pre-established neural pattern returned instantly. The initial firing patterns—which included a spike in neural activity at both the start and the end of the maze, with a lull during the run (that autopilot mode)—reflected that habits can be triggered with familiar cues.

Seek out healthy habits from the start. You don't want to get stuck in a cycle of bad behavior because of uncontrollable variables that essentially reset your brain, rekindling the fire of a negative routine. Fortunately, the fact that the brain is able to snap back from broken patterns means that it is easy to return to a good habit, even if you drop the ball. You have the power to take control of your life simply by creating and maintaining wholesome rituals that best serve you and your mind.

Neurological pathways generate memory habits in your mind due to the replication of patterns. The more you repeat any pattern, the deeper its imprint, much like walking through a crowded forest until you bend the shrubbery into a trail. If a ritual is revisited enough, your body creates an emotion established from that specific neurological pathway in the brain. The frequency of this ritual—whether it is daily or weekly—will determine its impact in your body, on your relationships, and in your life as a whole.

I talk a lot about how important it is to meditate daily and make it part of an anticipated routine in your life. But there is an aspect of meditation that is, in fact, strictly about the power of repetition: mantras. Mantras are sounds or words that help to tune or control the mind. By applying this yogic ritual into your meditation, you will be able to alter the mind's expected thoughts. Instead of turning to distracting thoughts (everything from feelings of inadequacy to wondering what to make for dinner), the mind is trained to focus on healing words. Mantras are healthy triggers for self-reflection and introspection.

Although Kundalini Yoga's mantras are typically in Gurmukhi, you don't need to know or understand the language to feel its full effects. You don't even have to use a Gurmukhi mantra at all. I have already mentioned working with a client who used a Bible verse as his mantra, which worked wonderfully for him. However, I know that traditional mantras work, and I implore you to at least try incorporating them into your Kundalini experience at some point.

You already have daily rituals in your life. We all do. We wake up, eat breakfast, check social media, take a shower, drive to work; some of us might have more specific routines, like ordering the same elaborate coffee beverage at a local café every afternoon. You might want to refer to these rituals as habits, instead.

The question I have for you is, are your habits healthy for your body, mind, and soul? When you are stressed at the end of a workday, what do you do to relieve the stress? We all approach this release differently, from having a beer to vegging out the couch. How does this ritual help your life? Think about each of your daily or situational practices and truly consider their effects.

In the moment, some of our most nefarious habits feel good; they can unburden us from the tension that stress and anxiety create. The primary problem with many of these habits is that we conduct them mindlessly. We may feel relaxed because we are checked out, but this is just because we are forcing our bodies to ignore the source of our pain. They are merely temporary distractions. For a brief while, they will serve their purpose of taking your mind off stress-inducing issues and tempering any bubbling anxiety.

It is not necessarily bad to have these short-lived remedies to ease yourself, but they cannot maintain a healthy lifestyle or heal your drama or trauma. They only mask the issues until your mental health worsens. In the end, certain ritualistic behaviors will not uplift you. They will not be the positive support your body and mind requires to be lit from the inside, inspiring change that in turn causes growth. You need that eternal movement forward in order to be truly healthy, happy, and whole. Do not let yourself be that still, algae-covered pond.

Meditation is a ritual that will help support your life. It will support the change that you seek by turning on that light within you, manifesting creativity and happiness. It will start a process of healing, inspiring you with the courage to grow. Implementing this new habit might not always be easy, but the good news is that anyone can get started: today, right now.

Because this habit might be something new you are introducing into your life, you might experience an internal struggle to practice each day. In that regard, it is not unlike setting a New Year's resolution to go to the gym every day. It might be hard because you find that spending a few extra minutes in bed each morning is just a little too tempting.

Keep in mind this mantra: "I am doing this for me." You picked up this book because you wanted to elevate your life through positive change. You knew that stress and anxiety were becoming too overwhelming, and so you wanted the ability to self-heal. Maybe everything else you've tried so far has not worked or met your expectations. Well, now you have the insight on how to set new habits that will change your life for the better. Using Kundalini technology, you will have the power to create the inner strength you need to help heal your own body and mind.

You can do it. You can start today. The beautiful part is that getting started on this meditative journey can take just three minutes, every day. I like to joke to my clients that a trip to the bathroom can take longer. Just three minutes. Go on, start small. You can build up your meditative stamina by practicing a little longer as each day passes. Eventually, you will find that you *want* to practice daily. Meditation will become your healthiest habit.

Finding Contentment and Building Trust

As human beings, we have a basic life goal of wanting to be happy—all the time. While this is an admirable goal, the truth is that long-term heightened happiness is not sustainable. Life, as it turns out, is a roller coaster; we must ride through its ups and downs. We cannot find clarity in life without the fog of issues to act as a contrast; otherwise, we would never know what we are seeking in the first place. Everything would exist in a gray area.

When we find we are unable to achieve this constant high level of happiness, we often become anxious or even depressed. Some of us might even feign happiness in order to mask the pain of life, which can result in a manic state of mind. This forced happiness is often seen in the form of consumerism (short-term satisfaction via purchases), stimulants (short-term relief through mind-altering drugs), and people (short-term dependence). When a permanent level of happiness is not achieved through these distractions, we can crash and become depressed.

What we can do is work toward a sustainable level of contentment.

While we bob on the unpredictable waves of life, contentment gives us an anchor to throw overboard. It is a manageable life goal, one that helps to ground ourselves in realistic expectations. By practicing meditation daily, you are able to tap into this emotional state as you work through your neuroses and fears. You can find contentment through your inner peace.

Feeling elated on a long-term scale is not attainable, but you can find the security you need to travel through life by embracing contentment. Every day will not be sunny, like every day will not be stormy. Knowing that each extreme variable is an option we might face—and learning how to respond to the variables—gives us the capability to move through life with dignity and grace, even in hard times.

Ultimately, it is contentment that clears space for us to assess and deal with any problems we encounter. It gives us a sense of inner safety, which allows us to self-reflect and self-correct. Being content means that we trust the process of life.

Trust is a powerful belief system that holds great importance in our lives. If we don't trust life and its processes, fear can sneak up and ensnare us with anxiety. As I have previously mentioned, anxiety stems from various levels of fear. Each level leads to a different form of anxiety that plays out in our lives, often to wildly damaging effects. The problem is that anxiety diminishes our trust, and the lack of trust aggravates our anxiety. It is often complicated for us to navigate out of this cyclical lose-lose situation.

Those who are happy or content have an inherent trust of life: they trust in the experience and how it plays out. They don't sit back and wait for life to be handed to them or for their problems to be fixed simply because it was their perceived fate. For many, that sense of entitlement is not feasible because of life's expectations and demands. Those who are content work hard to achieve a sustainable level of happiness, often in spite of their plights.

This level of happiness is found through their ability to trust. Because of its inherent requirement to relinquish control, trust is a powerful tool that allows us to have the courage to create. By freeing our mind, we can dive into our natural energy and listen to ourselves on the deepest levels. This can be intimidating, but don't feel vulnerable. When you have fear, it breaks the walls of trust and puts a fissure in your foundation of beliefs.

Although some blessed individuals are born with the gift of trust, it is not impossible to learn it for yourself. Think of religious faiths, for example. A fundamental belief in many faiths is trust; a trust that "it"— whether it is a divine energy or a spiritual God—will guide and take care of all.

I often tell people that we experience trust—the deepest, most pure form of trust—when we believe in something that we cannot see, hear, or touch. When we place faith in the unknown with confidence, we surrender ourselves with a belief system that assures us that *we* are ultimately *enough*. This is when we encounter *wowo*, trusting the process of life.

This innate sense of trust is a spiritual and emotional thread that can bind your life together. But like any thread, it can sometimes fray. I have this trust in my life, yet I still experience meltdowns. I still have my difficult days, and I sometimes question what I am doing. This inner thread of trust, however, gets me back on track every time. With a little mending, I can reconstruct my faith in life. I need it too. With that trust, I do more than dream; I have the courage to make those dreams come true. That trust fuels me to move and accomplish my goals.

If you are wondering how I mend that tattered thread of trust, you might not be surprised by my solution: meditation. Not only can it maintain trust, but it can also create it for those taking their first steps toward a deep trust in the process of life. This is because its different components—such as breathing patterns, mantras, mudras, and eye focus—build an internal support system within us. This, in turns, reinforces our connection to inner trust.

Meditation is the key to opening yourself to the belief that you—yes, *you*—can maneuver yourself away from pain, avoid feeling hurt, and diminish fear. By building trust, your body, mind, and soul become an energy source that awakens all that you are and all that you can be in life. With that energy, you can walk away from those cornerstones of anxiety.

Chapter 7

The Science behind Meditation

When the body, mind, and spirit are in balance, life works more harmoniously. You are at your best when you strike this delicate balance; life, you may find, tends to closely follow an idealistic path. By having insight into your greatest needs, you are able to set and achieve goals. Although this is basic yogic philosophy, there is actually scientific support behind the benefits of meditation, through the maintenance of cognitive function.

Think of meditation as exercise for the brain. When your mind hits the gym (through the meditative act), the brain and nervous system receive a top-to-bottom workout. Your nervous system speaks to your neurotransmitters through hormones, which are regulated by the hypothalamus, pineal, and pituitary glands. Through meditation, these neurotransmitters become trained to unite and communicate in harmony (*Ancient Science*, 2015). When you are no longer battling fragmented thoughts, your mind becomes unoccupied and free to reach its fullest potential.

By incorporating sounds (chanting), mental focus (mantras), body focus (mudras and posture), eye focus, and your own breath, meditation calls on your brain to think, feel, and act differently. It causes a shift in the frequency of your brainwaves through the act of regulated concentration, as confirmed from Brown University researchers in a study exploring the role of motor responses in relation to attentional training (*Journal of Neuroscience*, 2015).

Your brainwaves are divided into five bandwidths, each activating different centers in the brain. The slower the frequency of these bandwidths, the more time there is to process thoughts and make skillful decisions. Meditation allows you to consciously shift between these frequencies, often placing us within the alpha to theta range: slow activity patterns that promote relaxation, creativity, and even memory consolidation (when our brains file short-term memories into a permanent database).

Joining researchers from the Norwegian University of Technology and Science, Professor Jim Lagopoulos of the University of Sydney in Australia conducted a study measuring the changes in electrical brain activity when using nondirective meditation (*The Journal of Alternative and Complementary Medicine*, 2009). Their findings showed that the specific use of chanting-based meditation—rather than a controlled state of general calmness—caused a significant upswing of theta waves in the frontal and temporal-central regions of the brain, while alpha waves were abundant in the posterior region.

As a result, these neuroscientists discovered that meditation actively shifts your consciousness. This carries you toward a peace of mind as you enter into a relaxed, protective, worry-free state. When your brain is running on alpha frequencies, you move away from the critically thinking mind; external sensory information is diffused in exchange for reflective lucidity. It is the idle daydream you have as you stroll through a park. Many artists function out of this frequency, since it provides a mind-set for optimal creative insight.

The goal of Kundalini meditation, however, is to reach the theta frequency: the doorway to the subconscious mind. It is the trancelike state you enter when experiencing deep relaxation, felt just before falling asleep and just after waking up. Because it is on the threshold between the conscious and unconscious mind, it is often difficult for beginning meditators to remain in this state without drifting off to sleep. However, with regular practice, you can learn to explore this elusive state of mind with ease.

When functioning under theta waves, you are guided by your intuition. Actions are so automatic that you feel disengaged entirely, as you might feel during a hair wash routine. It allows you to access your deepest knowledge and tap into instinctual insight, giving the subconscious self a sense of clarity and understanding without analysis. While in meditation, you find answers within yourself. Because your mind is so open, you are receptive to new information and can generate creative concepts. If your best ideas come to you in the shower, it might be because you're in the theta state.

Low-frequency brainwaves can have an enormous impact on memory consolidation and emotional processing, aspects that are provided by your body when it naturally suppresses the norepinephrine hormone in the amygdala (which helps us experience emotions) during a specific phase in the sleep cycle. As you sleep each night, your brain enters into five different phases: 1, 2, 3, 4, and rapid eye movement (REM) sleep. It is the REM sleep cycle that operates under the influence of theta waves, and it is where you find your dreams: where your conscious and unconscious minds unite.

While studying brain functions during sleep, researchers found that REM sleep helps us to elude negative emotions (*Current Biology*, 2011). They deduced that amygdala reactivity was decreased during this phase in the sleep cycle due to the suppression of norepinephrine—which is usually activated during the fight-or-flight response—and that memories were simultaneously reactivated. Since stress-induced norepinephrine wasn't in abundance to negatively influence the mind, memories were revisited and reprocessed with better coherence. This means that REM sleep can gift you with subconscious introspection. By meditating, you can reach this essential dreamlike state by training your mind to run on the theta wavelength. These electrical currents in the brain eventually carry you to a place of ultimate relaxation and tranquility.

It's worth looking into the importance of intense mental repose, as experienced on low-frequency wavelengths. The relaxation you achieve through the meditative mind increases white matter in the brain (*Proceedings of the National Academy of Sciences of the United States of America*, 2010), which is vital for us sentimental human beings. This feature of the brain is where myelinated axons carry information gathered from the gray matter, where synapses occur. We want a lot of white matter because it regulates how our brain interconnects and supports us to process our emotions.

In chapter 4, "Stress versus Anxiety," I discussed a study conducted by Daniela Kaufer et al. that explored the impact chronic stress has on the brain (*Molecular Psychiatry*, 2014). In their findings, they concluded that a stress hormone (corticosterone in rodents; cortisol in humans) triggers an overproduction of a white matter cell (oligodendrocytes) that trips up the transmission of signals in the central nervous system. Under stressful situations, therefore, nerves can misfire and cause miscommunication in your brain circuits. When this happens, especially on a prolonged basis, you are left vulnerable to more serious mental afflictions, such as anxiety and even depression.

When you meditate, you remove yourself from acute stress. In doing so, you actively strengthen the white matter in your brain, ensuring that the information gray matter receives gets integrated and communicated properly. Despite white matter covering about 60 percent of the brain while gray matter fills the rest of the 40 percent or so, these two tissues must work together as equals, and meditation can serve you and your brain as the great unifier.

As I mentioned earlier, meditation can increase the volume of gray matter in the prefrontal cortex. Gray matter is the control board of your emotions. It is the regulator or processor. It governs your personality. In abundance, gray matter results in healthy brain functions, including the avoidance of anxiety and depression. Those with an expanded prefrontal cortex are generally calmer, more patient, and more rational. They feel inner peace with greater ease. In the deep state of relaxation that evokes the subconscious mind, you are able to properly process emotional issues without the threat of oppressive thoughts (like worries and fears).

Because meditation has the potential to mitigate stress levels, it can also slow down the aging process. This is because meditation actually increases telomeric activity in the body. Telomeres are compound caps that protect the integrity of DNA rods, allowing for continued cell replication. (They are often compared to aglets, the tips at the ends of shoelaces that prevent fibers from fraying.) This repetitive process naturally shortens our telomere length as we age, but stress can accelerate the speed at which the telomeres deteriorate (*Proceedings of the National Academy of Sciences of the United States of America*, 2014).

If this kind of information frightens you, then I am here to reassure you that all hope is not lost: we are capable of literally restructuring our DNA by slowing down this cellular degeneration, and this can be achieved through meditation.

In order to sustain cellular health in the body, we must increase an enzyme called telomerase. This enzyme not only prevents telomere shortening, it can also add telomeric DNA back into chromosomes and increase the lifespan of our body's cells. A study conducted by Tonya Jacobs, et al. was the first to link meditation's influence on telomerase activity. These researchers looked at participants who spent three months at a meditation retreat, practicing daily meditation. At the end of the investigation, it was discovered that retreat participants experienced "significantly greater" telomerase activity than those in the control group, affirming that meditation can promote "positive psychological change" (*Psychoneuroendocrinology*, 2011).

Elizabeth A. Hoge, a professor of psychiatry at Harvard Medical School, studied the effects meditation had on increasing telomere activity (*Brain, Behavior, and Immunity*, 2013). She and her team found that long-term meditators had longer telomere length overall and that this was especially true of women (who had significantly longer telomeres than the non-meditator control group). The stress reduction that coincides with mindful meditation has a direct impact on the body as a whole, as further proven by a study conducted at Howard University Medical Center (*Plos One*, 2015). Looking at a group of men and women with stage I hypertension, researchers found that meditative technology increased telomerase gene expression and lowered blood pressure.

By strengthening the protein caps at the ends of your DNA strands, meditation can prolong your life expectancy. But if you are to live a longer life, you want to experience happiness and contentment. There will always be dark days, but you want to have the capacity to find enjoyment on the sunny days in between the gloom. This can be achieved by giving your body and mind the tools to remain calm, even in the stormiest weather. One of those tools is called gamma-aminobutyric acid (GABA).

GABA is an amino acid that acts as a neurotransmitter in the central nervous system; it is produced in the brain and nervous system, specifically in the frontal lobe and hypothalamus. GABA transmissions in the brain lead to a calming sensation, mentally and physically. It is like a built-in tranquilizer. When you raise the level of GABA, you feel less impacted by trauma in your life.

Nutritionists and doctors often suggest GABA in chewable or vitamin form for individuals with anxiety and depression, but you don't need to spend money on this supplement. You create it within yourself for free. Your body was designed to naturally provide your mind with this self-protective armor, which can be increased through the use of mindful meditation.

A group of researchers from the Division of Psychiatry at the Boston University School of Medicine studied whether GABA levels in yoga practitioners changed after a yogic session (*The Journal of Alternative and Complementary Medicine*, 2007). They discovered that their subjects saw a 27 percent increase in GABA levels, allowing them to conclude that yoga "should be explored as a treatment for […] depression and anxiety." Three years later, that same group at BU returned to study yoga's influence on moods and anxiety (*The Journal of Alternative and Complementary Medicine*, 2010). They looked at a larger group of subjects who practiced yoga during a twelve-week intervention course and found, once again, that yoga asana (postures) led to improvements in mood. By increasing thalamic GABA levels, practitioners of yoga—including meditation—can expect to decrease their anxiety.

Meditation, therefore, can modify brain mechanisms that affect stress levels. By triggering the release of neurotransmitters, yogic technology can regulate psychological disorders of varying degrees, including anxiety and anxiety-related illnesses. Research scientists from Harvard Medical School's Wellman Center for Photomedicine encouraged the use of meditation to help grow new neurons and enhance the connection between existing neurons, allowing for strong and healthy communication within the body and mind (*Ancient Science*, 2015). "Our brains do not contain fixed hardwiring," Shanmugamurthy Lakshmanan concluded in the paper. "By tying together the neurobiological effects of neurotransmitters, brainwaves, mental exercise, and the empirical evidence from psychological experiments, it is evident that meditation is an effective treatment for anxiety."

All of the medical benefits of meditation can, at times, seem overwhelming. Pause for a moment to regather yourself. Take a deep breath, expanding out from your stomach, and note how calm it makes you feel. Establishing strong breath support aids us when relaxing. When you free your mind of distractions, you raise your overall cognition. This helps you to reconnect with the self, of course, but it also helps you process information, like the scientific support for meditation.

An enormous aspect of Kundalini meditation—and yogic technology in general—is diaphragmatic breathing. Whether it is segmented or patterned, long-deep breathing meditation stimulates the vagus nerve (located in the center of the chest, near the heart center), which is linked to our nervous system and brain. It increases our vagal tone, improving the health of our parasympathetic nervous system; this is the "rest and relax" part of our internal body. Research has proven that slow abdominal breathing reduces the body's fight-or-flight response (*The Journal of Alternative and Complementary Medicine*, 2010) and consequently lowers stress.

You must learn to connect to your breath. This helps you to connect to the sound of your voice. By incorporating mantras into your meditative routine, you can learn to listen to yourself in an intimate way. This gives you the power to change your deepest internal thought patterns, which will reflect outwardly in the way you react to experiences, including stress and anxiety.

Too many of us are lost in our own heads. As I've mentioned before, our thoughts control our stress levels; they affect our perception of ourselves, sometimes baselessly. Incorporating repetitive speech into our daily lives allows us to step away from negative, distracting, or otherwise unfulfilling ruminations. In fact, research has proven that using mantra—a relatively easy cognitive task, even for nonmeditators—helps prevent your mind from wandering by giving it purpose (*Brain and Behavior*, 2015).

According to a study published in *Brain and Behavior*, repetitive speech causes a widespread reduction in brain processes in what is known as the default mode network (DMN), which is responsible for self-reflection. DMN is the busy mind; it is where your thoughts go when you lack focus. Assigning your thoughts a job means less free time for it to daydream, which can lead to self-judgment and even catastrophic thinking like "No one will ever love me" or "I am not good enough." By performing a simple cognitive task—doing as little as repeating a single word—you can quiet the internal thoughts that plague you and threaten to introduce stress in your life.

Meditation triggers brain mechanisms that alter you on a cellular level. Through the use of mudras and mantras, you can harness the power of the human cortex in your favor by creating new neural pathways and strengthening those that you have. Its endless benefits prove that meditation is a thousand-year-old form of technology for good reason: it is a natural tool for you to feel good, happy, and peaceful. When you are calm, you have more clarity in life. This inner strength provided by your own body is a bountiful resource you should learn to properly utilize.

Despite there being thousands of Kundalini meditations, there are sadly very few studies on their effects and benefits. In fact, I hope to be involved with future research to help uncover the compelling truth behind meditation's potential. Until then, however, we can look at the work by a doctor named Dharma Singh Khalsa. Thankfully, he had the insight to explore Kirtan Kriya—a Kundalini meditation—which resulted in some remarkable discoveries.

Kirtan Kriya is a twelve-minute chanting meditation where the rhythm of the mantra breaks down negative thought patterns in the mind. By repeating "Saa Taa Naa Maa," practitioners create a positive relationship with the idea of change. The

> mantra fills the gap in your default mode network so that you can enrich your mind with positive thought patterns.

patterns in this mantra play over the neuroses of your life, guiding the mind away from those critical thoughts and irrational feelings that try to govern you. As mentioned before, the mantra fills the gap in your default mode network so that you can enrich your mind with positive thought patterns.

Because it is such a powerful meditation, I prescribe Kirtan Kriya to many of my clients who suffer from anxiety or even depression. To remove them from the rut in which they find themselves, I encourage them to perform Kirtan Kriya for a full thirty minutes each day. This has allowed my clients to mentally shift on a deep level within their conscious, removing them from a pit of despair. Once out of this hole, their pain becomes manageable because of a clear and thoughtful mind. Without those disturbing distractions, they can move forward in life.

Within four weeks of regular practice, Kirtan Kriya can cause some people to feel vulnerable. Thoughts may change too dramatically, including the subconscious dreamscape visited when asleep. As you are healing, you are more sensitive and often feel more raw. If you are looking to work through more acute trauma, I implore you to seek a licensed therapist to support you in your healing. You may also want to look into the Gunpati meditation; it helps you to disconnect yourself from the pain associated with traumatic experiences.

Dr. Khalsa has practiced Kundalini since 1978 under the guidance of Yogi Bhajan; he is an American physician who has extensively studied the benefits of meditation. As the president and medical director of the Alzheimer's Research and Prevention Foundation, he has been the leading researcher showing that Kirtan Kriya specifically can stop the process of cognitive aging. Kirtan Kriya reduces depression, which can set practitioners on a pathway toward lessened anxiety and overall better mental health.

After twelve intensive years of research, Dr. Khalsa found that meditation reduced the risk of Alzheimer's disease and acted as a form of brain exercise. It does this by breaking the pattern of negative past memories and replacing them with introspective, positive patterning in the brain. By utilizing specialized scans (such as SPECT and fMRI) and conducting both memory and blood tests, he found that Kirtan Kriya positively affected the body, mind, and spirit.

Meditation reduces stress by lowering cortisol levels in your brain (*Journal of the Medical Association of Thailand*, 2013). When these levels are too high, the loss of brain cells threatens to impede your cognitive skills in the hippocampus, the memory bank of your brain. Consequently, because of meditation's influence on the cortisol hormone, Kirtan Kriya can aid in preventing memory loss. Patients under Dr. Khalsa's supervision saw an increase of cerebral blood flow in areas of the brain that impact memory as well as concentration skills and mental resiliency. There was also an improvement in brain chemistry because it naturally increased neurotransmitters (which allow brain cells to communicate and function better).

When the mind is healthy, the body is anxious to follow its footsteps. Kirtan Kriya was noted as boosting the immune system and improving sleep, both of which are optimal for brain and body health. (Think of it as a medication that can help a range of different issues.) Dr. Khalsa also recorded a 44 percent increase in telomerase in his patients. As I mentioned before, when our telomeres are shorter, we are prone to accelerated aging and a shorter life expectancy; it can also result in Alzheimer's. By practicing Kirtan Kriya for twelve minutes a day for eight weeks, the stressed subjects experienced the largest increase of telomerase ever recorded.

Kirtan Kriya even saw a positive impact on the spirit of Dr. Khalsa's patients. Over half of his subjects (65 percent) saw an improvement on their depression. Patients performing this form of meditation discovered a sense of purpose during this study, promoting their well-being and self-growth. Meditators experienced a peace of mind, impacting their overall health.

It is important to keep in mind that meditation is merely one tool among many to find happiness. Kundalini cannot promise a fairy-tale ending where your mental ailments are entirely erased and negativity can no longer affect you. Although you may find a sense of inner peace, life will still happen. And with life comes new experiences, new possibilities for stress, and unexplored emotions. Using meditations like Kirtan Kriya as a tool, however, will give you a map to guide you away from darkness and toward an inner light. It is a technology that has given me inner peace and guidance in life, and it has helped many of my clients create the changes they needed. In addition, witnessing these positive changes in the self boosts confidence. This positive energy further helps you deal with life with optimism.

There are some Kundalini meditations—like Kirtan Kriya—which are very difficult to practice, even for experienced meditators. The reason for this is because we end up triggering our monkey mind, which is the fidgety part of our mind that is hard to pin down. It is distracted, often does not make sense, and can set off our emotions (especially regarding what is real or not real). Because we feel compelled to flee from these overwhelming thoughts, it activates our fight-or-flight response system. Through habitual meditation, however, we can reconfigure our learned behavior and teach ourselves to react differently to pain and trauma in our lives.

Ignoring this internalized behavior means we are more likely to repeat our reactions in certain high-pressure situations. We end up like a background character in the movie *Groundhog Day*, reliving an unhealthy pattern that only the protagonist can change. But remember that *you* are the protagonist in your life. You, and only you, can start the journey of meditation to produce positive change.

Many people don't know how to meditate or when to start. You might even feel this way too. The biggest step is making the choice to practice, and only you can decide on the reason why. Sometimes, the only thing stopping someone is that it feels unfamiliar and weird. This is a natural hesitation that will dissipate over time as you adapt to the new sensation. You'll find that feeling more relaxed, calmer, and happier in your life becomes a priority over any lingering feelings of awkwardness.

For me, my absolute favorite reason to meditate is that it creates a change in my brain. It is a way for me to resolve core stress in a natural, healthy manner. The worry and anxiety that I might otherwise experience is muted by the successful control of my cognitive processes and awareness. Through Kundalini technology, I can find and maintain that inner peace. By staying centered in meditation, I am more likely to remain centered in my everyday life.

This isn't an abstract belief, either; there is scientific proof for meditation's support on the mind. In an article for *Psychology Today*, Emma M. Seppälä presented a list of twenty different scientific reasons to meditate. Among them, she cited a healthier immune system due to an increase in immune function, a decrease in pain, and a decrease of inflammation (a hallmark of diseases) at the cellular level. Dr. Khalsa's studies back up these physical changes.

In terms of happiness, meditation works on improving your moods by increasing GABA levels and consequently decreasing stress, anxiety, and depression. This, in turn, can affect your social life. By making you feel less lonely, instilling compassion, and fortifying emotional intelligence, your external world—that is, the life beyond internal monologues—is greatly improved with meditation.

If you have a hot temper, Kundalini can help. This yogic technology regulates your emotions by tapping into the default mode network and bettering your ability to be introspective. Understanding your emotional outbursts gives you greater self-control. This is also related to the increase in gray matter, which causes you to be more calm and relaxed.

Meditating increases your cortical thickness and also your attention span. Although it seems like you're doing nothing by sitting and meditating, this habitual form of self-reflection ironically improves your productivity by altering your brain frequencies. It sharpens your focus and ability to multitask while honing your memory skills. Meditation is akin to a fun brain game, like Sudoku, where you ask yourself to be creative and think outside the box. It expands on both your cognitive and critical thinking skills. Overall, meditation makes us wiser.

And all of this yogic technology is free.

There are endless reasons why you might turn to meditation. What's yours?

Chapter 8

Meditation's Influence on the Mind and Body

Basic Characteristics of the Mind

Kundalini teachings share that the soul enters an infant's body and is immediately confined and defined by the physical form. Unfortunately, you did not arrive with a user's guide to living, so you become dependent on your caregivers and look up to them for guidance. In this vulnerable state, you still manage to collect conscious experiences from your caregivers and the environment around you. This builds your ego identity.

When you enter the tumultuous terrible twos, you experiment with your separate identity—away from your mother and father—and start to form the "little me" identity. This ego formation is meant to happen; it is a natural process of life.

Around your thirties, you usually experience another shift toward a new awareness. This is the soul me. It is when you truly acknowledge that there is something bigger than yourself (hence the alternative name, bigger me). In this new awareness, you recognize that there is a force that looms taller than your parents. At this stage in life, you can grasp the concept of an expanded energy force that supports us all.

Meditation can shift you from the little me to the bigger me, easing you away from a finite (small and limited) to infinite (open and connected) view of your reality. Anxiety and depression are decreased when this process happens due to the security of being supported by a greater force. This force is an energy pool you can tap into, as needed.

Human beings are curious creatures who want to understand the infinite view. You are programmed to constantly seek answers. Like a three-year-old always asking, "But why?" or an ancient civilization of voyagers, you desire to know the unknown. It is why you are so drawn to the internet: there is endless information at our fingertips. Simply reading something, however, does not give you wisdom; it just gives you facts, without experience. You end up knowing information, sure, but it comes without authentic depth. Human beings need knowledge plus experience to achieve true wisdom.

Meditation builds the relationship between the ego and the unknown by providing experience beyond the five senses. This gives you the personal experience of being connected to the soul, which drives you toward a keenly aware consciousness to the unknown. This experience is what gives you profound wisdom and stability.

By creating consciousness in your thought process, you can feel in balance with your life. You can make clear and healthy decisions to avoid bad habits or indulge in salacious gossip. I once worked with a young patient who, even at her age of eleven, had the proper insight to surround herself with positivity. Thinking their daughter might be depressed because of a disinterest in playdates, her parents sent her to work with me.

Curious, I asked her why she didn't like to be with her friends outside of school. Her response was simple and pure: "I don't like to hang out with them because all they want to do is gossip and talk about others. I don't like to do that."

To this day, I still think, *Wow, this is our next generation.* (Happily, she remains a dedicated meditator.)

Being a conscious being, this young woman was already finding the capability to discriminate situations while remaining connected with her own self. We can all learn something from her: once we start connecting to our own identity, we start feeling very empowered with our choices in life. Meditating regularly is key to cultivating your mind and connecting to your Soul Self, allowing you to forge that identity and guide you toward *shuniya*: internal happiness, calmness, and peace.

The mind functions best with contrasts. You think in terms of "good and bad," for example, or "happy and sad," or "positive and negative." Polarities help you make sense of life by allowing you to evaluate the dimensions. Training your mind to read these contrasts gives you access to the facts of any situation, allowing you to make mature decisions with more confidence.

Unsurprisingly, not all of your thoughts support you, your life, or your goals. Have you ever tried to change a certain habit but found that your thoughts kept getting in the way?

Your mind is full of unconscious identifications (who you think you are), emotions (feelings), projections (expectations), intentions (wants), and attachments (connections, real or imagined). These thoughts are perceived as larger than they are; their meaning or importance becomes inflated based on bias. When you believe your self-made biases, a new reality is formed. Because your belief is based on false judgments from your unconscious, this can cause a lot of trauma and pain. Understanding the soul means you must understand and relate to the mind and all of its thoughts.

But most of us aren't aware that our thoughts have a life of their own. Your thoughts and feelings are experienced so strongly that they can only be understood as irreversible reality. And your viewpoint, of course, will always differ from someone else's viewpoint based on your personal biases, life experiences, and knowledge. Even your own, self-contained thoughts come from different avenues—the subconscious and unconscious minds, which can each alter how they are created and how you approach them emotionally.

The path of a thought affects many parts of your life and the world around you. (Think of it like the butterfly effect, a concept that argues "small causes can have larger effects.") Educating yourself on the pathways of your thoughts gives you the ability to intercept that thought at any time, including before it can manifest itself into action energetically. When you allow yourself to be honest about your thoughts, you are able to change them. Meditation teaches you how to change and learn from your experiences in life, training the mind to serve the soul.

The mind is largely automatic. It is an organ, and the job of this organ is to orchestrate the functions of the body. The brain naturally wants to perform its duty, but it does not always have the right guidance. Kundalini meditation allows you to step away from the automatic reaction process by training the mind to operate in an observing process instead. This allows the mind to become the observer, functioning with less attachment. As you become more unattached, the space between your thoughts changes, as does the quality of your cognition.

Becoming an observer does not mean remaining silent in your introspection, however. Kundalini meditation does *not* teach that you should silence the mind. The mind does not stop, so the concept of silencing your thoughts is an oxymoron. Rather, you must listen to them.

By creating more room in your mind to study your thoughts, you become competent in recognizing the changes in life you need to make. When you enable the opportunity to make these positive changes, you can see your relationships, career, monetary situation, and even physical health all start to improve. Supporting the mind to focus itself through meditation, you can learn to harness its power to serve you and your higher self. This, however, is not an automatic process, like the brain's natural function. Meditation is not a permanent experience. Like going to the gym to maintain a fit physique, it is important to meditate daily to keep your brain in shape.

Producing one thousand thought impulses per blink of an eye, the mind is a fast-moving machine. Your mind unconsciously and constantly generates these thoughts. That is why, at times, it is hard to relate to what you are thinking at the moment. It feels like there is a disconnect between you, your thoughts, and your emotions, often resulting in confusion. Routine maintenance—through the practice of meditation—helps you to get on top of these thoughts and to continually regulate then, allowing you to make sense of feelings like stress and anxiety.

With self-awareness achieved through Kundalini technology, you can train your mind to have more peace within. You can learn to act more conscientiously in your relationships throughout life, with yourself and with individuals around you. This is especially important because it can often be difficult to improve the quality of your thoughts when your mind is influenced by other people—in part, due to random thought waves that surround you.

Quantum physics shares the theory that there is a universal consciousness, a frequency, which connects all living beings (*Physics of Life Reviews*, 2014). This can be experienced as a supportive connection, a sense of belonging. Adversely, if one aspect of the connection is unstable, the universal frequencies can be experienced as overwhelming. You must be self-assured in who you are, what you are thinking, and why you are feeling a certain way in order to process experiences and situations in a healthy manner.

Part of the reason why Kundalini is so effective is because it puts you on a path toward self-reflection and clarity. You learn to look at situations through the two lenses—both the positive mind and the negative mind—to activate the neutral mind. This allows you to make powerful, righteous decisions that best serve you, your life, and your purpose.

The Three Minds

In yogic tradition, there is a concept of destiny. Now, people often confuse the concept of destiny with fate. Fate is predestined; we cannot change anything. Destiny, however, is the challenge to realize who you are and why you are here. When following your destiny, you recognize your intended goal of life and utilize discipline to fulfill it. An example would be a man who was born to paint (fate) but loses the use of his hands, so he learns to paint with his feet instead (destiny).

Your destiny is influenced by your neutral mind, the lens you look through once you have processed your negative (protective) mind and positive (perspective) mind. Everyone goes through this process, consciously or unconsciously.

The *neutral mind* is also called the meditative mind. This mind-set allows you to become less attached to the outcome of human experiences in life. The *negative mind* creates a lens of protection in your life; it's that "trust your instinct" feeling. Courage and creativity are both born out of the *positive mind*, which also gives you the insight to make new decisions.

Meditation creates a stronger inner balance because it strengthens the connection between the two contrasting aspects of the mind—positive and negative—to awaken the neutral mind. When you view life through the neutral lens, you become more sublimely conscious of your thoughts, emotions, and behaviors. As you learn to process and understand these internal functions, you learn how to alter your thoughts and change how you feel. You respond instead of react. This, in turn, adjusts the focus on the lens of your mind and gives you control of your destiny.

The three aspects of the mind are developed differently in everyone.

For some, the negative mind could be more active (by having a thicker lens) or less active (by having a thinner lens), while others have a more active positive mind. (Either way, don't get confused over the common connotations behind positive and negative. In this context, a negative mind is not bad, and additionally, you would not want to have a strictly positive mind.) The neutral mind can be the strongest aspect for certain individuals; these people tend to have a strong sense of intuition. Luckily, anyone can achieve the neutral mind if they apply themselves.

In its cultivated state, the neutral mind exists as a servant to your soul. It processes your innermost needs by recognizing your feelings, consequently choosing the best option for you before you're even fully cognizant of your thoughts. Sadly, for the most part, you allow your positive mind and negative mind to alternately control—rather than serve—you and your life. You often feel stuck with chaotic thoughts and uncontrolled, unwelcome emotions. Many of us don't know how to let these emotions go, other than hoping we will disguise them with bad habitual distractions or by forgetting them over time.

Addressing unwelcome emotions through a meditative lens is vital for clarity in life. Many people feel inclined to suppress them, but eventually, these stifled emotions will creep back into the forefront of your thoughts. They can become distracting, even burdensome. The average age of my clients attending my therapy practice is the late forties, early fifties. At this time in life, the suppressed emotions of years past can no longer be contained; they begin to emerge as part of what many people call the midlife crisis.

For example, I have some clients who have suppressed the pain and sadness of physical abuse they experienced in childhood. Although they have worked hard to push through those haunting memories and now lead successful lives, the deep pain from these negative memories still cause physical and emotional distress. Decades after the trauma, they decided that they can no longer tolerate the painful memories and simply want to have a more peaceful life.

While sometimes unpleasant, even downward cycles are challenges you should accept for the opportunity to grow as a human being. The only time you will be without these challenges is when you are no longer alive, so you might as well learn something from them. This may prove hard to endure, but meditation can support you when persevering through your most chaotic emotions and difficult experiences.

As you learn to master your mind, it starts to serve you by generating prosperity and happiness. Otherwise, the mind can become a haunting monster. Our aim with Kundalini technology is to teach the mind to serve our real self, the atman (the soul), because our Soul Self is steady. It is connected to the greater energy force of the universe. Some call this God, others call this Mother Earth, and many conceptualize this essence as a general form of a higher power.

Unlike our Soul Self, our minds are malleable when considering the human experience. It has an identity of its own that is shaped by our experiences, which it then forms into our perceived reality. Consider how two people with a terminal illness can respond to their prognosis in vastly different ways: one open-minded and positive, the other afraid and angry.

This contrast highlights how each mind perceives a situation uniquely. By practicing meditation, your mind learns to behave in a way that supports your life intention instead of hindering your path. Meditating helps you to develop clarity within yourself so that you can embrace obstacles and activate the strength to create change in your life, even when the challenges are difficult. Meditation cultivates alignment within yourself, resulting in beautification of your true self.

Sometimes, you think you have achieved neutrality when you are in your intellectual mind because you feel logically balanced. This is not the same as intuition honed through the neutral mind. Intellectual thoughts can, in fact, block you from your spiritual self. It threatens to remove a mental security blanket, which can cause you to become mistrusting and fearful in all facets of life. On the other hand, strengthening your spiritual self will establish an internal experience that tells you, ultimately, that you are going to be okay, even if life is hard right now. This "keep it up" attitude is related to the nervous system, which supports you when you feel overwhelmed. When the nervous system is in peak shape, you can face hard times with a brighter outlook.

If you want your mind to serve you, then your mind must be in alignment with your higher self, your Soul Self. When this happens, you will experience fewer chaotic moments. Instead, you will find more peace and clarity as a human being and as a soul being. Meditation is a process of awakening and experiencing your divine energy. This energy is the root of your basic need to be good and kind and to have grace and compassion: the essentials of what makes you human.

Losing the experience of your divine energy causes you to feel disconnected, both with yourself and with others in your life. Feeling alone and out of control with yourself and your body, anxiety may form. As a result, your mental health can further deteriorate, unless you work to connect with your Soul Self and maintain a mindful attitude toward life.

Meditation creates inner balance. Those who achieve this may find true inner peace, or enlightenment. The Dalai Lama, for example, has practiced meditation for years and has been cloaked in divinity. Kundalini meditation trains the mind so that you can harmonize the three minds together into a euphonious song and allow you to realize your destiny, your greatest potential.

Meditation and Emotions

"Everyone is emotional, but our emotions can become commotion.
When emotions become commotion, then you enter a dangerous zone. Because commotion can create a pattern, and then patterns start governing your life."—*Kundalini Yoga Teacher Training Manual*, 2003

Many of us believe that all of our emotions are inherently real. We often experience something and automatically process it as *the* universal truth. That particular emotion—whether it is fear or anger or stress—then governs us. I believe that about 90 percent of what we feel is not reality. It may be real to your perception, but it is not a comprehensive reality. Our beliefs come from our interpretation of the situation. Our emotions are a by-product of our thoughts, which are formulated due to our learned personal scenarios, experiences, and biases. The mind produces a thousand thoughts per blink of an eye, so it is impossible for us to register and compartmentalize all of this commotion in our mind.

By meditating, we train the mind to recognize which thoughts we want to become involved with and to which we should attach ourselves. It helps us to decipher whether emotions are real (i.e., confronting danger) or imagined (i.e., unfounded worry), which we can then study as we scrutinize our emotions through the neutral lens.

When we strengthen the positive mind and the negative mind through the practice of meditation, we learn to view life through the all-powerful neutral mind. This strikes harmony within our bodies and souls, and this fusion creates a strength within us by grounding the self in reality. When we accomplish this, we can make wholesome decisions for ourselves. Meditation can help us release anxiety, for example, by changing how we look at our feelings and rationalizations (or lack thereof). It helps us understand not just what we are feeling but *why* we are feeling this emotion.

As Yogi Bhajan said, emotions can become devotion or commotion. When we experience devotion, or "oneness," fearlessness is triggered within us and causes us to feel no pain. We are free from the chaos inside ourselves, and we are less likely to be drawn into the commotion around us. In the hectic times we live in, mastering this skill of directing our emotions to devotion is worth exploring.

Alternatively, commotion is akin to drama in our lives. By allowing our emotions to become commotion, a pattern begins to form and set in our subconscious mind. This makes us feel pain more easily, internally (mentally) and externally (physically). When the subconscious mind is disrupted by commotion, our bodies are given permission to be governed by that dramatic state.

Habits bred from commotion can become part of our lives by taking root in our subconscious minds. If your mother always freaked out over you spilling milk, then you will learn a pattern of also freaking out over something simple. If you opened yourself up to your father and he responded by saying, "Toughen up and don't be a baby," then you will feel unsafe to share your feelings. Words are powerful, especially when spoken by someone we trust, love, and need. We then act out those habits unconsciously, whether they are healthy for us or not. The repeated patterns set an expectation within us (a neurological pathway dictates this behavior), eventually establishing who we are as human beings in our everyday lives. This helps form our personalities, for better or for worse, which starts from the moment we are born.

How we are raised sets the precedence for our lives and our behavior.

The values our parents taught us, consciously and unconsciously, affected our habits and emotions in the long term. That is why it is difficult for some to make sense of their thoughts and learn how to improve them. After all, we—as a society—have a tough time hearing negative feedback about ourselves. We often don't want to accept that we need help in bettering ourselves, which can be the hardest part when starting on this journey to self-discovery and inner peace.

Anyone can change negative habits, which is the good news. The bad news—or, at least, the hard news to accept—is that it takes some people a lot of practice to accomplish this goal. It is not necessarily out of stubbornness but rather the comfort of being set in their situation. Often, there are years' worth of bad thought programs and habits to adjust; undoing the damage on the psyche and physical body after prolonged mental stress can prove to be an especially difficult challenge. However, with focus, the commitment to healing, and the support from uplifting loved ones, this challenge can be fulfilled.

Take me, for example. As a teenager and young adult, it was hard for me to hear feedback about how I was impacting my own life, which I viewed as unfair. When I was sixteen, my mother wouldn't allow me to buy a revealing shirt from H&M in Hamburg, Germany. We got into a big fight over it—an argument so impactful, I still remember it to this day. We all have memories of rebelling against similar feedback—a nightly curfew, a disclaimer to stay away from drugs—that we process with better clarity as adults with life experience. Now, especially as a mother, I understand my mom's reluctance back then.

For me, meditation has been a big asset to being open. As I stabilized my meditation practice at the age of twenty-four, I started to feel strong enough to handle hearing critiques from others and was able to change as a result. I grew and matured. Meditation helped me build my self-worth, which is essential when facing challenges or negative life habits.

When we feel bad about ourselves, or if we are not comfortable with who we are as a person existing in society, then this process of introspection and correction is an overwhelming burden. We may feel like we are incapable of accomplishing something, or we might even shift the blame to the healing technology failing us. Whether it is meditation, group therapy, self-help books, or a therapist guiding us, we might find ourselves disagreeing with them before we find the capacity to self-reflect. We may judge harshly and walk away, feeling critical and jaded.

A chronic negative habit can affect our unconscious mind and lead us to trouble. We feel unhappy and view life as unfair, and a "This always happens to me" mentally kicks in. These patterns usually stem from our childhood, and we act out on them in our adult life. That is why the habits don't easily vanish; they have been etched into our deepest thoughts. Over time, some of us may learn to cover them, but that doesn't mean they are forever gone from our psyche. As we get older, bad habits start crowding into our lives in unexpected, even unwanted, ways.

Have you ever had a time when you reacted to a situation, and it felt like you were out of your own body? Have you ever felt like you lost control of your emotions? This could happen during an argument with your child for not eating her vegetables or as a result from a traffic incident that left you enraged. If you occasionally experience this, there's no reason to feel ashamed; losing control of emotions and reacting unfavorably happens to everyone. For some, it may happen more often, and that is why it is important to have a tool to teach you how to best respond. That is why I meditate.

Neutralizing the reactions of our mind clears the room for healthy self-reflection to take place. Eventually, we establish positive thought patterns that encourage good habits to form. The essence of meditation is to support the shift of our emotions from commotion to devotion, allowing us to understand and enhance this connection. We experience that oneness. When this happens, we awaken our connection to the soul by linking us to bhakti energy. We become accepting to the miracles of life and nature.

Committed meditation practice creates a sense of humility to honor the source of all beings, resulting in us living with grace. This is important because it teaches us to be humble in all of life's situations, both good and bad, and it also steers us away from insecurities and the notion of feeling like a victim. Ultimately, life is less painful and more fulfilling when we embrace this potential.

Anatomy of Meditation: Mudra

Thousands of years ago, yogis noticed that the fingers on our hands have a profound impact on the brain. I can confirm this, too, because I have witnessed endless clients benefitting from this ancient technology, which is called mudra (body movement and poses). This seemingly strange relationship has to do with how the hands connect to the brain. The link is similar to the concept of acupuncture and the meridians within our bodies.

According to yogic philosophy, the small finger relates to the frontal lobe; this is all about action and reaction, calmness and worry. The index, middle, and ring fingers each connect to the partial lobe; this governs how we process our emotional state and, therefore, our lives. The thumb connects to the back temporal lobe; this is where we hold our memories.

In addition to the finger-brain connections, Kundalini technology shares the philosophy that our fingers also connect to various aspects of human behavior: the small finger is communication; the ring finger is vitality; the middle finger is wisdom; the index finger is knowledge; and the thumb is our ego. Because these finger-brain connections work to subtly massage and activate the brain, Kundalini meditations use these mudras to help our various brain functions work together in harmony.

By stimulating different parts of the brain, mudras will actually help to reduce stress within the brain. This is because it helps us to set patterns and expectations within us, which I have already discussed is a powerful yogic tool when dealing with mental disorders such as stress and anxiety. I have seen the positive results from my clients who have utilized mudras in times they found it difficult to relax, and I also use this method regularly, so I know it can be effective and valuable. Truthfully, you won't know if it works for you unless you try it too. So let's take a moment to practice a simple mudra exercise:

Start by touching your thumb to each finger pad in a sequential pattern: thumb to index, thumb to middle, thumb to ring, thumb to small, and then back to thumb to index. Repeat the cycle for three minutes, breathing gently as you practice. When you are finished, write down how you feel.

Popular meditations like Kirtan Kriya and Gunpati use this simple sequence of mudras, so it is beneficial to add it to your repertoire. As you practice either of these two meditations in conjunction with the finger movements, you will condition yourself to associate the repetitive pattern with the connection to calmness you've established during the meditation. By creating this association pattern, you will be able to connect to the same feeling of mindfulness and serenity that you experience during meditation at any point throughout the day. All you will have to do is touch your fingers sequentially with your thumb to activate your positive memory and help put your mind back at ease.

Yes, I know the act of incorporating mudras with your meditation can seem daunting. Especially when used in conjunction with other Kundalini meditation directions (specific movements, chanting, breath patterns, holding difficult yoga poses, and so on), it is sometimes overwhelming. But I have seen repeatedly that Kundalini meditation in particular is an incredible tool for clients and students who are dealing with anxiety *because* of its labor-intensive qualities. The specific instructions of Kundalini meditations require a lot of focused effort, which allows you to harness and cultivate your mind functions.

Meditation forces you to be present. The procedure trains your mind to refrain from straying back to any haunting fears or worries. By meditating, you are reprogramming your brain patterns and altering the way you process your life in the healthiest manner possible, physically and mentally. This is part of Kundalini technology's intention: to harmonize the functions of the entire glandular and nervous system.

By incorporating hand postures—along with chanting, breathing patterns, and eye focus—we create specific effects in our body, mind, and spirit, like activating neurons (which occurs when making a movement or even observing movements). When these neurons are fired up, they bind together for long-term potentiation. On the other hand, when these neurons are not communicating proficiently in the brain, it can cause anxiety and depression.

The brain forms memory patterns based on what we do. If you commit to a regular daily time to meditate, you will gradually find your practice easier. If your brain learns to associate finger-brain movements with relaxation, gradually you can establish inner peace within yourself as you practice your mudra. And you can practice your meditation mudra at any time throughout the day. (Try moving your fingers into mudras at your work desk to help awaken a memory pattern of calmness.) The more you practice, the sooner mudras will become second nature to you as you meditate, and the faster a positive pattern will take shape in your brain.

Eye Focus during Meditation: Drishti

What we see—and, in contrast, what we experience when we *cannot* see—has a direct impact on our mental state. By feeling as if we are connected to something bigger than the little me, we feel safe and can more easily trust the process of our lives. Because of how influential it can be on our minds, it is no surprise that eye focus—along with mudras—is a big component of Kundalini meditation.

Our mind thinks, *Action!* when we see light. When the eyes take in light, it affects the pineal gland and stimulates the brain. In meditation, the different positions of eye focus (or *drishti*) control the level of light affecting your brain and determine which muscles are then triggered. The pull of these muscles—influenced by eye movements—helps to stimulate the brain. Each method, therefore, has a direct influence on a specific emotion. For example, focusing on the third eye activates the pituitary gland, which is connected to our hormones (which regulate our emotions) and our sixth sense (which is also known as our intuition).

Some Kundalini meditations will instruct you to close your eyes, which can be a difficult experience for some. This darkness can evoke fear and insecurity, especially if there are traumatic memories tied to nighttime or low lighting. If you feel emotional pain or discomfort when meditating with closed eyes, cast your eyes down and keep your lids half-closed. This will mimic a similar effect of closed eyes without triggering unwanted anxiety. Over time, try moving into an eyes-closed position. By learning to focus on your third eye, you will find that it helps you to hold on and connect to yourself. Being able to accomplish this will be a sign of how much you have healed, and you should find pride in that personal achievement.

For others, closing the eyes during meditation is comfortable and more relaxing. The reason we tend to prefer this method is because of the invasive light. When we close our eyes, we create more interaction between the prefrontal cortex and parietal lobes, which affect our emotions and thought processes. By enhancing this internal network, meditation can help support you if your life is overly governed by thoughts and emotions.

Let's try a brief eye focus lesson. Try looking straight ahead, preferably at a plain wall with no distractions. Make sure you are in moderate lighting: no direct sunlight but not pitch-black. Keeping your eyes open, bring your focus down to your lap without moving your head. You might note a tug on your eyebrows. In your journal, write down how this feels. Now, bring your focus to the tip of your nose; this is a common eye focus in Kundalini meditation. Does this feel different from the previous eye focus? Jot down your observations and notice how each affected you, physically and emotionally.

Kundalini technology extensively utilizes the various forms of eye focus in order to activate the glands and brain pathways. Each drishti has a different goal in its intended meditation. Some are considered high locks in Kundalini; locks are areas in your body where awareness is awakened through eye intention, muscle squeezing, and raising of energy. They are often difficult to master but can eventually be achieved with great patience and much practice.

Below, you can find a list of the standard eye focuses used in Kundalini meditation. I have provided brief information on their purpose as well as detailed instructions on how to achieve their objective. When you practice any of the Kundalini meditations listed at the end of this book, you will be able to reference this guide on how to properly master each eye focus.

Eyes Closed

When we say "eyes closed" in Kundalini Yoga and meditation, we often encourage you to focus on your third eye. This is the default drishti. However, sometimes, there are no further directions; you are simply meant to close your eyes and look through the eyelids or look at the tenth gate. The tenth gate is also known as the crown chakra; it is the top of your head, where you feel connected to the source, also known as God.

Although some are able to close their eyes with no focus, this is not always conducive to clearing your mind and aiding you in your journey toward self-healing. It requires a lot of mental strength to keep your mind from becoming distracted with unintended stimulation. When meditating from a point of focus, you are able to harness your mind with greater ease.

Instructions: Close eyes. Focus straight through the eyelids, or focus at the tenth gate (the crown of your head). For very disciplined or experienced meditators, you may remain unfocused.

Eyes Focused on the Third Eye

This is the most commonly used eye focus in Kundalini Yoga because it taps into our sense of intuition. When stimulated, the third eye creates more mental focus and clarity to the unseen and unknown.

The third eye focus stimulates the pituitary gland, which regulates our hormones and emotions. When focusing on the third eye, we create a deep awakening within us so that we can make better choices in our lives. When we suffer from anxiety, we often don't know what to do. We sometimes seek the help of others to make decisions for us. But we all have this knowledge inside us already; it is our intuition. The key is to get it functioning in a way that best serves the self.

Occasionally, you will see people focusing on the third eye with their eyes open. In general—unless the directions state otherwise—your eyes should be closed.

If you feel a physical pull when you first attempt this eye focus, remind yourself that this is normal. Your muscles aren't used to being used in such a way. Mild discomfort is also common. However, if you find that the discomfort is persistent or that there is even some pain involved in the practice, you may want to consult a doctor.

Instructions: Close eyes. Gently roll your eyes up and to the center of your eyebrows. Do not strain your eye or face muscles, and do not cross your eyes. Hold this eye posture throughout the meditation.

Eyes Focused on the Tip of the Nose

Although one of the most commonly used eye focus techniques, focusing on the tip of the nose can be challenging to many. This eye focus—also known as Agiaa Chakra Bandh—is recognized as one of the highest locks in Kundalini Yoga. In meditation, it is known as the Lotus Point.

By focusing on the tip of the nose, you harness the mind. It is the perfect tool to train the mind to serve you and your life in a healthy, happy manner. According to yogic philosophy, this eye focus brings balance to the self by stimulating the pineal gland and frontal lobe, creating new pathways in the brain.

When introducing this eye focus technique into your meditation, you may find it difficult. Initially, you may feel a pulling sensation at your eyebrows or brow point. This is a normal occurrence to new practitioners as they begin to strengthen the nerve endings. It will likely take time to be comfortable in this eye focus, so don't feel discouraged if you cannot hold it for a whole meditation. You can always relax your eyes and try again. Over time, you will find it easier and easier to employ; eventually, you will master the skill.

Instructions: Sit straight with your neck in neck lock (Jalandhara Bandha). Bring one of your index fingers in front of your stomach and cast your eyes downward, without moving your head. As you keep your eyes focused on your fingertip, slowly bring it to the tip of your nose. Once your finger arrives at the nose, pause for a moment, noticing the location of your finger. Then, take your finger away. Keep your eyes focused on the tip of your nose. Hold this eye posture.

Eyes Focused on the Top of the Head

The top of the head is also known as the crown center. It is the tenth gate, or the seat of the soul. When we bring our focus to the seat of the soul, we cultivate our ability to be more authentic. This is because the top of the head connects us to the pineal gland, which oversees all of our glands and emotional reactivity. Stimulating the pineal gland, we are able to feel more inner peace; therefore, we are able to live our lives with more sensitive awareness. This consciousness is the experience of our Kundalini energy rising and spreading through our bodies.

Instructions: Relax your face and close your eyes. Roll your eyes up and focus the eyes to look through the top of your head. Allow your mental focus to meet your eye focus at the crown center. Hold this eye posture.

Eyes Focused on the Chin

Our chin connects to the energy of the moon, which brings us balance. Therefore, yogically, it is no surprise that the chin is also known as the moon center. By focusing on the chin, we create a cooling energy; this guides us toward serenity and allows us to view life with more clarity. As you might have noticed, all of the eye focuses create a sense of clarity within us. This is because the eye focus activates and balances the pituitary and pineal glands: the glands of higher awareness.

Like the Agiaa Chakra Bandh (focusing on the top of the head), this eye focus can be particularly hard to master. It takes time to create the strength and stability necessary to hold your focus on the moon center. Do the best you can, for as long as you can, and relax when needed. Again, with practice, you will be able to experience the results you wish to achieve.

Instructions: Relax your face and close your eyes. Roll your eyes down, bringing your focus to your chin. Allow your mental focus to meet your eye focus at the moon center. Hold this eye posture.

Eyes One-Tenth Open

When we hold our eyes open one-tenth of the way, we actively control the amount of light entering into our system. As mentioned before, the amount of light we allow in will affect the brain in different ways. Holding the eyelids slightly open also encourages our system to stay awake due to the stimulation of the optic nerve. If you find that the closed-eye focus techniques cause you to feel sleepy, you may want to try the eyes one-tenth open option; its constant stimulation to the brain will help keep you sharp and concentrated on your self-reflection.

Yogi Bhajan teaches this eye focus in two different ways: one-tenth open or nine-tenths shut. The difference between these two options is strictly based on mental awareness: whether you are open as a person or are closed off. How you look at and deal with life will determine how you approach this particular eye focus. Physically, they have just about the same effect.

Once again, you may find this is a difficult eye focus. Your eyelids might have a tendency to flitter. It takes time and patience to relax in this eye posture. Mastering this eye focus will help you develop a calm intuition, helping to support your meditation of choice.

Instructions: Relax your eyelids. Allow them to fall closed, but not all the way. Retain the intention of holding your eyes one-tenth open or nine-tenths closed (based on your mentality). You may want to experiment by shifting between the two eye focuses to see which best affects your emotional self. Hold this eye posture.

Chapter 9

Meditative Breathing

I can immediately recognize when I am upset because my breathing changes, sometimes dramatically. You might also notice this happening to yourself. Occasionally, you may find it's hard to catch your breath during an argument or after giving a presentation at work; any emotionally trying situation can stimulate distress. When this happens to me, I try to focus on my breath to calm myself down. It slowly becomes easier for me to deal with my emotional issue.

Psychologically, when we hold our breath for longer than normal (whether inhaling or exhaling), it can trigger the feeling of fear and anxiousness. Worry strikes us as our brain registers, "Oh my God, I am not breathing." This can start a chain reaction where you feel unable to breathe normally, which—for some—might induce a panic attack. Even worse, many who are experiencing a panic attack think they are actually having a heart attack. This can eventually create an unhealthy negative pattern in the mind, as panic sufferers associate this physical compulsion with their weakened mental state. They feel shamed by the panic attack and fault themselves for the experience, making it difficult to address this feeling of anxiety.

Breathing should not—and, frankly, cannot—be associated with negative feelings. It is the most simple and pure process of the body. Most of us take it for granted. We don't think about our breath and how it relates to life. When was the last time you stopped to think about your breathing patterns? Take a moment to do so right now. Sit quietly in your chair, on your bed, or on the couch; somewhere comfortable, preferably with a back rest. Close your eyes and concentrate on the rhythm of your breathing. In and in, in and out. Keep doing this for three to five minutes as you appreciate the miracle of your breath.

Breath plays a big role in how we feel. Our thoughts create how we feel, and often it is the breathing pattern that kicks off our emotional patterns. This is why, in meditation, we use various breathing patterns to generate different effects on both the brain and body. Breath also plays a big role in chanting. Without our breath, we couldn't create sound. It is the first thing we do when we are born—we cry out, making noises—and our relationship with it should remain special, even paramount, throughout our lives.

When my youngest son was a baby, his restless witching hour was between 6 and 8 p.m. He was often unhappy during these hours. I used to hold him as he cried, and I noticed that my breathing quickened as I felt his irritation and unease. I decided that I should chant to support his emotional state: faster when he was frantic, slower to help him relax. After about five to ten minutes, I would slow my breath, and my chanting softened as a result. By the time I was calm in both my breathing and chanting, my son was no longer crying. Because I was able to control my emotions through chanting, I was able to help by son by handling the situation with more grace.

Telling someone to "just stop crying" or to "cheer up" simply doesn't work, and unsurprisingly, it can be hurtful for someone to hear. Feeling especially sensitive, they won't know how to seize their emotions. They might even find it physically impossible to control themselves. Sometimes, the body doesn't even realize that it is upset, like in the case of my young son. It's important to find the space between your breaths to build a relationship between you and your breathing patterns. This allows for greater clarity as you process information, including thoughts and feelings. The organs and glands naturally respond to your breath. By mastering this act, you take control of your own emotions.

Breath suspension is a type of meditation where you are holding your breath (in or out) longer than what feels comfortable. The benefit of this suspension is that it strengthens your nervous system (a result we see often throughout Kundalini yogic technology). Gradually, with practice, suspending your breath will help heal your mental state and change how you respond—rather than react—to various scenarios. It will allow you to make quicker decisions under pressure.

Holding your breath out means that after you have exhaled, you don't take another breath for five, ten, or even twenty seconds. This can apply when inhaling, as well. The sensation can feel abnormal, but it shouldn't be painful. You may feel some discomfort, but this is okay if it is mentally based; breathing meditations force you to face inner issues of real or imagined pain, so deep emotions surface as a result. With enough focus or a mantra incorporated into your yogic practices, you will be able to shift these old patterns into something new and promising.

If you ever feel light-headed while practicing this form of meditation, stop immediately. The reason this occasionally happens is due to carbon dioxide (CO_2) and oxygen becoming trapped in the lungs, causing a light-headed sensation. Breathe normally until you feel centered with your breath again and your head is no longer spinning. Reaching a state of dizziness is not a state of enlightenment.

Suspending your breath out affects the parasympathetic nervous system, while suspending your breath in affects the sympathetic nervous system. When you focus and emphasize your inhale, the sympathetic part of the autonomic nervous system boosts your heart rate, increases blood pressure, and makes you more alert by giving you additional energy. On the other hand, by shifting the focus onto your exhale, the parasympathetic nervous system slows the heartbeat; it relaxes your nerves and digestion. Emphasizing the exhale helps release emotional and physical tension in your body.

Because you can slowly raise your blood pressure when you suspend your breath, you must pay attention to your body's reactions and adjust accordingly. If you have serious blood pressure issues, consult your doctor before practicing this yogic technology. If you still want to incorporate this form of meditation into your life, then show your doctor what you want to do; you may want to practice in the doctor's office first, where you can be monitored.

This particular meditative technique not only affects you physically; it can also be mentally demanding, as well. Suspending breathing is hard for some practitioners, especially beginners. Often, this difficulty represents a certain mental state: feeling like one doesn't have enough in life or that one is shortchanged in money, relationships, or life in general.

So much of how you feel is impacted by the strength of your nervous system. With practice and time, you will be able to regulate your thoughts and emotions with dexterity and mindfulness through something as simple as your breath.

"Breath is the essence of being. In all aspects of the universe, we can see the same rhythmic pattern of expansion and contraction, whether in the alternating cycle of day and night, waking and sleeping, high and low tides, or seasonal growth and decay. Oscillation between two phases exists at every level of reality, even up to the scale of the observable universe itself, which is presently in expansion but will, at some point, contract back to the original, unimaginable point that is everything and nothing, completing one cosmic breath."—Andrew Weil

Physician Andrew Weil is a proponent of incorporating meditation into medical healing. He spent many years in his career looking at the use of this yogic practice—primarily breath suspension—as a tool to release stress. He concluded that our breath is the natural rhythm of meditation. It is an internal orchestra that conducts our lives. If we were to take one to two minutes each day to sit and focus on the simple yet magnificent experience of our breath, we would feel a deeper connection to stillness and peace. Our breath is our life.

You might have heard about the link between a healthy gut and a strong mind. The vagus nerve is responsible for this relationship. If you are attempting to heal your body—in this case, your gut—then you want your brain to know when you feel better. This would erase feelings of depression. It is important, then, that we keep our minds strong by giving our vagus nerves a good, regular workout. Luckily, scientific research (such as the 2010 international study published in *The Journal of Alternative and Complementary Medicine*) is confirming that the rhythm and pattern of breathing meditation helps to stimulate the vagus nerve.

Breath suspension allows us to increase the connectedness between mind and body, which brings us closer to a higher consciousness. Echoing Dr. Weil's quote provided above: breath is everywhere in our lives. The flow of our breath is a teacher in everything we experience, if only we slowed down enough to learn from it. We become more fully aware of the cycle of life, of birth and death, due to the inherent nature of breathing. Releasing our breath is an act of letting go, of change, and ultimately the death process, while the essence of inhaling is a new beginning, moving energy, and life.

I have found that breath control allows me to find trust in letting go and gives me the strength to start again. The space in between these two polarities allows for a pause in our function, giving us the opportunity to activate a shift (if needed) in life.

Breath and Chant

Breath plays a big role in meditative chanting, but it can also expand to professional careers. Most singers have amazing lung capacities because it takes healthy and expansive lungs to be able to hold a note and project it. Through this note, they can elicit joy or pain, just like chanting. With sound, we can create love and hate. We can shout war cries or croon romantic ballads. This is because sound is inherently connected to our breath, which is our essence. And although breath is important in both aspects, chanting is still a little different from singing.

When we chant during meditation, we are often repeating the same mantra or words over and over again. It is a rhythmic pattern. Sometimes, we are meant to repeat this chant with little to no pause in between words. This is why breath control is so important; if you are breathing incorrectly, then you may become light-headed due to the oxygen and CO_2 trapped in your lungs.

Unless the direction states to chant in one breath, it is perfectly acceptable to take breaths in between words while chanting. Adapt the meditation to your own skills and lung capacity, which you can work on as you practice over time. It's okay to slow down if you feel frustrated. Be patient with yourself. Understand that the process must involve you letting go of control, so work on relinquishing those reins. The more you practice chanting, the stronger your lungs will become. Eventually, you will be able to maintain the intended rhythm.

If there is a pause in between words, try focusing on taking a deep belly breath. Don't be shy to let your belly extend out. Sure, we all want flat stomachs, but I think having inner peace and contentment is far more life-sustaining. Do not let distractions get in the way of your meditation, especially if it involves the sort of mental blocks that threaten to paralyze you with insecurities.

As you chant, you'll be able to gradually let the breath out so that it becomes easier to gasp for that big breath again. Take your time. Don't feel like you have to get it right the first few attempts. It could take days or weeks. Ideally, you will be practicing the meditation of your choosing for at least forty days straight, so there should be plenty of opportunities for you to perfect your breathing in chanting meditation.

Long-Deep Breathing

Long-deep breathing has endless benefits. We can't function in life without our breath, so paying attention to our diaphragm's health and capabilities is vital. After all, we would be dead if we didn't breathe. It's a wonder why, then, that more people don't spend quality time with themselves each day, if only to focus on their own breath and enhance their well-being.

Breathing long and deep releases chemicals into our brain—like endorphins, which can aid in the fight against depression. It also helps reduce and clean the build-up of CO_2 in our blood. Oxygen entering into the body is like a natural detox system, cleaning out any excessive CO_2, which tends to accumulate when we don't have healthy breathing patterns. More oxygen in the body helps bring more spinal fluid to the brain, boosting our memory and warding off headaches in the same process.

By influencing the parasympathetic nervous system, long-deep breathing relaxes and calms practitioners. This, of course, directly affects the way we handle stressful situations. When we're relaxed, we can make informed decisions without stress; we tend to respond rather than react when our nervous system is placated. If you pair this meditative breathing with eye focus techniques, the pituitary gland—which supports intuition—is additionally stimulated.

With long-deep breathing, we feel more in control of ourselves. Our brain is more alert. It gives us the strength to act. If you are dealing with emotional or physical stress, breathing deeply will help you heal more quickly. This is reflected in the way it allows you to break patterns in your subconscious mind, especially those founded in fear and insecurities. You might even find that you have more overall energy simply by practicing this meditative tool. In yoga, we call this energy *prana*; it is a life-giving force.

Long-deep breathing is the basic breathing technique used throughout most forms of meditation, unless the meditation specifies a different breathing pattern or chant. For any beginner, it is the first technique to start practicing. Because it sounds quite simple, it may seem silly that the first thing we need to do is to work on breathing long and deep. The truth is that most people—especially those who experience stress and anxiety— do not breathe correctly or deeply enough.

So let's practice:

Pay attention to your breath: the way it enters into your body through your nostrils, and how it gently exhales back outward. Cyclical, all-encompassing, expanding, and contracting. It is life, death, and everything in between. Focus on your breathing pattern for one to two minutes.

Now, put your hands on your belly. Emphasize your inhale by expanding your belly, like you are filling a balloon. It should be enough when your belly, chest, and the top of your lungs feel like they are full of air. Exhale and slowly release your breath. Let it roll through your body; relax your shoulders and then your upper chest. At the end of the exhale, pull in your belly; it should be hugging your spine as closely as possible, like a string has pinched them together.

Keep your hand on your belly and repeat this process. Inhale and inflate your lungs like a big balloon, exhale and pinch the belly to the back of the spine. Put down this book and close your eyes. Continue this practice for one to two minutes.

How do you feel? Was this easy or hard to do? Do you feel more calm and relaxed—or more anxious? Do you feel light-headed? Write down your initial experiences in a journal.

If you felt that it was challenging, I suggest that you keep trying. After a week of daily practice, you will notice a shift in the way you approach a proper breathing technique.

If you felt that it left you anxious, you might have activated relaxation-induced anxiety. This is when anxious feelings surface because you have let go of a sense of internal control, and your stress energy hikes up. Many people experience this without understanding what it is. "I don't like to meditate because I can't relax" is a common qualm, though it's actually the best excuse to continue meditating. If you can't relax, you should give yourself more time to adjust. If left unaddressed, that internal stress and anxiety will manifest itself into other health issues. So keep practicing. Eventually, you will be able to relax, and you'll find that your stress will start to melt away. You can also look into chanting meditations to inspire relaxation and then shift back to breathing exercises once you are at ease and comfortable.

If you feel light-headed, then you are getting the breathing sequence mixed up. You are pulling your belly in on the inhale and letting your belly relax on the exhale. This will cause you to get oxygen and CO_2 trapped in your lungs at the same time, causing dizziness. Stop the exercise and go back to your normal breathing rhythm before trying again—slower, next time. You can also try this practice while laying down with your hand on your stomach. Attempt long-deep breathing in this position for three to seven minutes for a few weeks. Then, try it sitting up again.

If you practice long-deep breathing for an extended time and still find it hard or even impossible, then I recommend you speak to your primary doctor or a physiotherapist who can work with you on your diaphragm. Your diaphragm can tighten up, requiring special treatment from a physical therapist to help you relearn how to relax the muscle. Get the support you need to be successful in breathing deeply.

Long-deep breathing may feel robotic at first, but that is a normal initial impression to have. Practice will make it a more comfortable sensation over time. When you were born, you breathed correctly, the way this meditation promotes. We can all return to that pure state. Remember: breathing correctly and deeply is one of the most important functions your body has. It can literally change your life.

Segmented Breathing

Segmented breathing is a meditative act in which you inhale or exhale in parts (also referred to as segments). By doing this, you create an internal rhythm within the body. This rhythm has a direct connection to the vagus nerve, which—as I've mentioned before—directly aids in the release of stress in your body.

Imagine your lungs as you breathe. With each inhale, envision your lungs as you fill them up—little by little on each pulse of the segment. Depending on how many counts the segmented meditation asks for, you will create a different amount of breath. For example:

- 4/4 Segmented Breathing: four inhale parts, four exhale parts.
- 4/8 Segmented Breathing: four inhale parts, eight exhale parts.

Nowadays, medical science has started using transcutaneous electrical nerve stimulation (TENS) machines to stimulate the vagus nerve and lower inflammation. But we don't need fancy equipment in order to experience such positive changes in our lives. We don't need to invest in the expense of a hospital visit. The only thing we need to invest in is time for ourselves. There is an internalized power within all of us that gives us the strength to alter our bodies, minds, and souls in a healthy and natural way. This power is activated by mindfulness.

Sadly, so many in our society are experiencing anxiety and panic attacks because their vagus nerve is overstimulated. That is why it is especially important to give this system the means to defend itself against stress and all of its debilitating side-effects. A medical device is not a requirement to receive this form of therapy, nor is money. Meditation—especially segmented breathing found in the Kundalini method—can provide this fortitude, free of charge.

The sooner you start exercising the vagus nerve, the sooner you will see its results. Using sound and segmented breathing rhythms, meditation will give you the power to heal from the inside out … as long as you allot yourself the time to practice. A few minutes of this meditative technique each day can be enough to get started. Go ahead and try it. Whether you're sitting at your desk or sitting in traffic on the commute back home, there is no bad time to breathe well.

Alternative Nostril Breathing

We are able to affect our thoughts and feelings by practicing nostril breathing, another meditative breathing option that Kundalini Yoga offers. The nerves that connect the brain to the nostrils cross at our eyebrows. The left hemisphere is connected to the right nostril, while the right hemisphere is connected to the left nostril. Depending on which nostril you breathe through, you can influence your own emotions.

Although it might not be noticeable, many of us tend to breathe through one nostril at a time. Sometimes, when we are completely relaxed and grounded, the breath may be balanced between the two nostrils. But if you were to check every so often throughout any average day, you would find that the air flow switches back and forth. Your mood can affect this, as well as the condition of your hypothalamus and pituitary glands.

By breathing in different ratios, we affect the time of the inhale and exhale. This dictates how much oxygen enters into our body and how much CO_2 is released. As human beings, we inhale and exhale in equal parts if we are content or relaxed. However, when we become triggered by upsetting emotions, our breath is the first reaction to our plight.

Unfortunately, because so many of us experience anxiety and other health issues in our lives, our basic breathing patterns have drastically changed. Anxiety, anger, and sadness can all make a huge difference in the way our lungs function. If scared, whether the fear is real or imagined, we might take short and shallow breaths. Some people even find that they hold their breath when distressed, not fully realizing that they aren't breathing. This sometimes occurs during sleep, especially in those suffering from sleep apnea. Practicing daily meditation can support your body and build up internal relaxation, resulting in healthier sleep.

All of these breathing patterns—a direct reaction to our feelings—end up impacting our emotion and can make it worse. Over time, we believe that this behavior is normal; this outlook eventually becomes instilled within us as anxiety. Meditation changes these breathing patterns and helps to teach our minds a new way to react to life and all of its stressful encounters, environments, and experiences.

When we close the left nostril and breathe through the right, we become more alert. Full of vigor and fueled by willpower, we become ready for action. The right nostril connects us to the sun energy, which is outward and expansive. This heat warms us and projects us forward, establishing movement in our lives. With focus and concentration, we feel compelled to create change.

When we close the right nostril and breathe through the left, we imbue ourselves with sensitivity and the capability to better understand any given situation. By connecting to the energy of the moon, we become more receptive to others; this teaches us to be more empathetic to ourselves and with the people in our lives. This sense of grounding gives us calm and balanced minds, granting us the capacity to be relaxed and self-reflective.

There are a number of Kundalini meditations to help balance the left and right nostrils. Because they are so simple and discreet, they can be practiced in your home or anywhere you find comfort, even in public settings. It only takes one to three minutes of this meditation to transform your mind and body; they are also incredibly easy to implement into your daily life.

Try the following breathing meditation to get a taste of its effect:

- Sit still. This can be in a chair or on the ground, but try to have your back straight.
- Remain quiet. Silence will allow you to focus on your pinpointed breathing.
- Close your eyes, or leave them half-open (I call this "Buddha eyes").
- Plug one of your nostrils, using your index finger; see above for the importance of each nostril. Breathe long and deep through the open nostril. Do this for three to seven minutes.
- Write down how you feel immediately after this experience.

Chapter 10

Benefits of Chanting

"Why do you chant when you meditate?"

This is a question that I hear often, especially in the United States, where many feel uncomfortable with chanting or making sounds out loud. This timidity is what drives some to explore silent forms of self-reflection, like Transcendental Meditation. TM has become a common perception of meditation worldwide, reaching as far as southern China. After teaching a class there in 2016, I had a student ask me, "Why not focus on everything around you and concentrate solely on your thoughts?"

The truth is that for many who experience stress and anxiety, silent meditation is not enough to overcome the noise in their head. It is not a suitable form of healing. Because of neurological stagnation in the brain and a weakened nervous system, their minds are very strong and active—and they run the show. Sitting still and trying to focus on clearing their mind is often unachievable, causing frustration or anger; it might eventually inspire feelings of being a failure due to the lack of accomplishment. Agitated, the symptoms of anxiety that they were trying to release are increased as a result.

Very rarely do I teach silent, sitting meditations. Many people who come to me to learn how to meditate as a way of self-healing are discouraged by the notion of sitting silently. They have tried the method, and it didn't work for them. I've noticed that my patients benefit the most from practicing breathing patterns or chanting meditations.

Chanting is a tool used to entertain the mind, giving it focus. It assigns the mind a specific job: repeating a mantra, following a rhythm, and supporting long-deep breathing. For more elaborate distractions from overbearing thoughts, hand poses (mudras) and eye focus can also be implemented. While the mind is concentrated on the chanting, the healing occurs.

Not only is chanting an excellent method to move your thoughts out of the way, but there are also scientifically supported benefits to this yogic technique. Dr. Alan Watkins of Imperial College London found that chanting—Gregorian, to be specific—resulted in "significant and positive physiological impact" by lowering heart rate and blood pressure ("Chant: A Healing Art?" 2008), therefore reducing stress. This is likely due to the controlled breathing techniques required in chanting (which naturally calm the body) and even the communal aspect of performing as a group. Overall, Dr. Watkins concluded that chanting can "significantly improve [our] mental state, reduce tension, and increase [our] efficiency in the workplace" ("Gregorian Chanting Can Reduce Blood Pressure and Stress," 2008).

Yogically, it is believed that chanting during meditation directs the mind to create new, positive patterns due to the conscious rhythm and sound currents we produce. Rather than the Latin used in Gregorian chants, however, Kundalini technology uses old Sanskrit, called Gurmukhi. It is said that Gurmukhi is the universal DNA behind all language because it comes from one sound current.

According to Kundalini Yoga ideology, Gurmukhi can adjust the endocrine system and metabolism to create balance in the self. When chanted, this language can help us overcome depression by strengthening our intelligence and intuition. Repeating mantras in Gurmukhi helps us to cultivate our brain chemistry and raises our mind's potential.

You can also chant in other languages, including English and even Latin. As I mentioned earlier in this book, I worked with a Catholic client who didn't feel comfortable chanting in Gurmukhi. Keeping his faith in consideration, I was able to ease him into an alternative path of meditation. Chanting prayers and hymns is totally acceptable as long as they bring you inner peace.

If you are uncomfortable with chanting in a foreign language simply because you find it awkward to get past the unfamiliarity of the words and sounds, then I would actually encourage you to try to connect with Gurmukhi. Because you are forcing your hesitant mind to get out of your own way, stepping out of your comfort zone will help direct you out of your anxiety. I know you can forge a relationship with Gurmukhi because *I* have, and so have thousands of others who have never previously spoken this ancient tongue.

In fact, chanting in a language we think we don't know or understand is inconsequential to the overall meditative experience. We inherently know what the words mean because we understand their purpose: to dig deep into ourselves and free the mind. The sound currents—regardless of our grasp of the language(s) and its translation—teaches us to let go and simply be. The noise produced as a by-product of life and all its experiences is quieted down.

Chanting—or any self-made sound— tames the brain's activity in the default mode network. When the DMN is overactive, our minds run wild, often with negative or worrying thoughts. (It's the *Did I leave the windows open?* sort of thought that pops in your head as you lounge on a hammock while on vacation.) Repetitive thoughts and emotions formed by stress and anxiety can be altered by creating new, healthy patterns instead. A mantra will fill the space in your mind where you might think, *I am not good enough*, giving you the room to evaluate your needs and assess your ability to address them.

> Chanting—or any self-made sound—tames the brain's activity in the default mode network.

Because your thoughts control how you feel, you can actively change your emotions by practicing chanting meditation. This simple instruction can prove to be difficult, despite how easy it sounds. Many have held a certain thought or feeling for so long that they believe it to be true. Trying to stop that thought creates an argument with the mind, leaving one with a sense of defeat. However, even though some habits are hard to break, we are wholly capable of change.

Our brains are made of 73 percent water (USGS, n.d.), so it is quite a malleable organ that can be easily influenced. Rhythmic chanting changes the patterns and frequencies in the brain by activating our theta and alpha waves, putting our minds in relaxed attention. This seemingly contradictory state of mind does not always happen immediately, but we can gradually train our minds to reach this consciousness without falling asleep. With practice, you can change your brain and create a deep, lasting change in your life. But it also must be consistent practice. Think of it like housekeeping: If you thoroughly clean your home one day, it will not be clean forever. You need to maintain its cleanliness.

Kundalini Yoga is known as the householder's yoga due to its quick effects in everyday life. It tends to work more quickly than other forms of yoga, in part because of the chanting incorporated into the act. It asks us to direct our attention somewhere specific: our breaths, words, body poses, and so on.

When we feel like we can successfully quiet our minds, we feel secure in focusing on our needs. When we feel confident, we are more likely to accept necessary changes in our lives. When we can control our thoughts and shift our emotions, we find the inspiration to continue the healing process. And the cycle continues.

However, meditation's healing power still takes some time. We are trying to reconfigure the fragile mind, after all, including the way it addresses and processes thoughts and emotions.

Sometimes, when we are in excruciating emotional pain or dealing with anxiety, we crave immediate change. We are willing to try anything because we want to feel better as quickly as possible; that is why many turn to temporary distractions like food or drugs. Meditation asks us to be patient as our bodies adjust. I promise you that the wait is worthwhile. Knowing this, I hope that you are encouraged to embrace the act of chanting during your meditative journey due to its immense positive effects on the brain and body.

It may take some time to get used to chanting. Incorporating words into your meditation can feel overwhelming due to the unfamiliar language and how strange it feels to be vocal. Start slowly and casually build up your comfort level. You will know when it is time to graduate to chanting and breath-oriented meditations by listening to your own body.

New students in my meditation classes are often shy when it comes to chanting. Understandably, it makes them feel self-conscious or embarrassed or intimidated. Once they move past their nerves, many actually prefer the Gurmukhi-based chanting more than silent and breath-oriented meditations. They'll find that they think, hum, and chant mantras even when they are not in class, like while doing the dishes or driving home from work. This is a great step toward the shift in your brain and training your mind to serve your needs instead of ruminating on hurtful thoughts or memories. When meditation and chanting comes to you in such a natural way, your body treats it as an act so essential to living that it is no different from breathing.

Kundalini music and chanting music can help you get started when introducing chanting into your meditation. I find that simple music works best; restrained sounds and monotone voices allow for each mantra to be well-exposed to listeners, allowing them to better pick up the words. Once you feel at ease with chanting alongside music, then I encourage you to try meditative chanting without the music as a guide. By chanting on your own, you will be able to dig deeper into yourself and hear what needs your body, mind, and soul are asking of you. This helps you to build a solid relationship with yourself.

Physiological Aspect of Vibrations

Think of your body as a tuning fork. When struck, a tuning fork vibrates and emits a note of a specific pitch. This, too, happens within your body: the vibrations caused by mantras and sounds create a change within you that reverberates out from your meridians.

Most of us have heard of—if not actually tried—acupuncture. This alternative form of therapy works on all meridians in the body by pricking the skin with needles, alleviating both mental and physical ailments. Stimulating one meridian affects other parts of your body. Reflexology, a massage system that is based around the foot and how it connects to every part of the body, is another form of therapy focusing on the power of meridians.

You have these meridians in your mouth—eighty-four of them, according to Yogi Bhajan (*The KRI Aquarian Teacher 1 Lecture Manual*)— which connect to your brain. When you talk, chant, or sing, you activate the meridians with your tongue; in that respect, they are like a piano with different keys. This is common faith held in yogic ideology, but I know that science will soon be able to back up this long-held belief with studies.

Most people have heard of "om" (meaning "formless") in reference to meditation; it is as synonymous with yogic practice as the word *namaste*. In Kundalini practice, however, we chant "ong." This means "creation."

From the pressure it places on the upper back palate of your mouth, it sends a vibration straight to your pituitary gland and frontal lobe. Although the two mystic syllables seem similar, try chanting each for one minute and see how you feel. Was there a difference between the two? Did you notice the nasal feeling when chanting "ong"? This is the awakening of the pituitary gland.

These are some other common Kundalini mantras:

- Wahe Guru: "indescribable truth"
- Sat Naam: "true identity"
- Guru Guru Wahe Guru: "true miracle of truth"

By chanting, we are creating an internal pulse that starts at the tongue and continues to the brain. It travels to and eventually influences the hypothalamus—the switchboard for the endocrine system—which is responsible for our vital functions such as hunger, thirst, body temperature, and sleep. Hanging by a thin stalk off our hypothalamus is our pituitary gland. Also known as the "master gland," the pituitary gland regulates the functionality of the endocrine system by controlling the release of hormones that affect the thyroid gland, adrenal glands, and ovaries or testes.

The hypothalamus and pituitary glands govern our moods, emotional behaviors, creativity, and sexuality. By chanting, we can adjust any of these qualities in our lives. This is why those with stress and anxiety—even PTSD and forms of depression—should contemplate incorporating meditation into their daily habits. You can change the emotions in your life by choosing which patterns to follow, and you can change patterns by using meditation.

With diligent practice, you might even stimulate the release of amrit. According to Hindu mythology, Amrita—a nectar created by the churning ocean—was consumed by the gods in order to achieve immortality. Amrit is believed to be released with a special mudra called Kechari, or the tongue lock (*The Khecarīvidyā of Adinathā*, 2007). This is a very advanced mudra, since it asks the tongue to move beyond the uvula at the back of the throat and press into the nasal cavity. By awakening the meridians through vibrations, the pituitary gland secretes amrit; this is yogically known as "nectar." This sweet nectar is believed to energize the body and stave off feelings of thirst, hunger, and sleep (all of which are connected to the hypothalamus).

One of the reasons why I love Kundalini technology so much is that there are thousands of meditations, with each one affecting us in a different way. There is no one-size-fits-all in Kundalini; you are able to pick which methods fit you, your life, and what you hope to change or achieve. I have included meditations related to anxiety in this book, but you will see that most can cross over to quell feelings of depression, anger, fear, and more.

From experience, I know that chanting mantras has improved my mental health. But you will have to try it for yourself to know whether or not it works for you too. Like I have mentioned before, you may not find success the first time—and you might not even find it on the tenth attempt. Meditation involves a lot of patience. In the meantime, learn to submit to the experience and be present with yourself.

Psychological Implications of Setting Patterns

I love to sing. I might not be that good at it, but I still love singing—loud and proud. My favorite approach is belting out a song in the car with my sons. It creates such a wonderful feeling inside, even (or especially) if you are imperfectly toned and carefree. Chanting is not singing, but you can feel similar effects: they both open your heart.

During a twelve-hour meditation marathon at a woman's camp in Northern California, my friend told me that I had an amazing chanting voice. Previously, I had never thought that my voice was any good; as I just mentioned, I'm not a fan of my singing voice, either. But the truth is that anyone can chant, and I ultimately discovered that my voice worked in harmony with mantras. All I had to do was keep them simple and utter them in a monotonous voice.

If you watch any of Yogi Bhajan's meditation videos, you will hear that a majority of his chants are performed in an uninflected, monk-like way. They are not high in pitch, and this is done on purpose; keeping your voice flat affects your glands and neurological pathways due to vibrations. Chanting not only creates a physiological change inside your body (as established in the previous section); it also has deep psychological implications due to the rhythms being set. Over time, these patterns become internalized and create change in our minds, as well.

The patterns created by chanting's rhythms activate the nervous system (regulating stress and tension), the endocrine system (balancing hormone production), and the vagus nerve (reducing heart rate and blood pressure). By using chanting to strengthen these systems, your body learns to communicate coherently and address its most pressing needs. It takes neurotransmitters—like the release of serotonin (affecting mood and behavior) and dopamine (the "rewards" chemical)—to correctly relay that information without the threat of misfiring. Meditation trains your body and mind to unite.

If you feel overwhelmed by the idea of practicing chanting meditation by yourself, without guidance or outside encouragement, you may want to consider joining a Kundalini class. In fact, you could see even more benefits by incorporating group meditation into your life.

Like I mentioned above, I love singing in the car with my sons, and there might be an evolutionary reason for that. A study published in *The Journal of Personality and Social Psychology* (2013) posed the idea that the pleasure we gain from singing together is the result of "its innate connection to the basic social drives" that have guided humans through history. This could correlate with a separate investigation that looked at the heart rate variability (HRV) of singers performing as a choir. What these researchers found was remarkable.

As part of a group study, fifteen cardio-healthy young adults were asked to sing in three different styles: hum, hymn, and mantra. Scientists discovered that the heart rates of the participants accelerated and decelerated simultaneously during the hymn and mantra portion of the experiment, but it was especially pronounced during the latter. They ultimately determined that if the participants had been able to chant a mantra in unison for longer than the allotted five minutes, "all the hearts would have been totally synchronized in HRV phase and frequency" (*Frontier Psychology*, 2013). Even if we can't harmonize in tone, it seems our bodies want to harmonize with each other. We are all connected to the collective conscious of the universe.

Because of the sounds and group energy involved, performing in a choir can be a lot like group meditation. Choral singing can also help us feel connected by lessening feelings of loneliness and depression (*Music and Health*, 2010). In combination with the *Frontier Psychology* study, we can conclude that mantra chanting holds the same benefits of guiding meditators away from feelings of isolation.

The active performance of music—including singing and chanting—is thought to be an important aspect of community-building across various societies. It is no surprise, then, that I find such enjoyment when singing with my sons; it is a human bonding experience. Not only that, but being involved in the act of creating music can trigger the release of two beneficial hormones: endorphins and oxytocin.

When participants in a study were asked to perform music (singing, dancing, and drumming), researchers found that this active performance—rather than merely listening to music—triggered the release of endorphins (*Evolutionary Psychology*, 2012). Secreted within the brain and nervous system, endorphins are chemicals within the body that bring us to a natural euphoric state. We experience this after vigorous exercise ("runner's high"), following sex, and even after eating chocolate or spicy food. It is associated with feelings of pleasure, in addition to serving as a tranquilizer for pain.

Oxytocin, on the other hand, is a chemical produced in the hypothalamus and released from the pituitary gland. It is often referred to as the "love hormone" due to it serving humans during acts of affection and bonding, including sexual activity, childbirth, and lactation. Enhancing feelings of trust within a social function, oxytocin provides us with psychological stability that encourages pro-social behaviors. With this stability, our body feels contented and relaxed. Ultimately, our stress responses—including anxiety—are lowered. Researchers have found that amateur and professional singers alike saw a significant increase in oxytocin concentration during a singing lesson (*Integrative Psychological and Behavioral Science*, 2003). While only the amateurs reported feeling more joy after the lesson, both groups were more energetic *and* relaxed. This seems to imply that singing—and, by extension, chanting—can give you the zest to move through life while simultaneously easing your overworked mind.

When the brain creates a shift in your glands and neurological pathways, this inspires change in your mind. Your thoughts are affected as a direct result, meaning your emotional self is revealed and healed. Again, you have to incorporate this ritual into your everyday routine. As important as patterns are in chanting, so is the repetition of meditating in your daily life. Like exercise for the body, you can maintain your brain's health through meditation. You will soon be able to set a new pattern in your mind to change the old patterns of stress, anxiety, and panic.

If you don't know where to start with chanting, try something simple. Chant this out loud: "I will meditate daily ... I will meditate daily ... I will meditate daily."

———

When I began incorporating Kundalini meditations into my clients' therapy, I needed chanting recordings that would be easy to follow without my direction. My clients needed to have the capability to dive deep into their own experience with themselves (without my physical presence), whether they practiced by themselves or with family and friends. This is one of the reasons why I started creating my own chanting meditations: I wanted something simple that anyone, especially the householders, could use.

On my website (www.MadhurNain.com), you can find various mantra music and instrumental music to incorporate into your daily meditation. I have information on how to pronounce various mantras as well as explanations on their purpose. If you are unable to find a meditation group near you, you may want to use supplemental music to guide you on your journey. Providing a sense of support, this music will help you to soothe your nerves and raise your spirits, especially as you adjust to the new sensations—including heavy thoughts and emotions—brought onto you by Kundalini technology.

Although I offer additional instructions and meditations at no cost, I also have several albums available for purchase on my website. These include the following:

- Meditation Collection, Vol. 1
- Meditation Collection, Vol. 2
- Segmented Breathing
- Kundalini Affirmation Meditation
- Kundalini Savasana
- 2014 Kundalini Mantra Compilation
- 2015 Kundalini Mantra Compilation
- 2016 Kundalini Mantra Compilation
- 2017 Kundalini Mantra Compilation

Chapter 11

Introducing Kundalini Meditation into Your Life

A basic yet essential element to meditation is that it helps to strengthen your relationship with yourself. This is the key to finding and maintaining happiness. Members of Western society often look outside themselves—depending on distractions like television programs and stimulants—in an attempt to bring themselves joy. Although not all distractions are harmful, few are sustainable for long-term happiness, regardless of their benefits. By relying on outside sources in order to create and maintain happiness, we ignore the mind's potential to serve our emotional needs. As a result, anxiety can emerge in the space between our thoughts. That is why it is important to learn how to cultivate the mind, which will allow it to flourish like a well-maintained garden.

You might be asking yourself, "When is it time to start using meditation as a treatment for my stress and anxiety?" Well, I think you know what I am going to say to that. The answer is *now*. Because you have picked up this book, you must be curious about the Kundalini process and are seeking help for your distress. *Now* is the time to start exploring meditation. There should be no reason to delay getting started. Not only will meditation relieve you of your stress and anxiety, but it can also help to prevent it. You brush your teeth every day to avoid oral diseases; similarly, meditation can be used every day to avoid mental diseases.

When used correctly, meditation can be an incredibly powerful tool. Because of its influence over the body, mind, and soul, you do not want to meditate when in an altered state of consciousness. Please do not meditate after you have had any form of alcohol; mixing the two is counterproductive. Beer, wine, and spirits offer us an option to check out. Meditation, however, is all about checking within and connecting to yourself. Alcohol hinders that process.

Additionally, meditation is *not* compatible with recreational drugs, such as marijuana, cocaine, MDMA, meth, heroin, and others such as Ayahuasca. Some turn to these drugs as a form of escape to avoid life or in an attempt to discover a deeper meaning, but they should not be used in combination with Kundalini meditations. Both yield great power over the body and its processes, so merging their functions together can be very harmful to your mind and consciousness.

If you have been using recreational drugs but would like to practice Kundalini meditations, I suggest that you halt using these drugs. Try incorporating whole foods into your diet, along with plenty of water to flush out your body. Do this for about one month before attempting Kundalini meditation.

If you have chosen to use pharmaceutical drugs prescribed by a licensed doctor or psychiatrist, it is acceptable to implement Kundalini meditations into your life. Before doing so, however, please check with your health professional. Do not change your dosage or stop your medication altogether without supervision from your doctor. Stopping your medication cold turkey can be detrimental to your health, so proceed with caution.

Although some people might need to be more keenly aware of their physical and mental state before starting Kundalini meditation, anyone can practice this ancient technology, at any age, religion, culture, or economic state. At any and all stages of life, meditation is here for you. Incorporating this tool into your daily routine will enhance, develop, and heal you and your life.

The manner in which you introduce Kundalini meditation into your life depends on your comfort level. When and where you choose to practice has to do with when and where you feel the most secure; it must be done in a place where you feel safe with your thoughts, which will vary from person to person. Some might find public spaces adequate, while others will only want to meditate alone in the tranquility of their bedroom. If you commit to this yogic journey, the only thing you *can't* do is make excuses to avoid meditating altogether.

In a perfect world, we would all have a beautiful setting in our home or garden where we could meditate once or twice a day. Most of us have busy lives that we have to juggle, so locating a peaceful spot to meditate is hard. Making a sacred space may not be in your budget, you think, because it has to be an isolated location that is specially designed and pleasing to the eye, but you must not use this lack of space to justify avoiding practicing altogether.

The truth is, we do not need to find this kind of paradise to meditate. If you are meditating following a Kundalini technique, your eyes will either be closed or in a specific eye focus. Because the act of meditation is about building a relationship with yourself, you should be concentrated only on your own consciousness, your higher self, your soul identity. If you are looking around at your environment, you are being distracted, and the meditation won't be effective.

Over the years, I have meditated in many different (and sometimes absurd) places, such as the yoga room in San Francisco International Airport. I was on a thousand-day meditation challenge and did not want to miss a day, so in I went. A few different people came in as I was practicing, yet I continued chanting despite the potential distraction or embarrassment. These people would never see me again, so if they thought I was strange, their opinions didn't matter to me. Plus, I figured the frequencies caused by chanting's vibrations were good for everyone in proximity anyway. Maybe they, too, benefitted from meditation's ability to calm the mind preflight.

Another odd place for meditation happened when I was camping with my friend and our children. One evening, I went to a quiet section of the camper and meditated. This sparked a conversation with my friend and her son about the benefits of meditation. To this day, they still ask me about the practice.

As you can see, you can meditate anywhere. You don't need a yoga studio or a lush garden space in your backyard. It is only your mind that can stand in the way.

We are so easily distracted and can find any number of reasons as to why we can't complete any given task. Most of the time, this is just an excuse to avoid responsibility. Meditation should be treated like a daily routine, one that is naturally incorporated into your life in a way that is as effortless as stepping out of bed each morning.

Meditation is for any time of the day or night, for any reason under the sun or moon. There is no single right time to practice; to miss that window on a particular day does not mean you can't revisit it before bed, for example. Like there is no uniform location to meditate, there is also no specific time one must practice.

You must ask yourself these questions:

- When will you feel more comfortable to bring meditation into your life?
- When do you think you need meditation the most?
- Why would you need it at this time?
- What could keep you from meditating at this time?

> If you have a lot of unsettling thoughts at night or you feel as if you can't let go of your day's experiences, then evening meditation is a great tool to help you unwind.

Meditating at night helps you to relax and enables you to go to sleep faster. This can be incredibly helpful for those who have an overactive mind and find it difficult to fall asleep. If you have a lot of unsettling thoughts at night or you feel as if you can't let go of your day's experiences, then evening meditation is a great tool to help you unwind. By filtering out your thoughts, you can find a calmness in your mind that allows you to drift off with ease.

About nine years ago, when I made the commitment to meditate every day for the rest of my life, I started to meditate at night. I even put a sign up by my bed that asked, "Did you meditate?" This was a great time for me to start practicing regular meditation because it helped moderate my mind. However, there were still those nights when I would be up a little too late or I had enjoyed a night out a little too long. When I got home, I would be so tired that I would forget to meditate. The next day, I would always polish up my act and catch up practicing, but it made me realize that evening meditation is not always an ideal set time for a hectic lifestyle.

I have found that the morning is the best time for me to meditate because it determines the mood for my entire day. It fixes the energy frequency from which I will operate. And anyone can achieve this natural daily enhancer by practicing morning meditation. By tapping into this frequency, you will be mentally and spiritually supported to find your potential and be the best version of yourself that you can possibly be throughout the day.

Most people wake up and do one of two things: go to the bathroom or look at some form of technology. What you do first thing in the day will affect the state of your day as a whole. So why not meditate instead? Why not chant or say a prayer? If you turn inward and listen to your conscious self, you have the potential to deliver uplifting messages to yourself. Set the pace of positivity by being kind to your soul, which will reflect on your body and mind.

Like breathing, meditation is a tool for living. We need oxygen to stay alive, like we need meditation to stay sane. Using this yogic technology can be daunting at first due to its unfamiliarity, but starting slow—with diligent practice—will help build confidence. This will eventually reflect inward, allowing practitioners to feel courage in controlling their minds. When we have courage, we feel like we can face anything. This makes it easier to assess our mental state, eventually giving us the strength to conquer our stress and anxiety. Having courage is an important step in making strident changes in our lives.

Those interested in using meditation must consider when and where they will practice, as well as how long. It is also worth taking a moment to consider why meditation is the correct step in treatment for stress and anxiety. When you can answer that question with clarity, then you can determine what Kundalini meditation (or meditations) to explore; each one has a set purpose and effect on the body and mind.

Here are some questions to consider before getting started:

What Is Your Intention Behind Meditating?

Many studies have proven the benefits of meditation, like how it raises GABA levels in the brain: a natural remedy to feeling happier and more at peace. It impacts the physical body and the emotional self as a result. There are a few reasons why you may find you have gravitated to this form of natural therapy:

- You feel a connection to something greater—something bigger than yourself—and you want to tap into this intuition. By doing so, you hope to live your life in a more conscious manner. You know that there is something beyond your mortal existence, and you want to feel connected to this amazing universal truth.

- You are in so much pain that you don't know where else to turn. Your life has become burdened with stress and anxiety, paralyzing you in a way that makes decisions difficult or impossible. You feel you have reached the end of your rope, and you are willing to try anything to feel better—even this yogic form that may seem strange from an outsider's perspective. Meditation may have been suggested by your doctor.
- You are someone who would like to improve your mental (and, therefore, physical) health for one simple fact: enhanced happiness. You are seeking to build contentment in all areas of your life. Meditation is not only for those in crisis, after all; it is a tool that helps keep us from reaching this critical point.
- You might even find that you want to try meditation simply because of its buzzworthy name in our modern society and culture. This is acceptable, too, as long as you honor the requirements it places on you (such as daily practice, learning proper breathing patterns, and holding poses).

No matter how you discovered meditation and decided to start a spiritual journey, all paths will lead you to your inner self. When you feel connected to your identity in such a deeply divine way, you are able to make the changes you want and need in your life. The depth and creativity instilled within you through the act of meditation will bring you balance and happiness.

How Long Should You Meditate?

If meditating is new to you, pick a length of time that you feel is attainable as you adjust to the daily habit. I suggest starting with three minutes and gradually increasing your time. Here are some options of timing and why:

- Two and a half minutes changes the psyche in the subconscious mind and creates new patterns from which you live.
- Three minutes affects the electromagnetic field (your subtle energies around your body) and the circulation and stability of the blood (changing your blood pressure).

- Eleven minutes begins to change the nervous and glandular system, affecting your moods (like depression and general feelings of sluggishness).
- Twenty-two minutes balances the three minds (negative-protective, positive-perceptive, and neutral) and supports them to work together, building more clarity within your emotional state.
- Thirty-one minutes allows the glands, breath patterns, and concentration to affect all the cells in and rhythms of the body, influencing your emotional state of mind and how you relate to yourself and with others.
- Sixty-two minutes changes the gray matter in the brain, improving self-control, aiding in better decision-making, and integrating the subconscious "shadow mind" and conscious mind.

What Meditation Should You Practice?

New practitioners of meditation should start with the Beginner's Meditation, as it will open a relationship between the mind and your inner self—including your thoughts and emotions—through your breath. If you have more experience or feel like you are emotionally prepared to explore a more powerful meditation, then I recommend the Healing Meditation; this is especially good for those who are desperately seeking to de-stress their lives as quickly as possible.

There are different kinds of meditation within Kundalini, each of which might appeal to different people based on comfort levels. Each form will also affect the body and mind in a distinct manner, so you may choose which to practice depending on the kind of healing you seek:

- Silent Meditation: This is when you sit silently for twenty minutes, two times a day. Kundalini silent meditation uses eye focus and mudras as support. For Kundalini, it is not about sitting in silence and tuning out; you want to tune within, and using the physical body helps you to achieve that goal.
- Breathing Meditation: This is when you focus on your breathing. If your mind starts to wander, you can bring your thoughts back to your breath. Kundalini has a vast variety of breath meditations

with different patterns, each stimulating the vagus nerve. Breathing meditations are easy to use throughout the day, if you find yourself becoming stressed or anxious. No one will even know that you are connecting to your inner self through the use of meditative breathing techniques.

- Chanting Meditation: This is when you sit and focus on a mantra. There are different kinds of chants from different faiths or yogic paths. Kundalini chanting-meditation is typically easy to follow, so it is perfect for beginners. Many who attend meditation classes with an emphasis on chanting are shy at first. It is normal to feel self-conscious about using your voice in such a way. I like to remind people that you are not singing; you are chanting. There is a difference. Once people feel more comfortable about chanting, they often prefer this form of meditation to the silent or breathing-sequence forms.

You have seen an essential fact reiterated throughout this book, and that is, our minds create thoughts and feelings we believe to be true. These are only prejudices, flexible and

> Meditation is a tool that changes the kinds of thoughts that your mind produces.

malleable, with enough willpower and positive influence. Meditation is a tool that changes the kinds of thoughts that your mind produces; it asks for more distance between the clutter in your brain, prompting clarity, inner awareness, and calmness as a result.

It only takes forty days to break a habit and ninety days to create a new one. So what are you waiting for? Try meditation now.

Learning to Meditate

Meditation is a very simple act once you get past its apparent weirdness. You must remember that it is only different because you have never done it before. Once you start practicing regularly—every day is ideal, as I've stated numerous times—then you will feel more connected to the experience. Before you can decide if you enjoy meditating or determine whether it is working for you, you have to at least give it a serious chance with your full dedication.

When learning to meditate, I suggest starting your habitual practice upon waking up. Morning Sadhana is the morning daily practice of Kundalini technology. The best time to meditate is early in the morning, before the sun rises; this is known as the ambrosial time. During this time, the unconscious mind is at its most open and vulnerable stage. Because of this, it is able to dump information, allowing you to self-reflect and process thoughts with greater clarity.

In other meditative pathways, we are told to clear the mind. This is not the case in Kundalini Yoga. During the ambrosial hour, as you are meditating, permit the thoughts—good, bad, ugly, scary, painful, and so on—to pass through you. As you sit in your mudra, keep breathing and chanting and allowing these thoughts to move within you. In doing so, you can process information and emotions, giving you knowledge and insight. *This* is meditation.

I like to say that meditation is like washing your brain, and chanting is the spot remover. You don't wear the same pair of underwear every day, and so you should likewise not let your thoughts sit idle in your mind. Like changing your underwear and washing the old pair, you are cleansing and purifying your thoughts through the act of Kundalini Yoga.

It only takes three minutes for irritating thoughts to get triggered in your mind. Then they can become persistent and annoying, perhaps even distracting. The trick is to sit very still as you allow the art of meditation—including breathing work and chanting—to do its job. Those thoughts could keep bugging you for as much as fifteen or forty-five minutes. Remain devoted to meditation for as long as you feel necessary, until these thoughts subside through rationalization.

This exercise will also strengthen your nervous system. The weaker your nervous system, the harder it is to sit still. When you physically restrain your body, the mind is granted the space to filter thoughts; this is the start of connecting to your meditative mind. Once you come to this total stillness, you will feel a sense of internal coziness. This is called *shuniya*. It is difficult to describe this feeling, but you will recognize its warmth when you experience it—and you can, with practice.

Who Should Meditate?

When it comes to learning how to meditate, the most important step is being ready to receive. Once you are ready to welcome this technology into your life, then you will be open to learn its power and benefit from it. People who meditate must be open-minded and accepting.

Life is about making connections, but we tend to float through life, making these connections in various dysfunctional ways. Meditation will teach you how to deal with the most important relationship in your life: the one with yourself. People who meditate must be willing to acknowledge imperfections and be comfortable working on their selves.

There are scientific studies that show meditation's high success rate in healing anxiety. This does not mean you should quit any prescription medications when you start feeling better through meditation. Before making any medical decisions, please work

> Meditation will teach you how to deal with the most important relationship in your life: the one with yourself.

with your health care provider for advice. Some pharmaceuticals need to be weaned off slowly, letting your body and mind adjust to the change. Moving too quickly can cause adverse reactions, which is the opposite of what we hope to achieve through Kundalini technology. People who meditate must be able to listen to what their bodies need.

You have two options when introducing meditation into your life: start slow, or jump in. Based on your comfort level, you can decide which path is right you. The journey to success is to follow the path, whether it's a lolling stroll or a brisk jog. Either way, you will reach your destination—as long as you just get started. People who meditate must *want* to meditate.

Where Should You Meditate?

Regardless of how you start (fast or slow), you will need a place to meditate. This can be at home, on a couch, or on a chair. You could even sit on the ground with a pillow, which is what I do. To maintain correct posture, it may help to lean against a wall or a couch. Keeping your back straight is the preferred method for Kundalini meditation; this allows the energy to rise up through the spine, reaching your chakra centers.

You may want to dedicate a special room in your residence to yoga and meditation, complete with altar and spiritual symbolism. But do not feel limited to practicing meditation only at home. You can do so at your job, sitting at a desk. You only need three minutes to feel its effects. If you are feeling stressed over an assignment, those three minutes used to balance your mind would be time well-spent; it will allow you to clear the distractions and focus on your work again.

There are yoga classes that offer Kundalini meditation, which is an option for those who are financially secure. And, of course, you could always take your yogic technology to the outdoors, meditating in your backyard or under a tree at a public park. You could even meditate in your car. No matter where you choose to practice, it is crucial to be aware of your surroundings and to feel safe in this setting. If you are trying to complete a task while meditating (like driving), please keep your eyes open and remain focused. Mantra music will help you in this process.

When Should You Meditate?

Meditation can be practiced throughout the day. There is this preconceived notion that we must sit in a completely quiet place, once or twice a day, for at least twenty minutes, to constitute it as meditating. This is not true. Meditation works best when it is integrated into your daily life, of course, but there are no universal rules. You set the location, time, and duration of each practice.

If you have a daily routine of meditating each morning, do not feel pressure to strictly adhere to that time period in order to self-reflect. If you had an upsetting conversation with a friend or family member in the middle of the day, take a moment to stop and reconnect with yourself through meditation. Use a chant or breathing sequence in order to reforge this connection. This helps to bring you back to a clearer mind by balancing your equilibrium.

Similarly, if you are about to take an important test or engage with superiors during a high-pressure meeting, you can meditate. Find the time to gather your energies and tune into your higher self, your intuition; you only need seven to eleven minutes to achieve this. Through meditation, your brain learns to coordinate its functions in unison to help support your cognitive communication (or thought process).

Ultimately, you must listen to your body. When you feel tense or your heart is racing, your body is internally screaming for help. Relief can be found in the form of meditation. Three minutes will lower your blood pressure. Don't be afraid to try it because it is new and different. Giving meditation a chance can help you regulate your life by improving your body's functions and increasing your mind's strength. Don't forget to write down your experiences in a journey after each meditation so you can track your progress. You might be surprised just how supportive meditation can be in helping you find success throughout all aspects of life.

How Should You Meditate?

Whether you start slow or jump in, it doesn't matter how fast you travel through your meditative journey. What will bring you the most success with reducing stress and creating inner peace is consistency. Try to do whichever meditation you choose for forty days straight, without missing a single day. After three weeks, you might notice that you feel strange or more emotional. This is normal. Don't forget that meditation is the act of cleaning out your subconscious mind and all of the baggage—positive and negative—that is locked inside.

Depending on your comfort level, you will have to decide which path to take:

- Starting slow: If you are choosing this path, the best meditation to start with is the Beginner's Meditation. It is very simple. All you have to do is listen to your preferred audio or practice with your own internal mantra. When you think or hear the mantra "Sat," inhale (from your diaphragm, up to your shoulders) and hold your breath for a moment. When you think or hear the mantra "Naam," then you can exhale. Slowly release the breath out of your lungs in a rolling manner, from the shoulders downward, and end by pulling your diaphragm and navel inward to the back of your spine. This activates your Kundalini awareness energy and inner strength.

- Jumping in: If you feel ready or are desperate for quick changes in your life, then jumping into a more elaborate form of meditation is ideal. This means incorporating chanting into the technology. Chanting in meditation will activate the top part of the brain (known as the partial lobe) and create more white matter, which helps you to deal with emotional issues (such as acute anxiety or depression). Kirtan Kriya and 7 Wave Meditation are great places to start, as they are both simple yet powerful.

Although I occasionally use English mantras, most of the mantras used in the meditations that I teach are in Gurmukhi. These mantras contain the vibrations of peace, prosperity, balance, and connection (within us and around us). Even if the meaning of each word is not understood by the practitioner, they are inherently accepted by the body and mind through their set frequency in the universe.

Of course, knowing the meanings of the words adds another layer of effectiveness to the act of chanting. I would recommend studying each mantra and its translation as you move through this meditative journey. Correct pronunciation comes from repetition and by example, so try listening to mantra music in order to familiarize yourself with these foreign sounds. It is best if the mantra music is simple, like the audios I've produced. It is easy to understand and follow, yet still beautiful. My three-minute recordings are always free. There is no excuse to avoid meditating.

After a few days of merely listening to mantra music, graduate to mouthing along with the chants and then start whispering with the audio. Finally, once you feel comfortable, open your vocal cords to chant out loud. Learning and understanding the mantras on a deep level helps you to build a relationship within your own self.

Keep a journal to record how you feel as you progress through this journey. By tracking how you feel, you will be able to see all the positive impacts of meditation (initially, there may even be some negative effects, like wondering if you are doing it right). Each meditative experience could be totally different for you, and it is important to note how and why each one is affecting you. If you start feeling like you are entering into a darker mind-set, for example, you will instantly be able to recognize this undesired shift. If this happens, pause your journey and ask for greater support through a licensed professional.

Why Should You Meditate?

I have not always meditated every day. Until about eight years ago, I only meditated when I felt I needed it. This is normal behavior; we tend to seek help only when we are actively suffering, but that doesn't mean it is the healthiest behavior to adopt. It is when we regularly practice healthy habits, such as meditating or eating whole foods, that our bodies and minds thrive. I now meditate every single day, anywhere from eleven to thirty-one minutes. I have made this commitment to myself because I have seen the positive results in my life.

During a meditation workshop at a gym, I spoke about the benefits of meditation on the physical body with an emphasis on how it lowers our blood pressure. The next time we met as a group, a woman approached me. She told me that she suffered from high blood pressure but decided to try meditation after my first workshop. After just three minutes of practicing at home, she checked her blood pressure and was shocked by the results: it was normal.

Kundalini technology has seen consistent use, all around the world, since its inception around 1600 BCE (according to the Upanishads). That in itself is an amazing feat; one that speaks to the credibility of its application as a form of therapy. By utilizing meditation techniques, we can influence our brain to process awareness and creation in an advantageous, invaluable way. We learn to hone in on our health and address our deep-rooted needs. Stress and anxiety are no match for an ancient tool of healing that is both natural and free. It has stood the test of time.

At its core, meditation is learning how to change the dialogue with yourself. Usually, we are overly harsh to ourselves. We self-criticize and second-guess much of what we do, say, and think. Kundalini technology encourages us to be truthful yet open so that we can embrace new, healthy patterns in our lives. This includes giving ourselves permission to change worrying thoughts and feelings so that we can accept ourselves through the promise of unlocking our true potential.

Chapter 12

Other Natural Tools for Self-Healing

Meditation, as we have established, is a wonderful tool for self-healing. With diligent practice, you can relieve yourself of the stress and anxiety that threaten to hold you back from experiencing life. I hope that you are able to adopt a meditative routine into your daily life for the maintenance of your well-being, spiritually and emotionally.

But there's more where that came from.

If you are seeking ways to elevate your relationship with meditation, you may want to consider bringing in additional natural tools. They can either boost your morale or literally strengthen your body through good habits, such as exercising and following a healthy diet. Below, I have listed a few supplemental tools for those seeking help. Feel free to apply one or all of these methods into your life to aid in your healing process.

Aromatherapy

Aromatherapy is an increasingly popular form of natural healing. More and more people are discovering that it is a great resource for relaxation due to the strong emotional triggers that smells can conjure in the brain. Some even use aromatherapy in conjunction with their meditation, which can help put your mind at ease if you find yourself overstimulated.

There are several options in which you can incorporate aromatherapy into your life. Candles and incense are popular forms, but—to feel the most powerful impact—I suggest looking into essential oils. These are scents in their purest forms. With oils, you can add them to your bath or use as a perfume (just make sure the oil is not a skin irritant, like peppermint). If you're interested in this method of stress relief, you may even want to consider investing in a diffuser for your oils. This will disperse the pure scent into the air, giving you several hours' worth of benefits with minimal effort.

By inhaling an essential oil in its various forms, its molecules enter into your system and eventually cause your limbic system to fire off an emotional response. Ideally, the essential oil(s) of your choice will provide you with a sense of calmness and reduced stress; this can be anything from a regulated heartbeat and breathing pattern to a normal production of hormones or blood pressure. Each scent will have a different yet meaningful impact on your mind.

These are the best oils for the treatment of stress and anxiety:

- **Bergamot**, found in Earl Grey tea, reduces corticosterone (a stress hormone) responses and is used to treat depression. It can also produce hormonal secretions that release bile and insulin (aiding in the digestive system) as well as dopamine and serotonin (reducing tension and alleviating stress and anxiety).
- **Chamomile (Roman)** has high anti-inflammatory esters that promote inner harmony by reducing irritability, overthinking, worrying, insomnia, and anxiety.
- **Lavender** supports the brain by restoring the nervous system and enhancing mood, allowing for a multitude of treatments: headaches, insomnia (and restful sleep), anxiety, depression, and PTSD.
- **Lemongrass** offers sedative properties that help to relieve stress and headaches, while also giving a calming sensation beneficial for restful sleep.
- **Frankincense** is believed to communicate with the limbic system to reduce issues related to anxiety and depression, including heart rate and high blood pressure. It also provides a sense of tranquility that builds intuition, making it especially helpful during meditation.

- **Geranium** triggers cells that combat inflammation in neural pathways, resulting in a stronger mental capacity, which helps to ward off anxiety and depression.
- **Jasmine** influences the nervous system and helps to boost energy levels, which includes strengthening cognitive functions; this helps to improve moods. Its sedative properties affect the autonomic nervous system, bringing feelings of relaxation.
- **Rose** acts as an antianxiety agent that can relieve depression and bring contentment to the heart. It can help with grief-related stress, such as shock and panic attacks.
- **Vetiver** works on the nervous system to lower hypersensitivity, thus making it a great option for trauma-induced symptoms such as panic attacks and instability.
- **Ylang-ylang** reduces cortisol levels, blood pressure, and stress responses due to its calming properties. As a sedative, it can also aid in insomnia by alleviating palpitations and heart-related agitation.

Before using any form of aromatherapy, please conduct your own research on which essential oils you would like to use. You might find you have a sensitivity or even allergy to a particular scent, while others that are skin irritants should not be applied topically to the skin without first being diluted (suspended in another substance such as jojoba oil). In addition, some oils—like those derived from the geranium flower—can influence hormone secretion (not recommended for pregnant women) and affect the cardiovascular system (crucial for those with high blood pressure). If you have medical concerns, consult with your licensed professional before incorporating essential oils into your self-therapy.

It is not uncommon to find yourself attracted to a certain scent one day and then a different scent the next. Depending on your mood or emotional state, the aroma that you are drawn to can change over time. Instead of ordering online, I encourage you to visit a local shop that carries a selection of essential oils. Smell each one to determine which scent speaks to you.

If you are practicing meditation in a group, please make sure others are accepting of the scents. Because someone might suffer from an allergy, the additional smell can disturb their self-healing session. However, if you are home alone and tolerant to aromatherapy, you may want to experiment with it. You might find that it helps you reach a serene state that is perfect for Kundalini meditation.

Basic Yoga Poses

Meditation works to put your brain, mind, nervous system, and glandular system in harmony, but you also need your body to engage in some physical movement. Think of your body as a vehicle: it needs to keep moving and be maintained, lest it rusts. This is why simple yoga poses can be beneficial to incorporate into your daily life.

I would like to share some Kundalini Yoga poses that support the release of stress and anxiety. For many of us, we feel the physicality of these ailments in our bodies; it is not *all* mental. I have had clients who suffer from panic attacks that affect their stomach, brains, and nervous system. And almost everyone has experienced a stress-induced headache.

If you are burdened by the weight of severe anxiety, I recommend that you practice any of the following yoga poses daily—ideally, just after you wake up—for the first forty or ninety days (or four months) of your meditative journey. As you work on your mind, you cannot ignore the basic need to support your body, as well.

Spinal Flex

Sit on the floor or in a chair. Bring your hands to your ankles or your thighs. You will be leading your breath with your navel (or lower chest). As you inhale, flex forward; as you exhale, flex backward. Focus on your breath.

Try to keep your head, shoulders, and hips aligned throughout these motions. It is akin to riding a horse: you want to remain in control of your body rather than have it flop limply around.

If you find your mind wandering,

you can mentally chant "Sat" on the inhale and "Naam" on the exhale. This will guide your mind away from upsetting thoughts.

Spinal Twist

Sit on the floor or in a chair. Bring your hands up to your shoulders. Place your hands on your shoulders with your thumb facing the back of your body and the rest of your fingers facing the front of your body. As you inhale, twist to the left; as you exhale, twist to the right. Focus on your breath.

Similar to Spinal Flex, you do not want your movements to be jerky. Remain in control of your body as you move to a rhythm that matches your breath.

If you find your mind wandering, you can mentally chant "Sat" on the inhale and "Naam" on the exhale. This will guide your mind away from upsetting thoughts.

Cat and Cow

This particular yoga pose is only encouraged if you can easily get down on and up off the floor. If you are able to do so, you'll find that this is a great exercise for the whole spine. It is like an internal massage for each vertebra in the spine.

Come to all fours on the ground. Place your hands a little wider than your shoulders and your knees a little wider than your hips. Keep your heels parallel to each other and, if possible, touching and resting flat on the floor.

Inhale as you raise your head up and move your forehead forward. Your hips will tilt to open. Allow that to happen as your belly moves down and you fill your lungs with air.

Hold this pose for a moment and then exhale as you reverse the movement. Your chin will come to your chest as your head bows down. Your hips will move back inward, and your spine will curve as you pull your belly button into your back. Again, hold this pose for a moment.

Repeat this back-and-forth movement for three minutes, focusing on your breath throughout. End by resting in Child Pose, with your forehead on the ground and your buttocks against your heels. Breathe naturally.

If you find your mind wandering, you can mentally chant "Sat" on the inhale and "Naam" on the exhale. This will guide your mind away from upsetting thoughts.

Life Nerve Stretch

Like the Cat and Cow, this yoga pose should be attempted only if you can easily get down on and up off the floor. This is an ideal method to build your flexibility. Yogis believe that you are only as flexible in your life—both mentally and emotionally—as you are flexible physically.

Sit on the floor. Stretch your left leg in front of you. Bend your right leg so that your foot is close or tucked against your groin. This will create an "L"-shape with your legs.

Grab your toes, ankles, or shin—whichever you can comfortably reach. Close your eyes. As you inhale, begin sitting up straight; as you exhale, bend forward from your hips. Continue this seesaw motion, up and down, for three minutes. Switch legs and repeat the process.

Physical Therapy

As mentioned before, keeping your body in motion is crucial to the health of your mind and soul. Various forms of physical therapy can each provide different benefits to you and your life. Some suggested forms include the following:

- **Physical Exercise:** The Anxiety and Depression Association of America endorses exercise in order to reduce stress. Physical activity stimulates your brain to produce endorphins, a natural painkiller which also aids in sleep. It takes as little as five minutes of aerobic exercise to feel its benefits on your body, including lowered tension, stabilized mood, and even an improved sense of self-confidence.

- **Massage Therapy:** While massages are often viewed as a spa day treat, their notoriety for stress reduction comes with merit. The American Massage Therapy Association recognizes that "stress can be reduced significantly on physical and psychological levels" by utilizing massage therapy. A 2002 study found that trigger point therapy in particular results in decreased heart rate and blood pressure (*Journal of Advanced Nursing*, 2002). But it doesn't take much to see results: a fifteen-minute chair massage can also lower blood pressure as well as cortisol levels and oxygen consumption (*American Journal of Chinese Medicine*, 2001).

- **Acupuncture:** Although this ancient form of healing—in which meridians on the body are activated with fine needles (or, more recently, electronically)—is still mysterious to modern-day scientists, its benefits are being recorded and proven over time. Georgetown University Medical Center conducted a study observing the effects of acupuncture on rats after they endured stressful conditions. They found that the rats had lowered blood hormone levels and a decrease in NPY, a peptide secreted during the fight-or-flight response (*Journal of Endocrinology*, 2013). In Chinese medicine, acupuncture is viewed as a natural method to treat blockage in the organs, clearing our energy. By correcting this stagnation on your body, you can restore your balance. Like meditation, this helps to bring clarity and calmness to your mind.

Many of these therapies require financial support and usually don't come free. If money is tight for you, try going to a massage or acupuncture school; trainees often offer discounted prices for their services. A small or locally owned gym might also be able to provide a deal. It certainly doesn't hurt to ask for assistance if you are financially burdened.

Of course, one of the best ways to exercise is free: walking. Go on a walk every day for at least twenty minutes for a workout that supports your full body (don't forget to swing your arms). Many people will listen to music, a book, or podcast as they do this routine, but you can also incorporate meditation music if you want to place your mind in a peaceful state.

Whole Foods Diet

When shopping at a grocery store, you should buy most of your food from the outer part of the store. This portion of the market usually includes the fruits and vegetables, dairy, meats, and the bakery (with freshly baked goods). Most of what you'll find in the center aisles is prepackaged products that contain preservatives with plenty of salt or sugar. I encourage you to instead seek out whole foods. These are, as the name implies, foods that come whole from the earth. Your diet should consist primarily—if not entirely—of whole foods, as this will best support your body.

Eating healthy can impact your overall mental health. Some foods have even been explicitly linked to stress and, especially, anxiety. Unfortunately, dairy, gluten, and sugar are all culprits in disrupting your mental health at the same extent they damage your body ("5 Foods That Can Cause Depression," 2017). This has to do with your nervous system and inflammation in your body caused by these ingested irritants.

If you are suffering from severe anxiety or panic attacks, I suggest that you wean yourself off of foods that contain dairy, gluten, and sugar. Treat it as a trial run, for about three to six months, to determine whether or not you feel better after eliminating them from your diet. Once you get better, you can try adding one at a time back into your life. You may find that you can eat these foods with no adverse effects, or you may find that you can't. It is a deep process that is highly personal. Only you know exactly how your body feels. Reach a conclusion on what foods are right for you by listening to what your body wants, needs, and rejects altogether.

Dieting can be a complicated and complex process, even if you have the purest intentions of getting healthy. You may want to meet with a certified nutritionist to talk about your diet (based on whole foods or otherwise) and get support. They can even guide you toward approaching new foods and incorporating them into your life, including how to prepare them.

Herbal Supplements

Before I share some supplements that I have found are helpful for stress and anxiety, I would like to assert that I am not a medical doctor or certified nutritionist. I hold a degree in psychotherapy and am a licensed marriage and family therapist in the state of California, as well as a professional trainer of Kundalini Yoga and meditation as instated by Kundalini Research Institute (KRI).

I have done research on my own accord for myself, my family, and my clients to seek support in the release of stress and anxiety. Based on this research and my own experience, here are some supplements you may want to ask your licensed medical practitioner about:

- **GABA:** You produce this amino acid in the frontal lobe of your brain. It is a natural relaxer. You can buy this in a chewable form and take as directed on the bottle.
- **L-Theanine:** An amino acid found in green tea that helps transmit nerve impulses in the brain. It helps you to relax by lowering your blood pressure and is commonly used as a treatment for anxiety.
- **L-Tryptophane:** An amino acid derived from animal and plant-based proteins. It is eventually converted to the hormone serotonin within your body, which can reduce anxiety and regulate depression.
- **Ginger Tea:** Because it aids in healing nerves, this is an especially great supplement for your nervous system. I suggest that you make

this at home with fresh ginger. It is a fast, easy, and cheap method for stress relief. Boil four to five cups of water with as much peeled and grated ginger as desired. Let it boil for five minutes, and then let it simmer for twenty minutes. Because this tea is enjoyable hot or cold, you can find satisfaction in drinking this at any time of the day, during any time of the year. If you find the flavor is too strong, add a little honey.

If you would like to know more about using supplements for stress or anxiety, I suggest locating a naturopathic doctor, certified nutritionist, or molecular psychiatrist. Whoever you speak to needs to truly understand amino acids, the brain, and our moods/mental self. This can get expensive, so try to find someone who comes recommended or make sure to conduct research on your own.

Check with your doctor or certified medical practitioner before taking any supplements or vitamins. They may even encourage a blood test to ensure your body is capable of tolerating additional supplements. If this form of therapy is something you are interested in, I suggest you conduct your own personal research to educate yourself on the usage of supplements for mental issues. Here are several books and website I have used and found to be helpful:

- *The Mood Cure* and *The Diet Cure* by Julia Ross
- *A Mind of Her Own* by Dr. Kelly Borgan
- www.CassMD.com. Hyla Cass is a psychiatrist who uses supplements for mental illnesses. She even produces and distributes her own supplements.
- www.EveryWomanOver29.com. Judy Scott is a nutritionist who specializes in supplement usage for mental illness and diet change. She has a newsletter that supplies tons of helpful information on this subject. In addition, she often organizes summits on different topics related to diet and its effect on mental health.

List of Kundalini Meditations

In this section, you will find a list of Kundalini meditations to help you get started on your path toward a calmer and clearer life. I have provided detailed instructions—including translations for mantras—for each meditation. Truly understanding each method is extremely helpful to experience the greatest change within you. I hope this yogic tool serves you like a weapon to fight off your stress and anxiety, allowing you to heal and transform yourself.

With the purchase of this book, you can enjoy complimentary mantra and musical digital recordings for each meditation. Please visit **https://www.madhurnain.com/downloadmantras** and enter the code, "**StresslessBrainCollection**". You will need to provide your email address to access the free files. If you have any questions, do not hesitate to reach out: info@madhurnain.com. For some, mantra music can elevate their meditative experience. I hope you find it helpful and enjoyable for your own experience.

My dream in life is for my legacy to shine through meditative therapy. It is my goal to inspire the world to meditate. I can achieve this little by little, one person at a time; the web expands with each new discoverer. When people meditate and find they have altered their lives in a positive way, they feel compelled to teach it to a family member or friend. There is an instinctive reaction to pay the good deed forward. And the cycle continues.

Before you start each meditative practice, please begin by chanting, "Ong Namo Guroo Dayv Namo" three times. This translates to, "I bow to the creator, the divine teacher within." End each meditative practice with one long chant of "Sat Naam." These intro/outro chants can be said out loud, whispered, or silently spoken to yourself to open and close your mental space.

"Breathing keeps you alive.
Meditation keeps you sane" Madhur-Nain

Meditation for Beginners

A simple meditation to create inner peace
through a connection to your breath.
(Sat Naam mantra originally taught by Yogi
Bhajan; breath focus by Madhur-Nain.)

Posture: Sit on the floor or on a chair, making sure to keep the spine straight.

Mudra: Gyan Mudra. Touch the thumb's tip to the index fingertip while keeping the other fingers straight.

Eye Focus: Keep eyes closed to focus easily on your breath.

Mantra: "Sat Naam."
- Translation: Sat: truth. Naam: identity.
- Chanting Instructions: Silent (mental).
- Summary: A Bija (seed) mantra, Sat Naam contains all the knowledge of a tree. Words are like seeds; they can grow beauty or destruction. "The essence/seed is the identity of truth embodied

in condensed form. Mentally chanting or thinking this mantra awakens the soul and gives you your destiny."—Yogi Bhajan.

Breathing Pattern: Train your breath to be very still as you follow the mantra, Sat Naam. Inhale on "Sat," and exhale on "Naam."

End: Inhale and hold your breath for fifteen to twenty seconds. Repeat this three times and then relax. Sit silently for two minutes.

Timing: Eleven minutes daily.

Summary: This meditation is best for those who don't know where else to start. If you suffer from anxiety, unresolved emotions might come forth from this method. You might even find you cry while utilizing long-deep breathing; this is the effect of connecting with your inner self. Those dealing with a major crisis might want to consider a chanting meditation instead. Practice this meditation daily for a period of time to experience the greatest sense of inner peace with your body, mind, and soul.

- A straight back allows energy to flow up through the spine, centering the self.
- Closed eyes help you to connect with your breathing, bringing you closer to recognizing and building a relationship with your self-identity.
- Gyan Mudra stimulates the ability to understand your inner knowledge and wisdom, invoking receptivity and calmness.
- Mantras bring the mind into focus, connecting the subconscious and conscious mind to assist in reparative life changes.

Negative Mind Meditation

Clears and adjusts the mind of negative (protective) and fearful thoughts. (Originally taught by Yogi Bhajan, *The Mind*, p. 153.)

Posture: Sit on the floor or on a chair, making sure to keep the spine straight.

Mudra: Make a cup with your hands, resting your right hand in your left hand with the fingers crossing over each other. The left fingers will point at a 60 degree angle forward and the right fingers are about 60 degree angle forward and to the left. Hold this mudra at your heart center.

Eye Focus: Hold eyes slightly open, looking down at your cupped hands.

Mantra: Silent Sat Naam (Mantra added by Madhur-Nain, originally taught silent)
  • Translation: Sat: truth. Naam: identity.

Breathing Pattern: Inhale deeply and in a steady breath through the nose. Exhale in a focused release out of the mouth, allowing your breath to flow over your hands. As you repeat this pattern, notice your thoughts or desires that are negative or otherwise distracting. (These can be current or from the past, which still haunt you.) Hold this mental focus as you inhale, and release the thoughts as you exhale.

End: Exhale completely as you hold your focus. Squeeze each vertebra until you reach the base. Inhale powerfully, and then exhale again. Repeat three to five times before relaxing.

Timing: Three, seven, eleven, or twenty-two minutes daily.

Summary: This meditation is best for those seeking to develop self-protection. By bringing your protective mind into balance, the mind can give you clear signals on how to protect and support you. Severe anxiety can cause overthinking, especially with regard to safety. This meditation helps you to gather your thoughts and let them go. I prescribe this meditation to pessimistic clients (to halt negative thought patterns) as well as clients who are risk takers (so they can avoid getting into trouble). Practice this meditation daily for a period of time to help you live your life fully by bringing your negative mind into balance.

- A straight back allows energy to flow up through the spine, centering the self.
- Allowing light to come in through this open-eyed eye focus stimulates the pineal gland. This will help you regulate your hormones and emotions.
- The silence created from the lack of mantra will allow the monkey mind to unveil your negative thoughts so you can release your fears.

Positive Mind Meditation

Opens the heart center and feelings of the positive (perspective) self.
(Originally taught by Yogi Bhajan, *The Mind*, p. 154.)

Posture: Sit on the floor or on a chair, making sure to keep the spine straight.

Mudra: Extend your index and middle fingers straight up as you curl the ring and little fingers into the palm. Place your thumb on top of the ring and little finger to hold them down. Keep your elbows bent and at your side with your hands at shoulder level. Bring your hands forward at a 30 degree angle. Press your shoulders and elbows back.

Eye Focus: Keep eyes closed and focused on the brow point.

Mantra: Mentally chant "Saa Taa Naa Maa."
- Translation: The cycle of life. Sa: infinity. Ta: life. Na: death. Ma: rebirth.

- Chanting Instructions: Chant only if you feel you need additional mental support. This can help you stay focused during the meditation; your mind should serve your life.
- Summary: Also known as Panj Shabd, this mantra balances the hemispheres of the brain and creates a deeper understanding of the Self. Chanting or even silently thinking this mantra develops intuition.

Breathing Pattern: Create and maintain a steady, deep, slow, and complete breath through the nose.

End: Inhale and exhale deeply three time and then relax the breath. Open and close the hands three times and then relax the body.

Timing: Three, seven, eleven, or twenty-two minutes daily.

Summary: This meditation is best for those who are risk-takers in life. We all need the positive mind to have courage in our lives; however, if the positive mind is overactive, then we take too many risks without thinking. In general, this meditation is effective for people to expand their thinking; I often prescribe it to overly optimistic clients so they can see different perspectives and avoid troubling situations. Practice this meditation daily for a period of time to teach yourself how to think before you act so you can calculate your choices and make smart moves when proceeding forward in life.

- A straight back allows energy to flow up through the spine, centering the self.
- Darkness created by closing the eyes affects the action of the pineal gland, instilling you with vastness and wholeness, a sense of belonging and connectedness.
- Mantras bring the mind into focus, connecting the subconscious and conscious mind to assist in reparative life changes.

Neutral Mind Meditation

Teaches you to be unattached, allowing for less suffering.
(Originally taught by Yogi Bhajan, *The Mind*, p. 155.)

Posture: Sit on the floor or on a chair, making sure to keep the spine straight.

Mudra: Place both hands on the lap with the palms facing up. Rest the right hand in the left hand. You may choose to touch your thumb tips together, though it is not required.

Eye Focus: Keep eyes closed. Imagine seeing yourself full of radiance as you sit peacefully. Gradually let this energy collect as it flows to your brow point, and then concentrate (without effort) on your third eye.

Mantra: Mentally chant "Wha-hay Guru."
- Translation: Guru: teacher. Wahe is an indescribable wonderfulness.

- Chanting Instructions: Chant only if you feel you need additional mental support. This can help you stay focused during the meditation; your mind should serve your life.
- Summary: A Trikutee mantra, Wahe Guru helps to dispel darkness from your life. "Gu" is darkness, while "ru" is light. "Guru" is the process of transforming yourself by connecting to the divine. Try supplementing with mantra music.

Breathing Pattern: Let the breath regulate itself in a slow, meditative—almost suspended—manner.

End: Inhale and exhale deeply three times, and then relax the breath. Open and close the hands three times, and then relax the body.

Timing: Three, seven, eleven, or twenty-two minutes daily.

Summary: This meditation is best if you want a clear, compassionate, and strong mind. For that to happen, you need your positive mind and negative mind balanced so that you can view life through the lens of the neutral (or meditative) mind. This is where you want to make your decisions from, because it is where you think outside of the box; you see things for what they are. When you form this nonattachment, the desire to control is lessened, benefiting those who suffer from stress or high anxiety. Practice this meditation daily for a period of time to neutralize the mind, allowing for balanced thoughts and actions throughout life.

- A straight back allows energy to flow up through the spine, centering the self.
- Darkness created by closing the eyes affects the action of the pineal gland, instilling you with vastness and wholeness, a sense of belonging and connectedness.
- Mantras bring the mind into focus, connecting the subconscious and conscious mind to assist in reparative life changes.

4/1 Segmented Breathing

For healing, energizing, and uplifting the self.
(Originally taught by Yogi Bhajan, *KRI Aquarian
Teacher Level 1 Lecture Manual*, p. 97.)

Posture: Sit on the floor or on a chair, making sure to keep the spine straight.

Mudra: Gyan Mudra. Touch the thumb's tip to the index fingertip while keeping the other fingers straight.

Eye Focus: Keep eyes closed to focus easily on your breath.

Mantra: None. If required, mentally chant "Wha-hay Guru."
- Translation: Guru: teacher. Wahe is an indescribable wonderfulness.
- Summary: A Trikutee mantra, Wahe Guru helps to dispel darkness from your life. "Gu" is darkness, while "ru" is light. "Guru" is the process of transforming yourself by connecting to the divine (originally taught silently; Madhur-Nain added mantra music for focus).

Breathing Pattern: Inhale in four segments: "wha-hay guroo". Then exhale in the same four segments: "wha-hay guroo". Inhale and exhale in little sniffs of oxygen through the nose, keeping the mouth closed throughout. The nostrils should remain relaxed so that the breath is pulled deep into the nasal passage with the movement of the diaphragm.

End: Inhale and exhale deeply three times and then sit quietly for two to three minutes.

Timing: Three, seven, eleven, twenty-two, or thirty-one minutes daily.

Summary: This meditation is best for those seeking to uplift their spirits. Breathing in a specific rhythm helps activate the vagus nerve, supporting the nervous system and ultimately lowering your stress and anxiety. As a result, you feel rejuvenated. Practice this meditation daily for a period of time to bring energy into your life.

- Segmented breathing patterns are meant to relax you while stimulating the vagus nerve, supporting the nervous system.
- A straight back allows energy to flow up through the spine, centering the self.
- Closed eyes help you to connect with your breathing, bringing you closer to recognizing and building a relationship with your self-identity.
- Gyan Mudra stimulates the ability to understand your inner knowledge and wisdom, invoking receptivity and calmness.
- Mantras bring the mind into focus, connecting the subconscious and conscious mind to assist in reparative life changes.

4/4 Segmented Breathing

Creates clarity and alertness (energy) to find purpose or meaning in life.
(Originally taught by Yogi Bhajan, *KRI Aquarian
Teacher Level 1 Lecture Manual*, p. 97.)

Posture: Sit on the floor or on a chair, making sure to keep the spine straight.

Mudra: Gyan Mudra. Touch the thumb's tip to the index fingertip while keeping the other fingers straight.

Eye Focus: Close eyes and focus on the third eye, one inch above the center of your brows.

Mantra: None. If required, mentally chant "Wha-hay Guroo."
- Translation: Guru; teacher. Wahe is an indescribable wonderfulness.
- Summary: A Trikutee mantra, Wahe Guru helps to dispel darkness from your life. "Gu" is darkness, while "ru" is light. "Guru" is the process of transforming yourself by connecting to the divine (originally taught silently; Madhur-Nain added mantra music for focus).

Breathing Pattern: Inhale in four segments: "wha-hay guroo". Then exhale in the same four segments: "wha-hay guroo". Inhale and exhale in little sniffs of oxygen through the nose, keeping the mouth closed throughout. The nostrils should remain relaxed so that the breath is pulled deep into the nasal passage with the movement of the diaphragm.

End: Inhale and exhale deeply three times and then sit quietly for two to three minutes.

Timing: Three, seven, eleven, twenty-two, or thirty-one minutes daily.

Summary: This meditation is best if you find it difficult to make decisions or don't know which direction to take in your life. By working your vagus nerve, this method supports you to make necessary changes without feeling fearful. Practice this meditation daily for a period of time to experience the greatest sense of inner clarity, aiding in connecting you to your inner awareness and ability to make choices.

- Segmented breathing patterns are meant to relax you while stimulating the vagus nerve, supporting the nervous system.
- A straight back allows energy to flow up through the spine, centering the self.
- Focusing on the third eye activates your intuition.
- Gyan Mudra stimulates the ability to understand your inner knowledge and wisdom, invoking receptivity and calmness.
- Mantras bring the mind into focus, connecting the subconscious and conscious mind to assist in reparative life changes.

4/8 Segmented Breathing

For unblocking, calming, and letting go.
(Originally taught by Yogi Bhajan, *KRI Aquarian Teacher Level 1 Lecture Manual*, p. 97.)

Posture: Sit on the floor or on a chair, making sure to keep the spine straight.

Mudra: Gyan Mudra. Touch the thumb's tip to the index fingertip while keeping the other fingers straight.

Eye Focus: Close eyes and focus on the third eye, one inch above the center of your brows.

Mantra: None. If required, mentally chant "Saa Taa Naa Maa."
- Translation: The cycle of life. Sa: infinity. Ta: life. Na: death. Ma: rebirth.
- Summary: Also known as Panj Shabd, this mantra balances the hemispheres of the brain and creates a deeper understanding of the Self. Chanting or even silently thinking this mantra develops

intuition (originally taught silently; Madhur-Nain added mantra music for focus).

Breathing Pattern: Inhale in four segments with the slow mantra, "Saa Taa Naa Maa." Then exhale in eight segments, quickly repeating "Saa Taa Naa Maa Saa Taa Naa Maa." Inhale and exhale in little sniffs of oxygen through the nose, keeping the mouth closed throughout. The nostrils should remain relaxed so that the breath is pulled deep into the nasal passage with the movement of the diaphragm.

End: Inhale deeply three times and then sit quietly for two to three minutes.

Timing: Three, seven, eleven, twenty-two, or thirty-one minutes daily.

Summary: This meditation is best if you have a lot of fear in your life. Because fear stems from a lack of trust, it often leads to anxiety. This method will help train you to trust and calm yourself at the same time. Practice this meditation daily for a period of time to slow you down enough to experience clarity and peaceful mindfulness.

- Segmented breathing patterns are meant to relax you while stimulating the vagus nerve, supporting the nervous system. In particular, 4/8 segmented breath strokes on the exhale stimulate the pituitary gland, creating clarity, intuition, and the ability to make decisions.
- Focusing on the third eye activates your intuition.
- Gyan Mudra stimulates the ability to understand your inner knowledge and wisdom, invoking receptivity and calmness.
- Mantras bring the mind into focus, connecting the subconscious and conscious mind to assist in reparative life changes.

8/4 Segmented Breathing

For focusing and energizing the self.
(Originally taught by Yogi Bhajan, *KRI Aquarian Teacher Level 1 Lecture Manual*, p. 97.)

Posture: Sit on the floor or on a chair, making sure to keep the spine straight.

Mudra: Gyan Mudra. Touch the thumb's tip to the index fingertip while keeping the other fingers straight.

Eye Focus: Close eyes and focus on the third eye, one inch above the center of your brows.

Mantra: None. If required, mentally chant "Ong Namo Guroo Dayv Namo."
- Translation: Ong: creative conscious. Namo: "I call upon." Guru: inner truth. Dev: divine.
- Summary: This is an Adi mantra, used to tune into your soul consciousness. It creates a connection to the divine teacher within

you (originally taught silently; Madhur-Nain added mantra music for focus).

Breathing Pattern: Inhale in eight segments with the mantra, "Ong Namo Guroo Dayv Namo." Then exhale in four segments, repeating "Ong Namo Guroo Dayv Namo." Inhale and exhale in little sniffs of oxygen through the nose, keeping the mouth closed throughout. The nostrils should remain relaxed so that the breath is pulled deep into the nasal passage with the movement of the diaphragm.

End: Inhale deeply three times and then sit quietly for two to three minutes.

Timing: Three, seven, eleven, twenty-two, or thirty-one minutes daily.

Summary: This meditation is best if you are looking for more energy and focus in your life. When you feel you've lost track of life, you suffer from an internal imbalance; this can lead to more anxiety. This method helps you to refocus by slowing you down, allowing you to reevaluate before you exert yourself with positive movement. Practice this meditation daily for a period of time to bring you the balance necessary to have a productive life.

- Segmented breathing patterns are meant to relax you while stimulating the vagus nerve, supporting the nervous system. In particular, 4/8 segmented breath strokes on the exhale stimulate the pituitary gland, creating clarity, intuition, and the ability to make decisions.
- Focusing on the third eye activates your intuition.
- Gyan Mudra stimulates the ability to understand your inner knowledge and wisdom, invoking receptivity and calmness.
- Mantras bring the mind into focus, connecting the subconscious and conscious mind to assist in reparative life changes.

8/8 Segmented Breathing

For calming and centering the self by achieving balance in your life.
(Originally taught by Yogi Bhajan, *KRI Aquarian
Teacher Level 1 Lecture Manual*, p. 97.)

Posture: Sit on the floor or on a chair, making sure to keep the spine straight.

Mudra: Gyan Mudra. Touch the thumb's tip to the index fingertip while keeping the other fingers straight.

Eye Focus: Close eyes and focus on the third eye, one inch above the center of your brows.

Mantra: None. If required, mentally chant "Raa Maa Daa Saa, Saa Say So Hung."
- Translation: Ra: strong, bright, energy. Ma: calm, nurturing. Da: secure, grounded. Sa: oneness. Say: sacred. So: identity. Hung: real.
- Summary: A Siri mantra, meant for healing. The sound current Ra Ma Da Sa, Sa Say So Hung creates is a combination of energy

from the earth elements and ether. This brings balance to your inner self, eventually offering a form of healing (originally taught silently; Madhur-Nain added mantra music for focus).

Breathing Pattern: Inhale in eight segments: "Raa Maa Daa Saa, Saa Say So Hung." Then exhale in eight segments, repeating "Raa Maa Daa Saa, Saa Say So Hung." Inhale and exhale in little sniffs of oxygen through the nose, keeping the mouth closed throughout. The nostrils should remain relaxed so that the breath is pulled deep into the nasal passage with the movement of the diaphragm.

End: Inhale deeply three times and then sit quietly for two to three minutes.

Timing: Three, seven, eleven, twenty-two, or thirty-one minutes daily.

Summary: This meditation is best if you have stress that impacts your life, especially if you find it hard to concentrate and be productive. When suffering from stress or anxiety, you often feel disconnected from your self. This method helps you establish inner peace by resolving the imbalance. Practice this meditation daily for a period of time to heal yourself by balancing the mind and inspiring calmness within you.

- Segmented breathing patterns are meant to relax you while stimulating the vagus nerve, supporting the nervous system.
- A straight back allows energy to flow up through the spine, centering the self.
- Focusing on the third eye activates your intuition.
- Gyan Mudra stimulates the ability to understand your inner knowledge and wisdom, invoking receptivity and calmness.
- Mantras bring the mind into focus, connecting the subconscious and conscious mind to assist in reparative life changes.

Sitali Pranayam

Creates the power for the body to heal; additionally,
can aid in the digestive system.
(Originally taught by Yogi Bhajan, July 1975.)

Posture: Sit on the floor or on a chair, making sure to keep the spine straight.

Mudra: Gyan Mudra. Touch the thumb's tip to the index fingertip while keeping the other fingers straight.

Eye Focus: Keep eyes closed.

Mantra: None. If required, mentally chant "Sat Naam."
- Translation: Sat: truth. Naam: identity.
- Summary: A Bija (seed) mantra, Sat Naam contains all the knowledge of a tree. Words are like seeds; they can grow beauty or destruction. "The essence/seed is the identity of truth embodied in condensed form. Mentally chanting or thinking this mantra awakens the soul and gives you your destiny."—Yogi Bhajan.

(Originally taught silently. Madhur-Nain added mantra music for focus.)

Breathing Pattern: Roll your tongue and stick it out of your mouth; inhale through this space. Exhale out through your nose. If you can't curl your tongue, simply stick your tongue out half-way and breathe in through the mouth, around the tongue; continue exhaling through the nose.

End: Inhale and hold your breath. Stretch your arms above your head to open your spine. Relax your breath and shake your hands and arms for fifteen to thirty seconds.

Timing: Three minutes daily; lengthen timing as you build stamina through practice.

Summary: This meditation is best for those seeking power, strength, and vitality. When you start this method, it is not unusual to have a bitter taste in your mouth; this is a symptom of the body detoxifying itself. Practice this meditation daily for a period of time to instill yourself with a great sense of vigor.

- This particular tongue-based style of breathing can cool off the body, cleaning from the inside.
- A straight back allows energy to flow up through the spine, centering the self.
- Darkness created by closing the eyes affects the action of the pineal gland, instilling you with vastness and wholeness, a sense of belonging and connectedness.
- Gyan Mudra stimulates the ability to understand your inner knowledge and wisdom, invoking receptivity and calmness.
- Mantras bring the mind into focus, connecting the subconscious and conscious mind to assist in reparative life changes.

Inner Conflict Resolver

Resolves conflict by supporting your automatic reflex to protect yourself.
(Originally taught by Yogi Bhajan, October 1979.)

Posture: Sit on the floor or on a chair, making sure to keep the spine straight.

Mudra: Place your palms flat on your chest with your thumbs pointing up. Your fingers will be pointing toward each other, as a mirror image.

Eye Focus: Hold eyes one-tenth open.

Mantra: None (Silent). If required, mentally chant "Sat Naam."
- Translation: Sat: truth. Nam: identity.
- Instructions: Sat Naam mantra can help you stay focused during the meditation (originally taught silently; Madhur-Nain added mantra music for focus).

Breathing Pattern: Inhale deeply for five seconds, and then exhale completely for five seconds. Suspend the breath out for fifteen seconds; pull in the abdomen and navel point on this breath.

End: Inhale and hold your breath. Stretch your arms above your head to open your spine. Relax your breath and shake your hands and arms for fifteen to thirty seconds.

Timing: Three, seven, eleven, or twenty-two minutes daily.

Summary: This meditation is best for breaking an internal block of energy by using a strict breathing pattern. When you restructure the breath, you are able to respond with a critical yet clear mind. You are then able to break through the deadlock to confront inner conflict, restoring your prana (energy). Practice this meditation daily for a period of time to unbridle yourself from fear that threatens to paralyze you with anxiety.

- Segmented breathing patterns are meant to relax you while stimulating the vagus nerve, supporting the nervous system.
- A straight back allows energy to flow up through the spine, centering the self.
- A one-tenth open eye regulates how much light affects the brain, stimulating the pineal gland.
- Mantras bring the mind into focus, connecting the subconscious and conscious mind to assist in reparative life changes.

Aerobic Capacity and Efficiency

Strengthens the nervous system and builds inner
strength to help deal with issues.
(Originally taught by Yogi Bhajan, *KRI Aquarian
Kundalini Teaching Manual*, p. 58.)

Posture: Sit on the floor or on a chair, making sure to keep the spine straight.

Mudra: Place your hands on your knees. Keep your arms straight with your elbows locked.

Eye Focus: Keep eyes closed to focus easily on your breath.

Mantra: None. (Originally taught silently. Madhur-Nain added music for focus).
- This was originally taught with no sound. I created music for focus if desired.

Breathing Pattern: Inhale deeply. Press the tongue behind the teeth while flexing the spine. Exhale forcefully, and then quickly inhale. Repeat this process. Try holding your breath for as long as you can tolerate as you practice this pattern. The goal is to reach one minute of suspended breath without gasping for air.

End: Inhale and hold your breath, concentrating on your brow point. Exhale, and then relax.

Timing: Three, seven, or eleven minutes daily.

Summary: This meditation is best for those who feel helpless, especially those with anxiety. Because it strengthens the nervous system, you can teach your body to handle emotional and physical troubles through this method. It creates a richer understanding of life and, thus, promotes a positive outlook. This meditation moves your inner energy, giving you internal motivation, which is why I prescribe it to clients who feel they can't make the changes they are seeking in life. If you feel especially overwhelmed, you may want to pair this exercise with the Healing Meditation. Practice this meditation daily for a period of time to build inner and outer strength in your life.

- A straight back allows energy to flow up through the spine, centering the self.
- Darkness created by closing the eyes affects the action of the pineal gland, instilling you with vastness and wholeness, a sense of belonging and connectedness.

Meditation for Mental Control

A meditation to face your fear of death; helps
you release yourself from attachments.
(Originally taught by Yogi Bhajan.)

Posture: Sit on the floor or on a chair, making sure to keep the spine
straight.

Mudra: Cross your arms parallel to the ground at chest level. Keep your
fingers straight and touching as your right arm rests atop your left arm
(right hand on top of left elbow, left hand under right elbow). Allow
both arms to stretch away from your body as much as possible while
maintaining this posture. Restrain yourself from movement.

Eye Focus: Close eyes and focus on the third eye, one inch above the
center of your brows.

Mantra: None. If required, mentally chant "Sat Naam."
- Translation: Sat: truth. Nam: identity.
- Summary: I encourage you to stay in the experience of this
  meditation without a mantra. If you prefer sound currents during

your meditation, choose any of the mantra music provided with this book (originally taught silently; Madhur-Nain added mantra music for focus).

Breathing Pattern: Maintain relaxed diaphragmatic breath rather than a deep breathing pattern.

End: Inhale and hold your breath for fifteen to twenty seconds. Repeat this three times, and then relax. Sit silently for two minutes.

Timing: Three minutes daily; build stamina to eleven minutes daily.

Summary: This meditation is best for major anxiety that threatens to control your life. Also known as Brahm Kalaa, this method guides you away from unsavory behavior that stems from a fear-based anxiety (like a fear of death). This meditation for mental control will give you the strength to achieve goals that are hindered by fear. Practice this meditation daily for a period of time to let go of negative attachments and make positive changes in life.

- Focusing on your breath will train your brain to concentrate efficiently, helping you to move past stress and anxiety.
- A straight back allows energy to flow up through the spine, centering the self.
- Focusing on the third eye activates your intuition.
- Moving as little as possible in this mudra gives you greater focus on your long-deep breathing, which should also be still.
- Mantras bring the mind into focus, connecting the subconscious and conscious mind to assist in reparative life changes.

Meditation for a Calm Heart

Clears mental blocks so that you can act from a full heart.
(Originally taught by Yogi Bhajan, September 1981.)

Posture: Sit on the floor or on a chair, making sure to keep the spine straight.

Mudra: Place the left hand flat against the chest, on the heart center, with fingers pointing to your right. The right hand is in Gyan Mudra: touch the thumb's tip to the index fingertip while keeping the other fingers straight. Hold the right hand up, like reciting an oath, next to the body.

Eye Focus: Keep eyes closed.

Mantra: None. (Originally taught silently. Madhur-Nain added music for focus.)
- This was originally taught with no sound. I added some music for focus. Use with or without any of the recordings that come with this book.

Breathing Pattern: With each inhale, suspend your breath and raise the chest slightly. Hold this breath. Now, concentrate on your breath release as you consciously and slowly exhale. Once all CO_2 is released, suspend your breath out as long as possible. Continue with this pattern of breathing, paying close attention to the movement of your breath.

End: Inhale and exhale three times and then relax.

Timing: Three minutes daily; build up to thirty-one minutes daily.

Summary: This meditation is best for beginners because it creates an awareness between you and your breath; however, anyone can practice this method. It gives you the ability to create energy, or prana, from the focus on the heart center. Practice this meditation daily for a period of time to build and strengthen a relationship between body and mind.

- A straight back allows energy to flow up through the spine, centering the self.
- Darkness created by closing the eyes affects the action of the pineal gland, instilling you with vastness and wholeness, a sense of belonging and connectedness.
- Placing the left hand over the heart center in this mudra creates stillness. The right hand represents decision-making and action; when used in this mudra, it signifies peace.
- Mantras bring the mind into focus, connecting the subconscious and conscious mind to assist in reparative life changes.

Meditation for a Calm Mind and Strong Nerves

Guides you toward calm and rational thoughts.
(Originally taught by Yogi Bhajan, *Transformation Vol. 2*, p. 119.)

Posture: Sit on the floor or on a chair, making sure to keep the spine straight.

Mudra: For women: Keep your left hand by your left ear, with your elbow bent. Touch your thumb to the mound of your ring finger without touching the nail on your finger. Hold your right hand in your lap with your thumb touching the small finger. For men: reverse hand posture.

Eye Focus: Hold eyes one-tenth open.

Mantra: None. If required, mentally chant "Sat Naam."
- Translation: Sat: truth. Nam: identity.
- Summary: I encourage you to stay in the experience of this meditation without a mantra. If you prefer sound currents during your meditation, choose any of the mantra music provided with this book (originally taught silently; Madhur-Nain added mantra music for focus).

Breathing Pattern: Breathe deeply in long-deep breathing, remaining relaxed. Keep a steady rhythm that you can maintain.

End: Inhale deeply and raise both hands above your head. Keep fingers wide apart as you shake your arms. Exhale. Repeat three times, and then relax.

Timing: Three, seven, eleven, twenty-two, or thirty-one minutes daily.

Summary: This meditation is best for those with anxiety who feel as if they are stretched thin and especially those prone to anger. Many who experience anxiety can implode by reacting internally or externally, which shows up as angry outbursts and can lead to depression. Using the hand and finger mudras in this method, you can teach yourself to slow down and calm the heart center. Practice this meditation daily for a period of time to calm your mind and train your thoughts to be more rational.

- A straight back allows energy to flow up through the spine, centering the self.
- A one-tenth open eye regulates how much light affects the brain, stimulating the pineal gland.
- Each finger position during this mudra represents a potential: knowledge (index finger), wisdom (middle finger), vitality (ring finger), communication (small finger).

Tattva Balance beyond Stress and Duality

Builds an internal resistance to stress, trauma, drama, and illness.
(Originally taught by Yogi Bhajan, March 1979.)

Posture: Sit on the floor or on a chair, making sure to keep the spine straight.

Mudra: Touch all five fingers together in front of the heart center, with the thumb pointing to the heart center. Apply pressure. Keep fingers spread apart to create space between each digit. Elbows should remain extended out to the side as you hold this posture.

Eye Focus: Lotus Point. Keep your eyes focused on the tip of the nose.

Mantra: Mentally chant "Raa Maa Daa Saa, Saa Say So Hung."
- Translation: Ra: strong, bright, energy. Ma: calm, nurturing. Da: secure, grounded. Sa: oneness. Say: sacred. So: identity. Hung: real.
- Summary: This Siri mantra is called Sushmuna and is meant for healing. The sound current Ra Ma Da Sa, Sa Say So Hung

stimulates Kundalini energy from the earth elements and ether. This energy is carried through your chakras and spine, bringing balance to your inner self. (Originally taught silently. Madhur-Nain added mantra music for focus.)

Breathing Pattern: Inhale deeply through the nose. Exhale in eight parts (eight equal emphatic segments) through rounded lips; on each segment, pull the navel point in.

End: Inhale deeply and hold for ten to thirty seconds. Exhale. Inhale again and shake your hands for fifteen to thirty seconds. Then, relax.

Timing: Three minutes daily; build up to eleven minutes daily.

Summary: This meditation is best for those who feel burdened with conflict: between your heart and your head, spiritual and mental, fight and flight. As its name suggests, this method balances the five elements in your body to relieve stress. Practice this meditation daily for a period of time to build a resistance to stress and various forms of anxiety.

- The patterns created during this segmented breathing style strengthen the parasympathetic nervous system, which helps to neutralize stress levels.
- A straight back allows energy to flow up through the spine, centering the self.
- Focusing on the tip of the nose (the optic nerve concentration) stimulates the pineal gland and frontal lobe, which controls your personality by creating new brain patterns. It is the highest lock, or Bandha, in yoga.
- Touching the fingertips together in this mudra allows you to work on both hemispheres of your brain.
- Mantras bring the mind into focus, connecting the subconscious and conscious mind to assist in reparative life changes.

Four Stroke Breath to Build Intuition

Helps you to embrace experiencing life through
intuition rather than knowledge.
(Originally taught by Yogi Bhajan, *Transformation Vol. 2*, p. 16.)

Posture: Sit on the floor or on a chair, making sure to keep the spine straight.

Mudra: Interlace middle, ring, and small fingers, leaving the thumb and index fingers out. Touch index fingers together and cross your thumbs. Bring your hands below your nose so that you are able to observe your index finger.

Eye Focus: Hold eyes one-tenth open, looking at the top of your index fingers.

Mantra: None. If required, mentally chant "Wha-hay Guroo."
- Translation: Wahe Guru indescribable wisdom.
- Summary: This mantra allows you to raise your inner awareness and unite this consciousness through the use of visualization in

chanting. Focus on your energy spiraling up your spine (originally taught silently; Madhur-Nain added mantra music for focus).

Breathing Pattern: Hold your mouth in the shape of an "O." Inhale in four parts through the mouth with powerful strokes. Through your nose, exhale in one slow breath. Repeat as desired.

End: Inhale. Hold your breath for twenty seconds as you stretch your arms out and parallel to the ground, palms facing up. Exhale while repeating the same step, keeping arms stretched out. Repeat three times. On the third cycle, spread your fingers wide apart and squeeze your entire body. Exhale, then relax.

Timing: Three, seven, eleven, or sixteen minutes daily.

Summary: This meditation is best if seeking trust in the process of life. Trust is a key aspect in transitioning out of anxiety. Practice this meditation daily for a period of time to help you connect to your inner intuition.

- According to yogic technology, using an "O"-shaped mouth during breathing patterns stimulates the vagus nerve.
- A straight back allows energy to flow up through the spine, centering the self.
- A one-tenth open eye regulates how much light affects the brain, stimulating the pineal gland.
- The physical exercise required during the cooldown helps to balance the central spinal column. Additionally, your brain receives messages from your fingers.
- Mantras bring the mind into focus, connecting the subconscious and conscious mind to assist in reparative life changes.

Breath of Fire with Lion's Paws

Resets the brain's electromagnetic field to
strengthen your nervous system.
(Originally taught by Yogi Bhajan, *KRI Aquarian
Kundalini Teaching Yoga Manual*, p. 61)

Posture: Sit on the floor or on a chair, making sure to keep the spine straight.

Mudra: Extend your arms out to the sides. Bring your hands into a claw position, facing up with palms exposed. Move your arms up and down, starting with arms out from the shoulders and parallel to the floor and raising them over your head, where they will cross. The elbows and arms will bend like an arch, and the hands should alternate when crossing over the head. Continue this movement throughout the entire meditation.

Eye Focus: Keep eyes closed and focus on the brow point.

Mantra: None. (Originally taught silently. Madhur-Nain added music for focus.)

- This was originally taught with no sound. I added some music for focus. Use with or without any of the recordings that come with this book.

Breathing Pattern: Breath of Fire. Through the nose, inhale and exhale in a quick yet even pace. (If you become light-headed, pause for a moment and recenter yourself. The best way to learn this breathing technique is by panting like a dog. Practice this method, and then close your mouth and continue the same rhythm.)

End: Keep the breathing motion going, and stick the tongue out as far as possible for at least fifteen seconds. Inhale and suspend the breath for fifteen seconds while maintaining the Lion's Paw. Bring the tongue in and fix your arms in an arch around your head, keeping the palms facing down about six inches away from above your ears. Maintain this posture as you exhale and inhale, suspending the breath for thirty seconds (or as long as you can) as you breathe. Relax for three to five minutes.

Timing: Three, seven, or nine minutes daily.

Summary: This meditation is best if you feel stuck in life, especially because of anxiety. It will help you feel as if you can confront your issues. Practice this meditation daily for a period of time to regain your inner and outer strength.

- A straight back allows energy to flow up through the spine, centering the self.
- Darkness created by closing the eyes affects the action of the pineal gland, instilling you with vastness and wholeness, a sense of belonging and connectedness.
- Breath of Fire helps to open the heart center, releasing anxiety and supporting inner peace.
- Mantras bring the mind into focus, connecting the subconscious and conscious mind to assist in reparative life changes.

The Caliber of Life Meditation

A simple and deep meditation to strengthen your
nervous system and create inner calmness.
(Originally taught by Yogi Bhajan, October 1979.)

Posture: Sit on the floor or on a chair, making sure to keep the spine straight.

Mudra: Extend both arms straight in front of your shoulders and parallel to the ground. Bring your right hand into a fist, with the thumb out. Wrap your left hand's fingers around the fist of the right hand. Point both thumbs out and touch them together; a small "v" will form at the tips.

Eye Focus: Hold eyes at thumbnails and the small "v" formed. Look beyond and out of focus.

Mantra: None. (Originally taught silently. Madhur-Nain added music for focus.)

- This was originally taught with no sound. I added some music for focus. Use with or without any of the recordings that come with this book.

Breathing Pattern: Inhale five seconds in, and then exhale five seconds out. Suspend your breath out for fifteen seconds. (You can hold your breath out for a shorter amount of time, if it is easier; just be consistent with the time. Slowly try building up to fifteen seconds.)

End: Inhale and hold your breath for fifteen to twenty seconds. Repeat three times and then relax. Sit silently for two minutes.

Timing: Three to five minutes daily; build up to eleven minutes daily. Do not practice longer than eleven minutes.

Summary: This meditation is best for those who suffer from acute anxiety or depression. If you feel as if you have no sense of control in your life and consequently try to control everything (and everyone) around you, this method will help instill inner peace within you. Practice this meditation daily for a period of time to help you build a deeper inner connection with your self through the use of pranic breathing.

- A straight back allows energy to flow up through the spine, centering the self.
- By keeping the elbows straight, you help to strengthen your nervous system.
- Allowing light to come in through this open-eyed eye focus stimulates the pineal gland. This will help you regulate your hormones and emotions.
- Breath suspension is a trigger method that strengthens your fight-or-flight response.
- Mantras bring the mind into focus, connecting the subconscious and conscious mind to assist in reparative life changes.

Me within Me Meditation

Creates inner self-worth to support your
personal relationship with yourself.
(Originally taught by Yogi Bhajan, August 2, 2000.)

Posture: Sit on the floor or on a chair, making sure to keep the spine
straight.

Mudra: Venus Lock: interlace your fingers at your heart center, keeping
your elbows relaxed.

Eye Focus: Keep eyes closed.

Mantra: "Me within me is the purity. Me within me is the reality. Me
within me is the grace. I am the master of the space."
- Translation: Various; see below.
- Chanting Instructions: Out loud, in a monotone voice.
- Summary: Me within Me is 1) the purity: connecting you to
  feel whole within, 2) the reality: supports you in life instead of a

fantasy scenario, 3) the grace: reminds you to be compassionate no matter the situation. Master of this space: taking ownership for you and your emotions.

Breathing Pattern: Breathe as necessary while you chant the mantra. Be sure not to break the rhythm of the mantra as you repeat it.

End: Inhale and hold your breath. As you tighten every muscle in your body, silently listen to the mantra vibrating with you. Exhale, then repeat this process again (two times total).

Timing: Three, seven, or eleven minutes daily.

Summary: This meditation is best for those with low self-esteem, a common occurrence in people with anxiety. I prescribe this meditation to clients who are new to meditation due to the English words, which makes it easy to practice. Practice this meditation daily to build a sense of belief within yourself so that you can release the anxiety that is hurting your life.

- A straight back allows energy to flow up through the spine, centering the self.
- Darkness created by closing the eyes affects the action of the pineal gland, instilling you with vastness and wholeness, a sense of belonging and connectedness.
- The Venus Lock Mudra connects negative and positive frequencies to bring balance.
- Mantras bring the mind into focus, connecting the subconscious and conscious mind to assist in reparative life changes.

Basic Breath Series: Alternate Nostril Breathing—Left to Right

Supports you to feel calm by releasing stress
and recurring negative thoughts.
(Originally taught by Yogi Bhajan, June 1969.)

Posture: Sit on the floor or on a chair, making sure to keep the spine straight.

Mudra: Left hand is in Gyan Mudra, resting on your left knee. Using your right hand, press and close each nostril as you inhale through the left nostril and exhale through the right nostril. You can use your thumb and index finger or thumb and small finger for this breathing sequence.

Eye Focus: Keep eyes closed to focus easily on your breath.

Mantra: Silent "Sat Naam."
- Translation: Sat: truth. Naam: identity.
- Summary: A Bija (seed) mantra, Sat Naam contains all the knowledge of a tree. Words are like seeds; they can grow beauty or destruction. "The essence/seed is the identity of truth embodied in condensed form. Mentally chanting or thinking this mantra

awakens the soul and gives you your destiny."—Yogi Bhajan. (Originally taught silently. Madhur-Nain added mantra music for focus.)

Breathing Pattern: Bring your right hand to the nose. Using your thumb, close your right nostril and inhale through the left nostril. Then, using your index or small finger, close your left nostril and exhale through the right nostril. Continue this back-and-forth breathing pattern. The breath should always be full and relaxed.

End: Inhale and hold your breath for fifteen to twenty seconds. Repeat this three times and then relax. Sit silently for two minutes.

Timing: Three, seven, eleven, twenty-two, or thirty-one minutes daily.

Summary: This meditation is best if you have daily stress that impacts your life, making it hard to concentrate and be productive. Practice this meditation daily for a period of time to help you release the toxic negative thoughts from your mind.

- Alternative Nostril Breathing balances the left and right hemispheres of the brain.
- A straight back allows energy to flow up through the spine, centering the self.
- Closed eyes help you to connect with your breathing, bringing you closer to recognizing and building a relationship with your self-identity.
- Gyan Mudra stimulates the ability to understand your inner knowledge and wisdom, invoking receptivity and calmness.
- Mantras bring the mind into focus, connecting the subconscious and conscious mind to assist in reparative life changes.

Basic Breath Series: Alternate Nostril Breathing—Right to Left

Creates a positive mood pattern, helping you to focus
on what is most important in your life.
(Originally taught by Yogi Bhajan, June 1969.)

Posture: Sit on the floor or on a chair, making sure to keep the spine straight.

Mudra: Right hand is in Gyan Mudra, resting on your right knee. Using your left hand, press and close each nostril as you inhale through the right nostril and exhale through the left nostril. You can use your thumb and index finger or thumb and small finger for this breathing sequence.

Eye Focus: Keep eyes closed to focus easily on your breath.

Mantra: Silent "Sat Naam."
- Translation: Sat: truth. Naam: identity.
- Summary: A Bija (seed) mantra, Sat Naam contains all the knowledge of a tree. Words are like seeds; they can grow beauty or destruction. "The essence/seed is the identity of truth embodied in condensed form. Mentally chanting or thinking this mantra

awakens the soul and gives you your destiny."—Yogi Bhajan. (Originally taught silently; Madhur-Nain added mantra music for focus.)

Breathing Pattern: Bring your left hand to the nose. Using your thumb, close your left nostril and inhale through the right nostril. Then, using your index or small finger, close your right nostril and exhale through the left nostril. Continue this back-and-forth breathing pattern. The breath should always be full and relaxed.

End: Inhale and hold your breath for fifteen to twenty seconds. Repeat this three time and then relax. Sit silently for two minutes.

Timing: Three, seven, eleven, twenty-two, or thirty-one minutes daily.

Summary: This meditation is best for those who need more focus. It is especially effective if you suffer from stress, anxiety, or OCD. Practice this meditation daily for a period of time to build and maintain concentration skills in your life.

- Alternative Nostril Breathing balances the left and right hemispheres of the brain.
- A straight back allows energy to flow up through the spine, centering the self.
- Closed eyes help you to connect with your breathing, bringing you closer to recognizing and building a relationship with your self-identity.
- Gyan Mudra stimulates the ability to understand your inner knowledge and wisdom, invoking receptivity and calmness.
- Mantras bring the mind into focus, connecting the subconscious and conscious mind to assist in reparative life changes.

7 Wave

Unifies the self by creating internal balance.
(Originally taught by Yogi Bhajan, *KRI Aquarian
Teacher Level 1 Yoga Manual*, p. 123.)

Posture: Sit on the floor or on a chair, making sure to keep the spine straight.

Mudra: Pranam Mudra. Hold hands in prayer pose at your heart center. Touch both thumbs to the sternum.

Eye Focus: Keep eyes closed and focus on the brow point.

Mantra: "Sat Naam."
- Translation: Sat: truth. Naam: identity.
- Chanting Instructions: Chant "Sat" as it travels in six waves that represent the chakras in your body: 1st (rectum area), 2nd (sexual organs), 3rd (navel), 4th (heart center), 5th (throat area), and 6th

(third eye: pituitary gland) on the "t." Chant "Naam" at the 7ᵗʰ (top of your head: pineal gland) and 8ᵗʰ (aura). Continue this cycle.

- Summary: A Bija (seed) mantra, Sat Naam contains all the knowledge of a tree. Words are like seeds; they can grow beauty or destruction. "The essence/seed is the identity of truth embodied in condensed form. Mentally chanting or thinking this mantra awakens the soul and gives you your destiny."—Yogi Bhajan.

Breathing Pattern: Inhale deeply and chant "Sat." It should flow through you in six waves, each representing a chakra (see above). Take a little sip of breath and chant "Naam," and then exhale.

End: Inhale and exhale three times and then relax.

Timing: Three minutes daily; build up to thirty-one minutes daily.

Summary: This meditation is best for those who want to clear patterns of negative thinking. Because 7 Wave focuses on the chakras by traveling through them (from the base, up the spine, and out the top of the head), this method helps to unify the self and creates a genuine relationship with the whole body. Practice this meditation daily for a period of time to help create inner peace.

- A straight back allows energy to flow up through the spine, centering the self.
- Darkness created by closing the eyes affects the action of the pineal gland, instilling you with vastness and wholeness, a sense of belonging and connectedness.
- The Prayer Pose Mudra neutralizes your male (yang) and female (yin) energy.
- Mantras bring the mind into focus, connecting the subconscious and conscious mind to assist in reparative life changes.

Kirtan Kriya

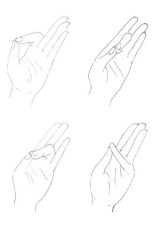

Heals depression by increasing gray matter and
breaking negative patterns in the mind.
(Originally taught by Yogi Bhajan, *KRI Aquarian
Teacher Level 1 Yoga Manual*, p. 99.)

Posture: Sit on the floor or on a chair, making sure to keep the spine
straight.

Mudra: Touch your thumb to each finger as you chant. Always start with
the index finger, then move through to the small finger. Start again at the
index finger and repeat.

Eye Focus: Close eyes and mentally focus on an "L"-shape with each pulse
of the mantra. Each syllable of the mantra enters in through the tenth gate
and comes out through the third eye.

Mantra: "Saa Taa Naa Maa."
- Translation: The cycle of life. Sa: infinity. Ta: life. Na: death. Ma:
  rebirth.

- Chanting Instructions: One, two, or five minutes out loud; one, two, or five minutes whispering; two, four, or ten minutes silent; one, two, or five minutes whispering; finish with one, two, or five minutes out loud.
- Summary: Also known as Panj Shabd, this mantra balances the hemispheres of the brain and creates a deeper understanding of the self. Chanting or even silently thinking this mantra develops intuition.

Breathing Pattern: Breathe as necessary while you remain silent or chant/whisper the mantra.

End: Sit silently for one minute. Then, raise your arms up and spread your fingers. Stretch the spine.

Timing: Six, twelve, or thirty minutes daily.

Summary: This meditation is best for those with anxiety, including PTSD and OCD. Several research studies have shown that Kirtan Kriya has aided in depression and prevented memory loss by increasing gray matter in the frontal lobe of the brain. Yogi Bhajan has even recommend this method to bipolar individuals. Please contact a medical professional before conducting this meditation. Otherwise, practice this meditation daily for a period of time to break negative patterns and guide you toward a more tranquil mind.

- A straight back allows energy to flow up through the spine, centering the self.
- Energy enters into you from the top of the head (top of the focused "L"-shape) and flows out of you through the frontal lobe (the bottom of the "L"-shape).
- Each finger position during this mudra represents a potential: knowledge (index finger), wisdom (middle finger), vitality (ring finger), communication (small finger).
- Mantras bring the mind into focus, connecting the subconscious and conscious mind to assist in reparative life changes.

Sodarshan Chakra Kriya

Builds your personal identity.
(Originally taught by Yogi Bhajan, December 1990.)

Posture: Sit on the floor or on a chair, making sure to keep the spine straight.

Mudra: Rest your left hand on your knee in Maha Gyan Mudra. You will use your right hand to hold the left and right nostrils throughout this meditation.

Eye Focus: Hold eyes slightly open and focus on the tip of the nose. It is important that this meditation is not done with the eyes closed.

Mantra: Silent "Wha-hay Guroo."
- Translation: Indescribable wisdom; a deep truth from within you.
- Silent (mentally chant); best practiced with mantra music.
- Summary: This mantra helps to strengthen your relationship to your sharpest self, also known as your identity. Because of the amount of navel pumps, this mantra is easiest to accomplish on an empty stomach or first thing in the morning.

Breathing Pattern: Inhale slowly and deeply through the left nostril. Hold your breath, keeping the right nostril closed with the right thumb. Relax your hand as you mentally recite "Wha-hay Guroo." Mentally chant sixteen times. Each pump is like a 3 part wave where you are pulling in the navel slightly three times with each repetition of the mantra. ("Wha," first wave. "Hay," second wave. "Guroo," third wave.) This will be a total of forty-eight navel pumps. Repeat this pattern for the full suggested time.

End: Inhale and hold your breath for five to ten seconds. Exhale. End by raising your hands and shaking every part of your body for one minute. Spread the energy over your body, and then relax.

Timing: Eleven minutes daily; build up to thirty-one minutes daily.

Summary: This meditation is best for those who find they do not trust themselves or the path of their lives. There is an old belief that this meditation can clear past karma and the subconscious reactions, which threaten to limit you. Practice this meditation daily for a period of time to support your capacity to reach the authentic you.

- The repeated navel pumps in this breathing pattern give you the pranic energy to heal.
- A straight back allows energy to flow up through the spine, centering the self.
- Focusing on the tip of the nose (the optic nerve concentration) stimulates the pineal gland and frontal lobe, which controls your personality by creating new brain patterns. It is the highest lock, or Bandha, in yoga.
- Mantras bring the mind into focus, connecting the subconscious and conscious mind to assist in reparative life changes.

Tershula Kriya

Brings together the three nervous systems, offering the ability to heal.
(Originally taught by Yogi Bhajan, *KRI Aquarian
Teacher* Level *1 Yoga Manual*, p. 125.)

Posture: Sit on the floor or on a chair, making sure to keep the spine straight.

Mudra: Hold your right hand over your left hand in front of your diaphragm. Thumbs are out from each hand. Keep hands about 10 degrees higher than your elbows, which are kept at your side.

Eye Focus: Keep eyes closed, looking at the back of the eyelids.

Mantra: Silent "Har Har Wha-hay Guru."
- Translation: Har is the creative energy of everything. Wahe is indescribable wisdom. Guru is truth.
- Summary: While you are chanting, visualize white light around your hands in your mind's eye. As you exhale, visualize life moving

out of your fingertips. This helps instill you with creativity and insight.

Breathing Pattern: Inhale through the nose and pull in the navel. Hold this breath and posture as you mentally chant the mantra for as long as you can manage. Exhale through the nose, and then hold your breath out as you mentally chant the mantra for as long as possible. Continue with this pattern, moving as slowly as you need to so that you don't run out of breath.

End: Inhale and hold your breath for five to ten seconds. Exhale, then relax.

Timing: Three, seven, eleven, twenty-two, or thirty-one minutes daily.

Summary: This meditation is best for those seeking a form of healing, especially in support of psychological disorders and phobias. Tershula Kriya brings balance to the three gunas: rajas, tamas, and sattya: the primary forces of life. Practice this meditation daily for a period of time to help balance your personality.

- A straight back allows energy to flow up through the spine, centering the self.
- Darkness created by closing the eyes affects the action of the pineal gland, instilling you with vastness and wholeness, a sense of belonging and connectedness.
- Mantras bring the mind into focus, connecting the subconscious and conscious mind to assist in reparative life changes.

Keeping You Steady and on the Path

Keeps you grounded and able to recognize
the silver lining in all situations.
(Originally taught by Yogi Bhajan, *Transformation Vol. 2*, p. 116.)

Posture: Sit on the floor or on a chair, making sure to keep the spine straight.

Mudra: Hold your arms up (with elbows bent) and parallel to the ground in front of the heart center. Place your right palm on top of your left hand.

Eye Focus: Hold eyes one-tenth open or focused on the tip of the nose.

Mantra: "Haree Naam Sat Naam Haree Naam Haree, Haree Naam Sat Naam Sat Naam Haree."
- Translation: "All this life is your gift; the pain and tragedy is as sweet as nectar."
- Chanting Instructions: Repeat three rounds of the mantra in one breath.
- Summary: The focus required during this mantra in relation to the breathing pattern gives you support on facing crises in life.

This is because you are creating a difficult situation through the meditation and learning to work through the struggle.

Breathing Pattern: Inhale and repeat three rounds of the mantra. (If this is hard for you, start with repeating the mantra twice in one breath and work your stamina toward three repetitions.)

End: Inhale and hold your breath. Exhale. Repeat three times, and then relax.

Timing: Three, seven, eleven, twenty-two, or thirty-one minutes daily.

Summary: This meditation is best to keep you focused and on your life path, as the name suggests. It helps to center you, teaching you to be a less reactive person by tapping into your inner sixth sense, or intuition. Practice this meditation daily for a period of time to achieve the greatest level of success in responding to life's hurdles.

- A straight back allows energy to flow up through the spine, centering the self.
- A one-tenth open eye regulates how much light affects the brain, stimulating the pineal gland.
- Mantras bring the mind into focus, connecting the subconscious and conscious mind to assist in reparative life changes.

Healing Meditation

Creates inner healing and awareness to shift
your mental health and emotions.
(Originally taught by Yogi Bhajan, summer 1973.)

Posture: Sit on the floor or on a chair, making sure to keep the spine straight.

Mudra: Bring your elbows close to your ribs and extend your forearms out to the sides at a 45 degree angle. Your palms should be flat, facing up, with all four fingers together and thumbs out.

Eye Focus: Keep eyes closed.

Mantra: "Raa Maa Daa Saa, Saa Say So Hung."
- Translation: Raa: strong, bright, energy. Maa: calm, nurturing. Daa: secure, grounded. Saa: oneness. Say: sacred. So: identity. Hung: real.
- Chanting Instructions: Out loud, in a monotone voice.
- Summary: This Siri mantra is called Sushmuna and is meant for healing. The sound current Raa Maa Daa Saa, Saa Say So Hung

stimulates Kundalini energy from the earth elements and ether. This energy is carried through your chakras and spine, bringing balance to your inner self.

Breathing Pattern: Breathe when you need to.

End: Inhale and hold your breath. Visualize the healing energy within you and around you, or for someone who needs strength. Repeat this three times.

Timing: Three, seven, eleven, twenty-two, or thirty-one minutes daily.

Summary: This meditation is best if you are suffering from a form of anxiety that is starting to affect your physical health. Like a prayer, you can even use this method for someone else in your life who has physical or mental health issues. This is because this meditation taps into the vast energy of the cosmos, including the light of the sun. Practice this meditation daily for a period of time to experience its fullest healing properties.

- A straight back allows energy to flow up through the spine, centering the self.
- A one-tenth open eye regulates how much light affects the brain, stimulating the pineal gland.
- Keeping the palms flat and open allows the healing energy to flow through you.
- Mantras bring the mind into focus, connecting the subconscious and conscious mind to assist in reparative life changes.

Bringing Mental Balance

Gives a sense of hope, especially to those who
feel as though all else has failed.
(Originally taught by Yogi Bhajan; *Transformation Vol. 2*, p. 121.)

Posture: Sit on the floor or on a chair, making sure to keep the spine straight.

Mudra: Interlace your fingers with your palms facing up and slightly out. Keep fingers open at a 60 degree angle; thumbs are straight forward and not touching. Hold your hands in front of your diaphragm/solar plexus area.

Eye Focus: Hold eyes one-tenth open.

Mantra: "Gobinday. Mukanday. Udaaray. Apaaray. Hareeang. Kareeang. Nirnaamay. Akaamay."
- Translation: Gobinday: sustainer. Mukanday: liberator. Udaaray: enlightener. Apaaray: infinite. Hareeang: destroyer. Kareeang: creator. Nirnaamay: nameless. Akaamay: desireless.

- Chanting Instructions: Chant quickly and try to maintain the quick pace for the duration of the meditation.
- Summary: The sounds of this mantra should create an internal sound current that helps bind you to hope and contentment.

Breathing Pattern: Breathe as necessary while you chant/whisper the mantra as quickly as possible.

End: Inhale and hold your breath. Repeat three times, and then relax.

Timing: Three, seven, eleven, twenty-two, or thirty-one minutes daily.

Summary: This meditation is best if you feel as though you have lost all hope. It will bring you back into balance with yourself. With anxiety, you often feel out of control. The goal of this method is to teach you to be focused while letting go at the same time, which is an important aspect to life: we all have free will and choices, but we need to remain relaxed and active. Practice this meditation daily for a period of time to help guide you away from the governing forces of anxiety.

- A straight back allows energy to flow up through the spine, centering the self.
- A one-tenth open eye regulates how much light affects the brain, stimulating the pineal gland.
- Mantras bring the mind into focus, connecting the subconscious and conscious mind to assist in reparative life changes. Chanting quickly allows you to tune into the mantra.

Anxiety Release Meditation

Supports you to be calm and centered throughout the obstacles of life.
(Originally taught by Yogi Bhajan; orally taught
to me by Shiva Kaur in 1992.)

Posture: Sit on the floor or on a chair, making sure to keep the spine straight.

Mudra: Interlace middle, ring, and small fingers, leaving the thumb and index fingers out. Touch thumb and index fingers together with tips pulled apart. Hold thumb tips to the center of the chest.

Eye Focus: Close eyes and focus on the third eye, one inch above the center of your brows.

Mantra: "Guroo Guroo Wha-hay Guroo, Guroo Raam Daas Guroo."
- Translation: Guru: teacher/truth. Wahe: indescribable. Ram Das: miracle of miracles.
- Chanting Instructions: Out loud, in a monotone voice.
- Summary: Wahe Guru is the indescribable process of transforming the self from darkness to light, from fear to courage, from anxiety

to contentment. Ram Das calls on miracles to aid in the process of this healing; it opens the door to what is needed. This mantra acts as an internal blessing to give your life comfort and support.

Breathing Pattern: Breathe as necessary while you remain silent or chant/whisper the mantra.

End: Inhale deeply and hold your breath, and then exhale. Repeat three times. Relax.

Timing: Three, seven, eleven, or twenty-two minutes daily.

Summary: This meditation helps keep you steady and moving forward. It allows you to be stable as you experience life's ups and downs, even when the process of life is plagued with pain, fear, and anger. Practice this meditation daily for a period of time to experience the greatest sense of inner stability and security, although long-term practice (I have been using it since 1992) is strongly encouraged.

- A straight back allows energy to flow up through the spine, centering the self.
- Focusing on the third eye activates your intuition.
- Mantras bring the mind into focus, connecting the subconscious and conscious mind to assist in reparative life changes.

Meditation to Remove Conflict

Offers internal problem-solving by establishing a
conscious communication pattern with the self.
(Originally taught by Yogi Bhajan, October 1979.)

Posture: Sit on the floor or on a chair, making sure to keep the spine straight.

Mudra: Venus Lock: interlace your fingers at your heart center, keeping your elbows relaxed.

Eye Focus: Keep eyes closed.

Mantra: "Humee Hum, Brahm Hum."
- Translation: "We are we; we are God."
- Chanting Instructions: Out loud.
- Summary: Yogically, "GOD" means Generate, Organize, and Deliver or Destroy. This mantra teaches you how to let go of what you believe to be true in your mind. Through this, you

can make changes in your life. Chanting "Humee Hum, Brahm Hum" creates a feeling of being connected to something bigger than yourself.

Breathing Pattern: Breathe as necessary while you remain silent or chant/whisper the mantra.

End: Inhale and hold your breath. Assess how you are feeling, and then exhale. Repeat two times. Relax.

Timing: Eleven minutes daily.

Summary: This meditation is best if your anxiety makes it hard for you to communicate with yourself or with others. Often, stress and anxiety end up controlling your life, which can affect your job or relationships. This method guides you away from the fragmented self that makes you feel separated and alone. You learn to understand exactly what you need to make positive changes. Practice this meditation daily for a period of time to teach your mind to serve your higher conscious and reconnect yourself with what is happening around you.

- A straight back allows energy to flow up through the spine, centering the self.
- Darkness created by closing the eyes affects the action of the pineal gland, instilling you with vastness and wholeness, a sense of belonging and connectedness.
- The Venus Lock Mudra connects negative and positive frequencies to bring balance.
- Mantras bring the mind into focus, connecting the subconscious and conscious mind to assist in reparative life changes.

Meditation for Stress or Sudden Shock

Balances the two sides of the brain to maintain equilibrium under stress.
(Originally taught by Yogi Bhajan, January 1979.)

Posture: Sit on the floor or on a chair, making sure to keep the spine straight.

Mudra: Rest your right hand in your left hand. Press your thumb tips together and pull toward your body. Hold hands one inch above your navel point.

Eye Focus: Lotus Point. Keep your eyes focused on the tip of the nose.

Mantra: "Sat Naam, Sat Naam, Sat Naam, Sat Naam, Sat Naam, Sat Naam, Wha-hay Guroo."
- Translation: Sat: truth. Naam: identity. Wahe: indescribable. Guru: truth.
- Chanting Instructions: Out loud, in a monotone voice, with music or by yourself.
- Summary: This mantra calls on the identity of your truth to help shift yourself from darkness to light. Because it is a fast mantra,

the chanting will feel intense; you will have to find your own pattern of when to breathe.

Breathing Pattern: Chant 3 repetitions of the mantra on one breath. You can start with 1 repetition and build up to 3 repetitions. Mantra music is continuous.

End: Inhale and exhale completely and quickly a total of five times. Then inhale deeply and stretch your arms above your head. Exhale, and relax.

Timing: Three, seven, eleven, or twenty-two minutes daily.

Summary: This meditation is best for those suffering from immense stress or sudden shock, such as a car accident or a natural disaster. These experiences rattle your nervous system so deeply that stress and anxiety can quickly overwhelm your feelings. By using this method, you can bring the nervous system back into balance and functioning in a healthy manner. Practice this meditation daily for a period of time to bring balance back into your life.

- A straight back allows energy to flow up through the spine, centering the self.
- Focusing on the tip of the nose (the optic nerve concentration) stimulates the pineal gland and frontal lobe, which controls your personality by creating new brain patterns. It is the highest lock, or Bandha, in yoga.
- Mantras bring the mind into focus, connecting the subconscious and conscious mind to assist in reparative life changes.

Gunpati

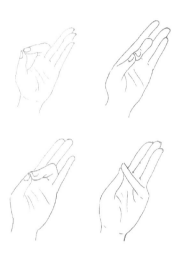

Helps clear the blocks from the past, evoking knowledge and happiness.
(Originally taught by Yogi Bhajan, November 2, 1988.)

Posture: Sit on the floor or on a chair, making sure to keep the spine straight.

Mudra: Touch your thumb to each finger as you chant. Always start with the index finger, then move through to the small finger. Start again at the index finger, and repeat.

Eye Focus: Hold eyes one-tenth open.

Mantra: "Saa Taa Naa Maa, Raa Maa Daa Saa, Saa Say Ho Hung."
  • Translation: Various; see below.

- Chanting Instructions: Out loud, in a monotone voice.
- Summary: Saa Taa Naa Maa is the mantra for breaking old patterns. Raa Maa Daa Saa is the universal energy for healing. Saa Say So Hung is the spiritual energy for change.

Breathing Pattern: Chant mantra on a single breath. Your thumb should move to a new finger with each new syllable in the chant. For example: "Saa" (index), "Taa" (middle), "Naa" (ring), "Maa" (small), and so on.

End: Inhale deeply, and then hold your breath and twist your body back and forth wildly. Do this three to five times total. Then sit quietly and focus your eyes on the Lotus Point (the tip of your nose) for two to three minutes as you relax.

Timing: Three, seven, eleven, or twenty-two minutes daily.

Summary: This meditation is best if you have anxiety that stems from a traumatic experience, especially those deeply imbedded within you from childhood. It is my most prescribed meditation for clients (who then see amazing results with daily practice). Gunpati supports you to cut the pain binding you to the trauma. This helps to break overemotional thinking and patterns born from worry. Practice this meditation daily for a period of time to experience the greatest sense of transformation to your body's whole system.

- Inhaling on "Hung" during the breathing pattern activates inner awareness, or Kundalini energy, which is based three inches below your navel.
- A straight back allows energy to flow up through the spine, centering the self.
- A one-tenth open eye regulates how much light affects the brain, stimulating the pineal gland.
- Each finger position during this mudra represents a potential: knowledge (index finger), wisdom (middle finger), vitality (ring finger), communication (small finger).
- Mantras bring the mind into focus, connecting the subconscious and conscious mind to assist in reparative life changes.

Laya Yoga Kundalini Mantra

Adjusts and establishes your soul to awaken you to your destiny.
(Originally taught by Yogi Bhajan, *KRI Aquarian
Teacher Training Yoga Manual*, p. 101.)

Posture: Sit on the floor or on a chair, making sure to keep the spine straight.

Mudra: Gyan Mudra. Touch the thumb's tip to the index fingertip while keeping the other fingers straight.

Eye Focus: Keep eyes closed and focused on the brow point.

Mantra: "Ek Ong Kaar-(UH), Saa Taa Naa Maa-(UH), Siree Wha-(UH), Hay Guroo."
  • Translation: Ek Ong Kar: one creator. Sa Ta Na Ma: true identity. Siri Wahe Guru: great indescribable wisdom.

- Chanting Instructions: Visualize energy as you chant the "(UH)" sections.
- Summary: This mantra allows you to raise your inner awareness and unite this consciousness through the use of visualization in chanting. Focus on your energy spiraling up your spine.

Breathing Pattern: Pull your navel in on "Ek," (hold until Siree) and lift the diaphragm with powerful movement on all "(UH)." Relax your whole navel and abdomen on "Hay Gur-Roo." (The sound "UH" should come from the lifting of the diaphragm, rather than actually saying it.)

End: Inhale and exhale three times and then relax.

Timing: Three minutes daily; build up to thirty-one minutes daily.

Summary: This meditation is best if you long to let go of the past and elevate yourself. It supports your need for nonattachment by increasing inner awareness, allowing you to be less controlling. Over time, this helps you release anxiety. Practice this meditation daily for a period of time to help you realize what you can and cannot control, easing you into an eventual sense of inner peace.

- A straight back allows energy to flow up through the spine, centering the self.
- Darkness created by closing the eyes affects the action of the pineal gland, instilling you with vastness and wholeness, a sense of belonging and connectedness.
- Gyan Mudra stimulates the ability to understand your inner knowledge and wisdom, invoking receptivity and calmness.
- Mantras bring the mind into focus, connecting the subconscious and conscious mind to assist in reparative life changes.

Master's Touch Meditation

Creates an understanding of the infinite energy
to accept it as part of your life.
(Originally taught by Yogi Bhajan, July 2000.)

Posture: Sit on the floor or on a chair, making sure to keep the spine straight.

Mudra: Touch the pads of your index fingers together at the heart center. Curl your other fingers in, with thumbs on top, and create a 45 degree angle with your index fingers. Face your left hand toward the body, and face your right hand away from the body. Keep shoulders relaxed.

Eye Focus: Hold eyes slightly open and focus on the tip of the nose.

Mantra: "Aad Such, Jugaad Such. Hai Bhee Such, Naanak Hosee *Bhee* Such."
- Translation: Aad Such: true in the beginning. Jugaad Such: true throughout the ages. Hai Bhee Such: true at this moment. Naanak Hosee Bhee Such: oh wise one, forever true.

- Chanting Instructions: Out loud, in a monotone voice.
- Summary: Also known as Kundalini Shakti Mantra, this chant helps you to create a connection to the authentic you. Your internal soul matches your outside.

Breathing Pattern: Breathe as necessary while you remain silent or chant/whisper the mantra. With each "Such," pull the navel in as you breathe.

End: Inhale and hold your breath, and then relax your posture. Sit with eyes closed for two minutes.

Timing: Three, seven, eleven, or twenty-two minutes daily.

Summary: This meditation is best to "achieve your Self for yourself. That is honey, your sweetness" (Yogi Bhajan). Through the combinations of chanting, mudra, and eye focus, you can unlock grace, respect, love, and satisfaction for yourself. I often prescribe this meditation to clients who have trust issues or problems with overthinking. Practice this meditation daily for a period of time to discover the true you and guide you toward the infinite energy.

- A straight back allows energy to flow up through the spine, centering the self.
- Focusing on the tip of the nose (the optic nerve concentration) stimulates the pineal gland and frontal lobe, which controls your personality by creating new brain patterns. It is the highest lock, or Bandha, in yoga.
- Maha Gyan Mudra creates an understanding of the infinite energy.
- Mantras bring the mind into focus, connecting the subconscious and conscious mind to assist in reparative life changes. Chanting out loud stimulates the upper palate through the tip of your tongue, activating the thalamus and hypothalamus.

Sarab Gyan Kriya

This meditation connects you to your inner awareness
by cutting into the duality of your life.
(Originally taught by Yogi Bhajan, April 2001.)

Posture: Sit on the floor or on a chair, making sure to keep the spine straight.

Mudra: Keep elbows relaxed at the sides of your body as you bring both hands into Gyan Mudra (index finger and thumb tip touching) at the front of the heart center. Rest right hand in the left hand, holding both palms up as the right hand's fingers cross over the left hand's fingers.

Eye Focus: Keep eyes closed and focused on the brow point.

Mantra: "Ek Ong Kaar, Sat Gur Prasaad, Sat Gur Prasaad, Ek Ong Kaar."
- Translation: "We are all one (connected) as we shift our negative thoughts from darkness to light with grace."

- Chanting Instructions: Out loud, in a monotone voice. Two repetitions take about fifteen seconds.
- Summary: A mantra to bring the mind into focus.

Breathing Pattern: Breathe as necessary while you chant the mantra. Be sure not to break the rhythm of the mantra as you repeat it.

End: Inhale deeply. Raise your arms up, bringing your palms together as you tighten your whole body for the length of the breath. Then, powerfully exhale. Repeat this process three more times.

Timing: Three, seven, eleven, or twenty-two minutes daily.

Summary: This meditation is best if you find your mind is spiraling out of control. The mantra is meant to help you connect with your mind, bringing focus and clarity back into your life. It is essentially putting a break on frenzied thoughts, allowing you to restore balance. Practice this meditation daily for a period of time to help you to reconnect with yourself.

- A straight back allows energy to flow up through the spine, centering the self.
- Darkness created by closing the eyes affects the action of the pineal gland, instilling you with vastness and wholeness, a sense of belonging and connectedness.
- Gyan Mudra stimulates the ability to understand your inner knowledge and wisdom, invoking receptivity and calmness.
- Mantras bring the mind into focus, connecting the subconscious and conscious mind to assist in reparative life changes.

Praan Naadi Shabad Guni Kriya

Balances your breath and meridian points through the
breath and sound to bring focus to the self.
(Originally taught by Yogi Bhajan, November 2, 1973.)

Posture: Sit on the floor or on a chair, making sure to keep the spine
straight.

Mudra: Place your right hand into your left hand, keeping both palms up
at the level of your solar plexus (without touching your body). Connect
thumb tips together and apply light pressure. Hold this pose while keeping
your elbows relaxed.

Eye Focus: Lotus Point. Keep your eyes focused on the tip of the nose.

Mantra: "Sat Naam, Sat Naam, Sat Naam, Sat Naam, Sat Naam, Sat
Naam, Wha-hay Guroo."

- Translation: Sat: truth. Nam: identity. Wahe: indescribable. Guru:
  truth.

- Chanting Instructions: Mentally chant "Sat Naam" with each segmented breath. Only chant "Wha-hay Guroo" in a strong whisper.
- Summary: The segmented breathing required in this mantra stimulates the vagus nerve by the rhythm and pattern you set. The vagus nerve is connected to all organs and glands (except the adrenals), so it supports the function of the entire body. By chanting "Wha-hay Guroo," we connect to the ethereal part of life.

Breathing Pattern: Inhale six times with each set of "Sat Naam," filling your lungs. Exhale as you whisper the chant, "Wha-hay Guroo."

End: Inhale and hold your breath as you focus all your attention to your brow point. Then, exhale powerfully through your mouth. Inhale again and reach your hands up, stretching your arms. Exhale, and repeat this stretch two more times. Relax.

Timing: Three, seven, eleven, or twenty-two minutes daily.

Summary: This meditation is best if you find you are often lost in your own thoughts. It will help teach you to be neutral in your life, restoring balance to your self. Practice this meditation daily for a period of time to shift yourself from darkness to light, bringing your mind's focus back to you.

- The patterns created during this segmented breathing style strengthens the parasympathetic nervous system, which helps to neutralize stress levels.
- A straight back allows energy to flow up through the spine, centering the self.
- Focusing on the tip of the nose (the optic nerve concentration) stimulates the pineal gland and frontal lobe, which controls your personality by creating new brain patterns. It is the highest lock, or Bandh, in yoga.
- Mantras bring the mind into focus, connecting the subconscious and conscious mind to assist in reparative life changes.

Kundalini Yoga Terminology

81 Facets of the Mind. As taught by Yogi Bhajan, the various parts of the mind that you must learn to harness in order to enrich your lives. When you can control them, you can master inner and outer harmony.

Ahangkar. The ego of the self and how it relates to the rest of the world.

Ajna chakra. The Third Eye point, or the sixth chakra, associated with the pituitary gland; also Agya chakra.

Akaal. Undying.

Alternative nostril breathing. A yogic technique that teaches you to breathe out of a single nostril (right or left) at a time, resulting in a harmonization of the brain hemispheres and balancing your mental, emotional, and physical well-being.

Ambrosial hour. Between 4 and 6 a.m., before the sun rises. This is a very special time and a great time to meditate.

Amrit. Also "amrita." Spiritual or sweet nectar; the ceremony in which one takes vows as a baptized Sikh.

Amrit Vela. Literally, "ambrosial time." It is the two and a half hours before the sun rises. During this special time, you are most receptive to your soul and can clear the subconscious of wrong habits and impulses. This is the ideal time to connect with teachers and saints from all traditions. It is encouraged to perform sadhana (spiritual discipline) during the ambrosial time.

Aquarian Age. The next in a succession of astrological ages, each lasting roughly two thousand years. Fully inaugurated in 2012, the Aquarian Age will witness a radical change in consciousness, human sensitivity, and technology. The central change of this new age emphasizes an increased sensitivity and evolution of our power of awareness and a new relationship to our mind.

Arc-line. One of the ten bodies, sometimes referred to as the halo. The arc-line goes from ear to ear and is the seat of the *akash* (the ether) in the body. Its color varies with the health and the mental or psychic condition of the person. Women have a second arc-line reaching across the chest, from nipple to nipple, which Yogi Bhajan says gets imprinted with the sexual experiences they have had in their lives.

Ardas. Prayer; the traditional formal prayer of the Sikhs.

Aryan. A name of God in the aspect of Sustainer and Preserver; also a name of Lord Vishnu.

Asan (Asana). Position, seat, yogic posture.

Ashram. A learning center for spiritual growth. Means "house of the teacher."

Atman. A person's soul or finite form of the infinite in consciousness; the essential self. It is transcendental in nature; it is not a product of the mind but a part of pure awareness. It is a witness of everything and can only be revealed through itself.

Aura, Auric body. There are seven chakras (energy centers) in the body, and the eighth is the aura: the electromagnetic field of energy that surrounds every living creature. A strong, radiant aura can protect us from many misfortunes and strengthen our mental, physical, and spiritual bodies. Kundalini Yoga kriyas and pranayams increase the auric field, thus increasing awareness.

Awareness. The pure nature of existence; the power to be consciously conscious without an object or need. A fundamental property of the soul and true self, it is Kundalini as it folds and unfolds itself in existence.

Bandha (Bandh). Body locks used in yoga meditation. These are areas in your body which, when stimulated with intention (like through muscle squeezing), will allow you to raise your energy and become more aware.

Bhakti. Self-purification. The devotional form of yoga practiced by a bhakta; a devotee.

Bija Mantra. "Sat Naam" is known as the seed mantra, also the Beej Mantra.

Breath of Fire. Breathing technique that challenges and strengthens the nervous and endocrine systems, testing the will of practitioners beyond the limitations of their egos.

Buddha. An enlightened one; founder of the Buddhist faith.

Buddhi mind. The part of the mind that perceives and understands reality.

Chakra. An energy center of consciousness associated with the seven nerve centers of the body.

Chitta. The universal mind, also known as the basic mind.

Devas. Gods.

Devtas. Angels.

Dharana. Concentration.

Dharma. Path of righteous living; the law of the universe that binds all things in relationship.

Dhiaan. Meditation.

Dog Breath. A pranayam that boosts the immune system. It is a diaphragmatic breathing exercise that asks you to stick the tongue all the way out, hold it, and breathe rapidly through the mouth (for three to five minutes).

Drishti. See "Eye focus."

Eye focus. A meditation technique that asks you to focus your eyes on different positions, each causing the optic nerve to stimulate major glands and gray matter. It causes you to have better mental focus so you can reach a meditative state of still awareness.

Fingers. Each finger on the hand has a special name and is associated with a different energy in yogic science: index finger (the Jupiter Finger, associated with the quality of knowledge and intuition); middle finger (the Saturn Finger, associated with wisdom, intelligence, and patience); ring finger (the Sun Finger, associated with the physical body and physical health); little finger (the Mercury Finger, associated with communication); thumb (the id, associated with the ego).

G-O-D. G means Generate, O means Organize, D means to Deliver or Destroy. We can do good in God consciousness, or we can destroy in God consciousness.

Ganesha. The Hindu elephant god; a symbol for prosperity.

Golden Chain of Teachers or the Golden Link. The long line of spiritual masters who have preceded us. When you chant "Ong Namo Guru Dev Namo." you tune into that flow of spiritual energy and become one with the universal teacher.

Gunas. The three conditions of matter: sattvaa (pure essence; saintliness), raajaas (active, creative, or initiating energy; imperial), and taamaas (inertia or decay).

Gurbani. Word of the Guru. Refers particularly to the words from the Siri Guru Granth Sahib.

Gurbani Kirtan. Devotional singing of Gurbani.

Gurmukh. One whose face is always turned toward the guru, or one whose mouth always repeats the guru's words; a perfectly devoted person.

Gurmukhi. Literally, "from the Guru's mouth"; refers to the script in which the Siri Guru Granth Sahib is written.

Guru. A spiritual teacher.

Guru Gobind Singh. The last of the tenth Sikh gurus. A poet, philosopher, and spiritual master, he was also a warrior who founded the Sikh warrior community, Khalsa, in 1699.

Guru Nanak. The founder of Sikhism and the first of the ten Sikh gurus.

Guru Ram Das. The fourth of the ten Sikh gurus. Yogi Bhajan often spoke of Guru Ram Das, saying he was the holder of the Golden Chain and was the Lord of Miracles. Because he reached such a spiritual enlightenment through a state of consciousness, Yogi Bhajan declared that Guru Ram Das had been bestowed the throne of Raaj Yog.

Gyan Mudra. A common hand position used in many meditations in Kundalini Yoga. Curl the index (Jupiter) finger under the thumb, and hold the other three fingers straight.

Hukam. An order from the guru.

Humanology. A complete system of psychology to promote human excellence and spirit. It incorporates the technology of Kundalini Yoga and meditation, the use of the Shabd guru, and the principles of spiritual counseling.

Ida. Left nerve channel (nadi); relates to the left nostril; moon energy.

Ji. Literally meaning "soul"; used as a term of endearment or sign of respect.

Jalandhar Bandh. Neck lock: a basic body lock used in meditation.

Karma. The cosmic law of cause and effect, action and reaction.

King Janaka. Considered a God-realized king, he ruled Videha around the seventh century BC. Despite his access to luxury and riches, he did not find joy in material goods and was focused on spiritual discourse. His teachings included to follow the pure intentions of the dharma and spirit.

Kirtan. Devotional singing God's praises.

Kirtan Kriya. A powerful meditation that brings balance to one's psyche.

Kriya. Literally, "completed action." A Kundalini Yoga Kriya is a sequence of postures and yoga techniques used to produce a particular impact on the psyche, body, or self. The structure of each kriya has been designed to generate, organize, and deliver a particular state or change of state, thereby completing a cycle of effect. These effects have been codified and elaborated by Yogi Bhajan and form the basic tools used in yoga and its therapeutic applications.

Kundalini. Comes from the word *kundalin*, or coiled energy; the creative potential of an individual.

Kundalini Yoga. A system of meditation directed toward the release of Kundalini energy.

Long-deep breathing. One of the most common methods of breathing in meditation. It asks you to utilize the entire capacity of the lungs in both inhalation and exhalation.

Mala. Meditation beads.

Manas. Part of the mind that records your life.

Manipura. The third chakra, or the solar plexus/navel chakra.

Mantra. Sounds or words that tune or control the mind. *Man* means "mind." *Tra* is "a wave" or the movement of the mind. Mantra is a wave: a repetition of sound and rhythm that directs or controls the mind. When you recite a mantra, you have impact on the mind through the meridian points in the mouth, the mantra's meaning, its pattern of energy, its rhythm, and its nada (energetic shape or sound current in time). Recited correctly, a mantra will activate areas of the nervous system and brain and allow you to shift your state and the perceptual vision or energetic ability associated with it.

Master. A person held in high esteem, considered to be an authority in his or her field.

Maya. The illusion of the reality of sensory experience of one's self and the world around us. Usually thought of as what takes us away from, or blinds us from perceiving, God.

Meditation. The act of thinking deeply or focusing on one's mind for a period of time, in silence or with the aid of chanting, for religious or spiritual purposes or as a method of relaxation.

Meridian(s). Each of a set of pathways in the body along which vital energy is said to flow; there are twelve such pathways associated with specific organs.

Monkey mind. Also referred to as "mind monkey," it is a Buddhist term that references our unsettled mind. In the Buddha's words, "Just as a monkey swinging through the trees grabs one branch and lets it go only to seize another, so too, that which is called thought, mind, or consciousness arises and disappears continually both day and night."

Mool Mantra. The first words of the Siri Guru Granth Sahib.

Morning Sadhana. When you rise early in the morning (between 4 and 6 a.m.) to practice yoga and meditation. See also "Amrit Vela."

Mound of Mercury. The fleshy portion or mound on the palm, just underneath the little finger (Mercury).

Mudra. Yogic hand position. These hand positions are used to seal the body's energy flow in a particular pattern.

Mul Bandh. Literally, "root lock." It is a body lock used to balance prana and apana (see "Prana") at the navel point. This releases reserve energy, which is used to arouse the Kundalini. It is a contraction of the lower pelvis: the navel point, the sex organs, and the rectum.

Muladhara. The root chakra, located in the base of the spine (where it is believed our Kundalini energy is stored). It is the first chakra.

Naad. Translated as "the cosmic sound" or "vibrations of the cosmos." The inner sound that is subtle and all-present. It is the direct expression of the absolute. Meditated upon, it leads into a sound current that pulls the consciousness into expansion.

Nadi. Energy channels for the flow of prana.

Nam. The vibration or essence of God; identity.

Nam Simran. This refers to the state and act of deep meditation by dwelling and merging into the names of the infinite, of God.

Navel point. The sensitive area of the body near the umbilicus that accumulates and stores life force. It is the reserve energy from this area that initiates the flow of the Kundalini energy from the base of the spine. If the navel area is strong, your vital force and health are also strong.

Negative (protective) mind. The part of our mental self that—as the name suggests—serves to protect us as it calculates the risks in our lives. When this mind is weak, we make poor decisions.

Neutral (meditative) mind. The balance between the negative/protective and positive/projective mind, resulting in harmony.

Nitnem. Literally, "repeated every day"; referring to the daily Sikh prayers.

"O" breath. A special breath used in Kundalini Yoga. Make a "O" of the mouth, and breathe through it.

Ojas. Spinal fluid.

One-minute breath. A simple yet challenging Kundalini meditation that strengthens the glandular system. There is one breath cycle per minute: twenty seconds to inhale, twenty seconds to hold, twenty seconds to exhale. It is often used as a calming mechanism.

Patanjali. Rishi Patanjali wrote the famous yoga teachings, *The Yoga Sutras*, thousands of years ago. He wrote the *Push Puran*, predicting the coming of Guru Nanak, and first recited the mantra, Wahe Guru.

Pauree. Literally, "step" or "ladder." Refers to a particular poetic form used in the Siri Guru Granth Sahib.

Pingala. Right nerve channel (nadi); relates to the right nostril; the energy of the sun.

Positive (perspective) mind. The part of our mental self where we weigh the risk versus reward ratio. When this mind is weak, our impulsive energy takes over in order to see quick results. When it is strong, we have a great sense of humor and view of hope.

Prakirti. The creation, the creativity, the matter that has been created by the creator. Earth is Prakirti.

Prana. Subtle ambient life energy; incoming breath of life given by God. It is the subtle breath of the purusha as it vibrates with a psychophysical energy or presence. Prana regulates the modes and moods of the mind.

Pranam Mudra. Also known as "Anjali Mudra," it is the prayer pose hand gesture used in meditation.

Pranayam. Yogic system of breathing exercises.

Pratyahar. One of the eight "limbs" of yoga, as described in *The Yoga Sutras of Patanjali.* Yogi Bhajan says on pratyahar: "Pratyahar is the control of the mind through withdrawal of the senses. The joy in your life which you really want to enjoy is within you. There is nothing more precise than you within you. The day you find you within you, your mind will be yours. In pratyahar, we bring everything to zero (*shuniya*), as pranayam brings everything to Infinity."

Pundit. A Hindu who is learned in the scriptures.

Purusha. The unmanifested spirit.

Raag (Raaga). A traditional melodic mode of the Indian classical music.

Raagi. Musician skilled in the Indian classical music system of Raag; Radha, beloved of Lord Krishna.

Raaj Yog. The Royal Path of yoga.

Raajas. One of the three conditions of matter-creative (see "Gunas").

Raja Yoga. A form of Hindu yoga intended to achieve control over the mind and emotions.

Rajas. The element or mode of prakriti associated with passion, energy, and movement.

Sadhu. A disciplined spiritual person.

Sahasrara. The seventh chakra, viewed as the highest spiritual center. It is at the crown.

Samadhi. The state of consciousness in which the mind is free from reacting to thought waves.

Samskaras. The patterns of thoughts and behaviors that are formed from your subconscious mind, brought from past lives, defining your character and who you are.

Sanskrit. An ancient Indic language of India, in which the Hindu scriptures and classical Indian epic poems are written and from which many northern Indian languages are derived.

Sant Hazara Singh. Yogi Bhajan's spiritual teacher; a former Mahan Tantric.

Sat Naam Rasayan. Healing technique.

Shabd. Sound current, or word of God. Refers to the poems in Siri Guru Granth Sahib.

Shakti. Universal creative energy; one's self-projection; feminine aspect of God; God's power in manifestation; woman. The creative power and principle of existence itself; without it, nothing can manifest or bloom. It is feminine in nature.

Shuniya. A stage of consciousness wherein you bring your ego to a zero state. It's not quite the act of surrender, which is involving you using your energy to engage in the act of surrendering. But once you become shuniya, or zero, then the one will carry you. There are certain rules of Mother Nature. When you fold your hands, God will open up his arms. It's a natural law. The first principle of a teacher is, "I am not." The power of a teacher of Kundalini Yoga is in his zero, in his shuniaa.

Shushmanaa. Central spinal channel.

Sikh. Means "a seeker of truth" and refers to one who follows the Sikh religion.

Simran. Constant remembrance and repetition of God's name. Replacing a negative thought with a positive one, specifically as a meditative process.

Sitali Pranayam. A Kundalini Yoga tool that cools the spine due to the method of inhalation.

Spiritual name. A name that describes the spiritual destiny a person should strive for in life.

Spiritual warrior. Term used in Tibetan Buddhism for someone working on their life's purpose, pushing aside their ego in exchange for ethical impulses.

Subtle body. The subtle body is one of the ten bodies; this body carries the soul to God at the time of death.

Sukhmani. "Peace Lagoon"; a prayer written by Guru Arjan; Song of Peace.

Suspended breath. A method of breathing that requires you to relax the muscles of the diaphragm, ribs, and abdomen.

Sutra. Section from scripture.

Swami. Master.

Syadisthana. The second chakra.

Tantra. Hindu or Buddhist texts and the doctrines that adhere to these texts (involving mantras, meditation, and yoga).

Tattvas. The elements of fire, air, earth, ether, and water, which all creation—including the human body—is composed of.

Ten Bodies. According to yogic science, we consist of ten bodies: (1) Soul Body, (2) Negative Mind, (3) Positive Mind, (4) Neutral Mind, (5) Physical Body, (6) Arc-line, (7) Auric Body, (8) Pranic Body, (9) Subtle Body, (10) Radiant Body. For an explanation of the Ten Bodies, see chapter 25 of *Kundalini Yoga: The Flow of Eternal Power* by Shakti Parwha Kaur Khalsa.

Tenth gate. The center of consciousness, located at the top of the skull.

The Eight Limbs of Yoga. An eightfold path of living that acts as a guideline for a meaningful life filled with purpose. It consists of (1) Yama: ethics and integrity, (2) Niyama: self-discipline, (3) Asana: yogic postures, (4) Pranayama: breath control, (5) Pratyahara: withdrawal from sensory experiences, (6) Dharana: concentration, (7) Dhyana: uninterrupted concentration, (8) Samadhi: ecstasy.

Third Eye Point. Ajna, the sixth chakra, associated with wisdom and intuition.

Trinity herbs. Onion, ginger, and garlic.

Trinity of God. Father, Son, and Holy Ghost; or Brahma, Vishnu, and Shiva; or One who Generates, Organizes, and Destroys or Delivers (G-O-D).

Upanishads. A series of sacred Hindu treatises written circa 800–200 BC.

Venus Lock. A mudra used to connect the negative and positive sides of the body.

Vishuddha. Located in the throat, it is the fifth chakra.

Yam. Yams/Niyams are "dos and don'ts," the ethical precepts defined by Patanjali.

Yatra. Pilgrimage.

Yoga. A discipline that includes breath control, simple meditation, and the use of certain body postures that is used for health or relaxation.

Yogi. One who has attained a state of yoga: mastery of one's self. One who practices the science of yoga.

Yogi Bhajan. A yogi, spiritual leader, and entrepreneur who introduced Kundalini Yoga to the United States.

Psychological and Medical Terminology in Relation to Kundalini Yoga

Adrenal gland. A pair of glands located at the top of each kidney, responsible for controlling the secretion of hormones (including cortisol). Norepinephrine and epinephrine (aka adrenaline)—which contribute to the fight-or-flight response—are produced by the adrenal gland.

Adrenaline. Another term for epinephrine, adrenaline is a hormone secreted by the adrenal glands that prepares us for a fight-or-flight response. It increases blood circulation and breathing in anticipation of exertion during conflict.

Alpha waves. The normal electricity signal of the brain when conscious and relaxed.

Amino acid. Considered the building blocks of protein, amino acids occur naturally in plant and animal tissues. GABA—a neurotransmitter that reduces neuronal excitability—is an amino acid.

Amygdala. A mass of gray matter inside each cerebral hemisphere. It helps us to experience emotions.

Anxiety. A nervous disorder associated with excessive uneasiness and apprehension. Compulsive behavior and even panic attacks are often experienced by those suffering from anxiety.

Brainwaves. Electrical impulses in the brain.

Catastrophic thinking. The irrational thought process that involves obsessing over worst-case scenarios. When left unchecked, these baseless fears can manifest themselves into stress and anxiety.

Cognitive behavioral therapy (CBT). A type of psychotherapy in which negative thought patterns are challenged to alter unwanted behavior. Often used as a treatment in disorders such as depression.

Cortisol hormone. A steroid hormone (also known as hydrocortisone) that is responsible for regulating body processes such as metabolism and the immune response. It is often referred to as the "stress hormone" due to its close connection to the stress response; it is often released in excess when dealing with stressful situations.

Dopamine. The "rewards" chemical. It acts as a neurotransmitter and a precursor to other substances, such as epinephrine.

Endocrine system. The glands and related system that secrete hormones (or other products) directly into the blood and keep them balanced. It is responsible for our vital functions such as hunger, thirst, body temperature, and sleep.

Endorphins. Hormones secreted in the brain and nervous system that serve a number of physiological functions, including the opiate receptors. These bring us to a euphoric state, but they can also act as a natural painkiller, so endorphins help ward off depression.

Epinephrine. Another term for adrenaline, epinephrine is a hormone secreted by the adrenal glands that prepares us for a fight-or-flight response. It increases blood circulation and breathing in anticipation of exertion during conflict.

Fight-or-flight response. An instinctive physiological response to threatening situations: our bodies naturally decide to face the threat or to run away, depending on the variables.

Gamma-aminobutyric acid (GABA). An amino acid that helps inhibit the transmission of nerve impulses in the central nervous system. With increased GABA—which can be achieved naturally or through supplements—we can experience a tranquilized state of mind. It helps us to relax.

Gray matter. The darker tissue of the brain and spinal cord, consisting mainly of nerve cell bodies and branching dendrites. This area of the brain is where synapses occur and allows us to process information; having increased gray matter generally means having more intelligence.

Hippocampus. Thought to be the center of emotion, memory, and the autonomic nervous system. Although commonly regarded as the memory bank of our brain, it also aids in communication.

Hypothalamus. A region of the forebrain below the thalamus, responsible for coordinating the autonomic nervous system and activity of the pituitary gland. It essentially acts as a switchboard for the endocrine system.

Nervous system. The network of nerve cells and fibers that transmits nerve impulses between parts of the body; the **autonomic nervous system** is the part of the nervous system responsible for control of the body functions not conscious directed, such as breathing, the heartbeat, and digestive processes; the **central nervous system** is the complex of nerve tissues that control the activities of the body; the **peripheral nervous system** is the nervous system outside the brain and spine.

Neurons. Specialized cells transmitting nerve impulses. They allow us to store and access information, resulting in strengthened communication within the nervous system.

Neurotransmitters. A chemical substance released at the end of a nerve fiber by the firing off a nerve impulse. It causes the transfer of cerebral information.

Norepinephrine. A hormone released by the adrenal gland and sympathetic nerves, usually activated during the fight-or-flight response. It functions as a neurotransmitter.

Panic attack. A sudden and often debilitating fear response stemming from acute anxiety. It manifests itself in physical reactions such as heart palpitations, shaking, sweating, and shortness of breath. Panic attacks are often triggered even when there is no real danger or threat; there does not have to be an apparent cause to experience a panic episode.

Parasympathetic nervous system. A term relating to the autonomic nervous system that counterbalances the action of the sympathetic nerves. It is responsible for the rest-and-relax part of our internal functions, neutralizing stress levels and allowing for a decreased heartbeat.

Parietal lobes. Paired lobes of the brain (located at the top of the head) that concern sensory information, including the reception and correlation of such information.

Pineal gland. A pea-sized mass of tissue in the brain that secrets a hormone-like substance. It overseas our emotional reactivity.

Pituitary gland. Despite its small size, the pituitary gland is the major endocrine gland. It oversees the growth and development of our bodies by controlling the release of hormones that affect the thyroid gland, adrenal glands, and ovaries or testes.

Psychotherapy. Treatment of a mental disorder by psychological rather than medical means.

Relaxation-induced anxiety (RIA). A phenomenon in which we experience anxiety while trying to relax. It often occurs when we feel as if we have lost some sense of control, throttling us into a state of anxiety or panic.

Serotonin. Acting as a neurotransmitter, serotonin is a compound that acts to constrict blood vessels. It leaves us with a "feel good" sensation due to its influence on our mood and behavior.

Stress. A state of mental or emotional strain resulting from an adverse circumstance. When extremely stressed, our bodies can lose a sense of normalcy in its functions. Over time, stress can lead to other illnesses, both mental (acute anxiety) and physical (heart disease).

Sympathetic nervous system. The part of the autonomic nervous system that consists of nerves arising from the ganglia that helps to balance the parasympathetic nervous system. Because of its influence on the internal organs, blood vessels, and glands, the sympathetic part of our nervous system controls our energy levels (through increased heart rate and blood pressure).

Telomeres. Compound structures at the end of a chromosome protecting our DNA rods, which naturally shorten over our lifespan due to the replication of cells. Stress is responsible for telomere deterioration.

Theta waves. Electrical activity observed in the brain under certain conditions.

Vagus nerve. The tenth cranial nerve, the vagus carries sensory information related to the heart, lungs, and upper digestive tract. When our vagal tone is increased, so is the health of the parasympathetic nervous system because of its ability to reduce heart rate and blood pressure.

White matter. The paler tissue of the brain and spinal cord, consisting mainly of myelinated axons that carry information gathered from the gray matter.

Mantras

Aad Such, Jugaad Such, Hai *Bhee* Such, Naanak Hosee *Bhee* Such.
This *Bhee* version is for creating trust within you and around you; trust
about the process of life.

Aad Such, Jugaad Such
Hai Bhee *Such*
Nanak Hosee Bhee *Such*
Aad Such, Jugaad Such
Hai Bhee *Such*

Gobinday. Mukanday. Udaaray. Apaaray. Hareeang. Kareeang.
Nirnaamay. Akaamay. "Sustainer, Liberator, Enlightener, Infinite,
Destroyer, Creator, Nameless, Desireless," the eight attributes of God.
Brings stability to the brain by training it to unite with the infinite.

Gobinday, Mukanday
Udaaray, Apaaray
Hareeang, Kareeang
Nirnaamay, Akaamay

Guru Guru Wahe Guru. Used for protection and for miracles. Chanting
this mantra calls upon Guru Ram Das, the fourth Sikh guru.

Guroo Guroo Wha-hay Guroo
Guroo Raam Daas Guroo

Hari Nam Sat Naam. A prosperity mantra as it manifests the spirit into
form. Hari Nam is the name of God; Sat Naam translated as "Truth is
His Name."

Haree Naam Sat Naam

Haree Naam Haree
Haree Naam Sat Naam
Sat Naam Haree

Har Har Wahe Guru. The mantra of ecstasy, used to balance yourself between the earth and ether.

Har Har Wha-hay Guru

Humee Hum Brahm Hum. Translated as "We are we, we are God," this mantra helps us feel connected and not alone. It helps us to remember we are connected to the source: God.

Humee Hum, Brahm Hum

Ong Namo. Translated as "I bow to the Divine Creator; I bow to the Divine Teacher Within." This is the mantra always used to tune in before teaching a Kundalini Yoga class.

Ong namo
Guroo dayv namo

Ra Ma Da Sa Say. This mantra creates healing energy for yourself or someone else.

Raa maa daa saa
Saa say so hung

Sa Ta Na Ma. Also known as Gan Pattee, this mantra helps you make the impossible possible by cutting through blocks.

Saa taa naa maa
Raa maa daa saa
Saa say so hung

Sa Ta Na Ma. This is referred to as Panj Shabd. It is the "atomic," or naad, form of the mantra, Sat Naam. It is used to increase intuition, balance the hemispheres of the brain, and create a destiny for someone when there was none.

Saa taa naa maa

Sat Naam. This seed (or Bija) Mantra is widely used in Kundalini Yoga. It is sometimes translated as "Truth is my identity" or "I call upon my eternal truth." When someone says, "Sat Naam" to another person, it means, "Your truth is your soul."

Sat Naam

Sat Naam, Sat Naam. Creates a deep awareness of knowing who you are.

Sat Naam, Sat Naam, Sat Naam, Sat Naam, Sat Naam, Sat Naam, Wha-hay Guroo

Wahe Guru. A mantra of ecstasy (Wahe is equivalent to "Wow!") expressing the excellence and magnificence of God.

Wha-hay Guroo,
Wha-hay Guroo.
Wha-hay Guroo,
Wha-hay Guroo.

Acknowledgments

First and foremost, thank you to my curious clients who have inquired about less traditional methods of psychotherapy.

Thank you to my husband, Julian, who has supported me through anything and everything that I have wanted to embark on throughout this journey we call life, including my career. Your love and constant presence have offered me consistent stability and support.

Thank you to my parents, who have walked their own path and found the strength to grow. Together, we have learned from our past pains and healed our old wounds. I love our adult relationship and know that you can love me unconditionally.

Thank you to my personal editor, Kristina Sigler, who helped me bring my book to life. I feel like you tapped into my brain with the way you helped me convey my message of Kundalini Yoga's influence on the body and mind.

Thank you to Alex Dolven, who—since he was sixteen years old—has helped me create the most simple yet beautiful mantra music to go with my Kundalini meditations. I am so appreciative of all the recordings and creations of each mantra piece you have done for me.

Thank you to my dear friends who have supported me in one way or another on this journey of writing my book. Lynn Lee, Cathy Hill, Sheila Jordan, Cindy Chavoen and many more. Thank you

Thank you to Yogi Bhajan, who brought the Kundalini Yoga teachings to the West fifty years ago. You said you didn't come here to make followers; you came to make teachers. I hope to carry on your legacy by bringing Kundalini's yogic technologies to the mental health world.

Thank you to my graphics team: Guru Amrit Kaur Khalsa from

Norway, who illustrated the meditation and yoga poses, and Christophe Genty, who photographed my headshot for the sleeve.

Thank you to everyone who has ever believed in me and supported me. Because you have picked up this book and made it this far, that means I want to thank you too.

Meditate daily and be well.

Bibliography

"About Addiction." National Council on Alcoholism and Drug Dependence. www.ncadd.org/about-addiction.

"America's #1 Health Problem." *The American Institute of Stress*. www.stress.org/americas-1-health-problem/.

"Anti-Aging Market Is Estimated to Be Worth USD 191.7 Billion Globally by 2019." Globe Newswire, Transparency Market Research, May 21, 2015. globenewswire.com/news-release/2015/05/21/737992/10135534/en/Anti-aging-Market-is-estimated-to-be-worth-USD-191-7-Billion-Globally-by-2019-Transparency-Market-Research.html.

"APA Survey Raises Concern about Parent Perceptions of Children's Stress." *American Psychological Association*, November 3, 2003. www.apa.org/news/press/releases/2009/11/stress.aspx.

Barnes, Terra D., et al. "Activity of Striatal Neurons Reflects Dynamic Encoding and Recoding of Procedural Memories." *Nature* 437, 7062, 2005, pp. 1158–1161, doi:10.1038/nature04053.

Berkovich-Ohana, Aviva, et al. "Repetitive Speech Elicits Widespread Deactivation in the Human Cortex: The 'Mantra' Effect?" *Brain and Behavior* 5, no. 7, 2015, doi:10.1002/brb3.346.

Boldt, Ethan. "The Top 7 Essential Oils for Anxiety." *Dr. Axe*, September 22, 2017, draxe.com/essential-oils-for-anxiety.

Boone, Tommy, et al. "Effects of a 10-Minute Back Rub on Cardiovascular Responses in Healthy Subjects." *The American Journal of Chinese Medicine* 29, no. 01, 2001, pp. 47–52, doi:10.1142/s0192415x0100006x.

Kelly Brogan Team. "5 Foods That Can Cause Depression." February 2, 2018, kellybroganmd.com/5-foods-that-can-cause-depression.

"Chant: A Healing Art?" *The Washington Times*, June 25, 2008, www.washingtontimes.com/news/2008/jun/25/chant-a-healing-art.

Chapman, Sandra B., et al. "Shorter Term Aerobic Exercise Improves Brain, Cognition, and Cardiovascular Fitness in Aging." *Frontiers in Aging Neuroscience* 5, 2013, doi:10.3389/fnagi.2013.00075.

Chetty, S, et al. "Stress and Glucocorticoids Promote Oligodendrogenesis in the Adult Hippocampus." *Molecular Psychiatry* 19, no. 12, 2014, pp. 1275–1283, doi:10.1038/mp.2013.190.

Chopra, Deepak. "Why Meditate?" DeepakChopra.com. March 5, 2017, www.deepakchopra.com/blog/article/4701.

Clift, Stephen, and Grenville Hancox. "The Significance of Choral Singing for Sustaining Psychological Wellbeing: Findings from a Survey of Choristers in England, Australia and Germany." *Music and Health* 3, no. 1, 2010. pp. 79–96.

Cummings, Nicholas A., et al. *The Value of Psychological Treatment: The Collected Papers of Nicholas A. Cummings*. Zeig, Tucker & Co., 2000.

Delaney, Joseph P., et al. "The Short-Term Effects of Myofascial Trigger Point Massage Therapy on Cardiac Autonomic Tone in Healthy Subjects." *Journal of Advanced Nursing* 37, no. 4, 2002, pp. 364–371, doi:10.1046/j.1365-2648.2002.02103.x.

DiSalvo, David. "Breathing and Your Brain: Five Reasons to Grab the Controls." *Forbes*, May 14, 2013. www.forbes.com/sites/daviddisalvo/2013/05/14/breathing-and-your-brain-five-reasons-to-grab-the-controls.

Dunbar, Robin, et al. "Performance of Music Elevates Pain Threshold and Positive Affect: Implications for the Evolutionary Function of Music." *Evolutionary Psychology* 10, no. 4, 2012, doi:10.1177/147470491201000403.

Duraimani, Shanthi, et al. "Effects of Lifestyle Modification on Telomerase Gene Expression in Hypertensive Patients: A Pilot Trial of Stress Reduction and Health Education Programs in African Americans." *Plos One* 10, no. 11, 2015, doi:10.1371/journal.pone.0142689.

Epel, E. S., et al. "Accelerated Telomere Shortening in Response to Life Stress." *Proceedings of the National Academy of Sciences* 101, no. 49, 2004, pp. 17312–17315, doi:10.1073/pnas.0407162101.

Eshkevari, L., et al. "Acupuncture Blocks Cold Stress-Induced Increases in the Hypothalamus-Pituitary-Adrenal Axis in the Rat." *Journal of Endocrinology* 217, no. 1, 2013, pp. 95–104, doi:10.1530/joe-12-0404.

Fosar, GrazÌyna, and Franz Bludorf. *Vernetzte Intelligenz.* Omega, 2006.

Grape, Christina, et al. "Does Singing Promote Well-Being?: An Empirical Study of Professional and Amateur Singers during a Singing Lesson." *Integrative Physiological & Behavioral Science* 38, no. 1, 2002, pp. 65–74, doi:10.1007/bf02734261.

"Gregorian Chanting 'Can Reduce Blood Pressure and Stress.'" *Daily Mail Online*, Associated Newspapers, May 2, 2008, www.dailymail.co.uk/sciencetech/article-563533/Gregorian-chanting-reduce-blood-pressure-stress.html.

Griffin, R. Morgan. "10 Health Problems Related to Stress That You Can Fix." *WebMD*, April 1, 2014, www.webmd.com/balance/stress-management/features/10-fixable-stress-related-health-problems.

Hameroff, Stuart, and Roger Penrose. "Consciousness in the Universe." *Physics of Life Reviews* 11, no. 1, 2014, pp. 39–78, doi:10.1016/j.plrev.2013.08.002.

Hofmann, Stefan G., et al. "Loving-Kindness and Compassion Meditation: Potential for Psychological Interventions." *Clinical Psychology Review* 31, no. 7, 2011, pp. 1126–1132, doi:10.1016/j.cpr.2011.07.003.

Holmes, Lindsay. "The Difference between Stress and Anxiety." TheHuffingtonPost.com, February 25, 2014, www.huffingtonpost.com/2014/02/25/stress-anxiety-difference_n_4833172.html.

Hölzel, Britta K., et al. "Mindfulness Practice Leads to Increases in Regional Brain Gray Matter Density." *Psychiatry Research: Neuroimaging* 191, no. 1, 2011, pp. 36–43, doi:10.1016/j.pscychresns.2010.08.006.

Hutchison, Isabel C., and Shailendra Rathore. "The Role of REM Sleep Theta Activity in Emotional Memory." *Frontiers in Psychology* 6, 2015, doi:10.3389/fpsyg.2015.01439.

"In-Depth Discussion." *Alzheimer's Prevention: In-Depth Discussion*, 21 July 2017, alzheimersprevention.org/research/discussion.

Jacobs, Tonya L., et al. "Intensive Meditation Training, Immune Cell Telomerase Activity, and Psychological Mediators." *Psychoneuroendocrinology* 36, no. 5, 2011, pp. 664–681, doi:10.1016/j.psyneuen.2010.09.010.

Johnson-Groh, Mara. "NASA Studies Cosmic Radiation to Protect High-Altitude Travelers." *Phys.org.* January 27, 2017, phys.org/news/2017-01-nasa-cosmic-high-altitude.html.

Jung, C. G., and Sonu Shamdasani. *The Psychology of Kundalini Yoga: Notes of the Seminar Given in 1932.* Princeton University Press, 1999.

Kasser, Tim, and Richard M. Ryan. "A Dark Side of the American Dream: Correlates of Financial Success as a Central Life Aspiration." *Journal of Personality and Social Psychiatry* 65, no. 2, 1993, pp. 410-422.

Kaufman, Marc. "Meditation Gives Brain a Charge, Study Finds." *The Washington Post*, January 3, 2005, p. A05, www.washingtonpost.com/wp-dyn/articles/A43006-2005Jan2.html.

Kaur, Ramdesh. "All About Kundalini Yoga: A Brief History of Yoga & Patanjali's Sutras." *Spirit Voyage*, September 7, 2012, www.spiritvoyage.com/blog/index.php/all-about-kundalini-yoga-a-brief-history-of-yoga-patanjalis-sutras.

Khalsa, Dharma Singh. "3 New Ways Kirtan Kriya Helps Keep Your Brain Sharp." TheHuffingtonPost.com, July 22, 2013, www.huffingtonpost.com/dharma-singh-khalsa-md/meditation-alzheimers_b_3625181.html.

Konturek, Peter C., et al. "Stress and the gut: pathophysiology, clinical consequences, diagnostic approach and treatment options." *Journal of Physiology and Pharmacology* 62, no. 6, December 2011, pp. 591-9.

Krishnakumar, Divya, et al. "Meditation and Yoga Can Modulate Brain Mechanisms That Affect Behavior and Anxiety: A Modern Scientific Perspective." *Ancient Science* 2, no. 1, 2015, p. 13, doi:10.14259/as.v2i1.171.

Lagopoulos, Jim, et al. "Increased Theta and Alpha EEG Activity during Nondirective Meditation." *The Journal of Alternative and Complementary Medicine* 15, no. 11, 2009, pp. 1187–1192, doi:10.1089/acm.2009.0113.

Liou, Stephanie. "Meditation and HD." Huntington's Outreach Project for Education, Stanford University, June 26, 2010, web.stanford.edu/group/hopes/cgi-bin/hopes_test/meditation-and-hd.

Loersch, Chris, and Nathan L. Arbuckle. "Unraveling the Mystery of Music: Music as an Evolved Group Process." *Journal of Personality and Social Psychology* 105, no. 5, 2013, pp. 777–798, doi:10.1037/a0033691.

Luders, Eileen, et al. "Forever Young(Er): Potential Age-Defying Effects of Long-Term Meditation on Gray Matter Atrophy." *Frontiers in Psychology* 5, 2015, doi:10.3389/fpsyg.2014.01551.

Lutz, A., et al. "Long-Term Meditators Self-Induce High-Amplitude Gamma Synchrony during Mental Practice." *Proceedings of the National Academy of Sciences* 101, no. 46, 2004, pp. 16369–16373, doi:10.1073/pnas.0407401101.

Mallinson, James. *The Khecarīvidyā of Adinathā: A Critical Edition and Annotated Translation of an Early Text of Hathayoga.* Routledge, 2007.

Mertz, Howard. "Stress and the Gut." *UNC Center for Functional GI and Motility Disorders.* https://www.med.unc.edu/ibs/files/educational-gi-handouts/Stress%20and%20the%20Gut.pdf.

Park, Alice. "Parental Stress Increases Kids' Risk of Asthma." *Time,* July 22, 2009, content.time.com/time/health/article/0,8599,1912184,00.html.

"Physical Activity Reduces Stress." *Anxiety and Depression Association of America,* adaa.org/understanding-anxiety/related-illnesses/other-related-conditions/stress/physical-activity-reduces-st.

Real, Terrence. *The New Rules of Marriage: What You Need to Know to Make Love Work.* Ballantine Books, 2008.

Sacchet, M. D., et al. "Attention Drives Synchronization of Alpha and Beta Rhythms between Right Inferior Frontal and Primary Sensory Neocortex." *Journal of Neuroscience* 35, no. 5, 2015, pp. 2074–2082, doi:10.1523/jneurosci.1292-14.2015.

Schulte, Brigid. "Harvard Neuroscientist: Meditation Not Only Reduces Stress, Here's How It Changes Your Brain." *The Washington*

Post, May 26, 2015, www.washingtonpost.com/news/inspired-life/wp/2015/05/26/harvard-neuroscientist-meditation-not-only-reduces-stress-it-literally-changes-your-brain.

Streeter, Chris C., et al. "Effects of Yoga versus Walking on Mood, Anxiety, and Brain GABA Levels: A Randomized Controlled MRS Study." *The Journal of Alternative and Complementary Medicine* 16, no. 11, 2010, pp. 1145–1152, doi:10.1089/acm.2010.0007.

Streeter, Chris C., et al. "Yoga Asana Sessions Increase Brain GABA Levels: A Pilot Study." *The Journal of Alternative and Complementary Medicine* 13, no. 4, 2007, pp. 419–426, doi:10.1089/acm.2007.6338.

Turakitwanakan, Wanpen, et al. "Effects of mindfulness meditation on serum cortisol of medical students." *Journal of the Medical Association of Thailand* 96, no. 1, June 2013, pp. 90-5.

Twenge, Jean M., et al. "More Happiness for Young People and Less for Mature Adults." *Social Psychological and Personality Science* 7, no. 2, 2015, pp. 131–141, doi:10.1177/1948550615602933.

United States Congress, U.S. Geological Survey. "The Water in You." water.usgs.gov/edu/propertyyou.html.

Van Der Helm, Els, et al. "REM Sleep Depotentiates Amygdala Activity to Previous Emotional Experiences." *Current Biology* 21, no. 23, 2011, pp. 2029–2032, doi:10.1016/j.cub.2011.10.052.

Vannucci, Anna, et al. "Social Media Use and Anxiety in Emerging Adults." *Journal of Affective Disorders* 207, 2017, pp. 163–166, doi:10.1016/j.jad.2016.08.040.

Vickhoff, Björn, et al. "Music Structure Determines Heart Rate Variability of Singers." *Frontiers in Psychology* 4, 2013, doi:10.3389/fpsyg.2013.00334.

Wang, Shu-Zhen, et al. "Effect of Slow Abdominal Breathing Combined with Biofeedback on Blood Pressure and Heart Rate Variability in Prehypertension." *The Journal of Alternative and Complementary Medicine* 16, no. 10, 2010, pp. 1039–1045, doi:10.1089/acm.2009.0577.

Weil, Andrew. Spontaneous Healing: How to Discover and Enhance Your Body's Natural Ability to Maintain and Heal Itself. Ballantine Books, 2000.

Winerman, Lea. "The Mind's Mirror." *Monitor on Psychology*, October 2005, p. 48, www.apa.org/monitor/oct05/mirror.aspx.

Yamamoto, Noriko, and Jun Nagano. "Parental Stress and the Onset and Course of Childhood Asthma." *BioPsychoSocial Medicine* 9, no. 1, 2015, doi:10.1186/s13030-015-0034-4.

Yogi Bhajan. *The Aquarian Teacher: KRI International Teacher Training in Kundalini Yoga*. Kundalini Research Institute, 2003.

Yogi Bhajan. "Happiness." October 11, 1989, Los Angeles, California.

Yogi Bhajan. "Mind and Meditation: Level 2." KRI International Kundalini Yoga.

Yogi Bhajan. "Stress and Vitality: Level 2." KRI International Kundalini Yoga.

Yogi Bhajan. "The Pranic Body." August 31, 1982, Stockholm, Sweden.

Yogi Bhajan. *The Teachings of Yogi Bhajan: The Power of the Spoken Word*. Arcline Publications, 1977.

Yogi Bhajan and Gurucharan Singh Khalsa. *The Mind: Its Projections and Multiple Facets*. Kundalini Research Institute, 1998.

Zeidan, F., et al. "Brain Mechanisms Supporting the Modulation of Pain by Mindfulness Meditation." *Journal of Neuroscience* 31, no. 14, 2011, pp. 5540–5548, doi:10.1523/jneurosci.5791-10.2011.

Zelano, Christina, et al. "Nasal Respiration Entrains Human Limbic Oscillations and Modulates Cognitive Function." *The Journal of Neuroscience* 36, no. 49, 2016, pp. 12448–12467, doi:10.1523/jneurosci.2586-16.2016.

About the Author

Madhur-Nain Webster was born into an ashram in Amsterdam and raised by spiritual parents; she has always had a life balanced by the traditions and practices of Kundalini Yoga. Her genuine love of humanity and fascination with the human mind guided her toward a career where she could influence people and enrich their lives through the use of meditation.

After receiving her master's degree from the University of Oregon State, Madhur-Nain moved to California and became a licensed marriage and family therapist. She currently runs a successful private psychotherapy practice in Napa, California, where she is focused on helping clients work through their stress, anxiety, panic attacks, life transitions, and couples-related issues. Her therapy is supplemented with training in cognitive behavior therapy (CBT), eye movement desensitization and reprocessing (EMDR), internal family systems (IFS) therapy, and Relational Life Therapy (RLT). She is convinced that meditation has a positive influence on our psychology and well-being, and this conviction plays a major role in her approach to therapy.

Certified by the Kundalini Research Institute (KRI), Madhur-Nain is a Kundalini teacher and Lead teacher trainer who has traveled the world to share her yogic experience and knowledge. One of her goals is to bring meditation and chanting—a basic tenet of Kundalini technology—into the mainstream. In addition to her five CDs (and over forty-five singles), Madhur-Nain releases a new mantra on her website every month, in hopes of inspiring others to discover how a simple meditation and chant can be a powerful tool for self-healing.

Madhur-Nain fully believes that we should do things with love. She not only loves her work, she also loves designing clothes, creating new meditation products, and traveling. After growing up traveling with her parents and Yogi Bhajan, she is still passionate about visiting places all over the world and carrying her message of unity through the power of Kundalini Yoga. She encourages you to embark on your own journey to find peace and joy on earth.

www.MadhurNain.com